THREE BEHAIM BOYS

Three Behaim Boys

Growing Up in Early Modern Germany

A Chronicle of Their Lives Edited & Narrated by

STEVEN OZMENT

Yale University Press ❦ New Haven & London

Designed by Richard Hendel
Set in Joanna type by Brevis Press,
Bethany, Connecticut
Printed in the United States of America

The paper in this book meets the guidelines
for permanence and durability of the
Committee on Production Guidelines for
Book Longevity of the Council on Library
Resources.

10 9 8 7 6 5 4 3 2 1

Library of Congress Cataloging-in-Publication
Data

Three Behaim boys : growing up in early
modern Germany : a chronicle of their lives /
edited and narrated by Steven Ozment.
        p. cm.
    Includes bibliographical references.
    ISBN 0-300-04670-7 (alk. paper)
    1. Behaim family—Correspondence.
2. Germany—Biography. 3. Youth—
Germany—Correspondence. 4. Youth—
Employment—Germany—History.
5. Youth—Travel—Germany—
History. I. Ozment, Steven E.
CT1097.B44T47   1990
943'.32403'0922—dc20
[B]   89-27312
                                CIP

To the memory of my dear son

MATTHEW

19 October 1960–12 July 1987

CONTENTS

🐛 🐛 🐛 🐛 🐛 🐛 🐛 🐛 🐛 🐛 🐛 🐛 🐛 🐛 🐛 🐛 🐛

Preface	ix
Introduction	1
MICHAEL V BEHAIM	11
Milan, 1523–1527	15
Breslau, 1527–1528	21
Breslau, 1529	39
Breslau, 1530–1531	55
Breslau, 1532–1533	64
Breslau, May–July 1533	75
Breslau, October 1533–January 1534	83
Epilogue	92
FRIEDERICH VIII BEHAIM	93
Altdorf, 1578–1581	97
Venice and Padua, 1581–1582	155
Epilogue	160
STEPHAN CARL BEHAIM	161
Altdorf, 1628–1629	165
Dresden, January–March 1630	187
Altenburg, March 1630–February 1631	195
Thirty Years War, 1632–1634	227
Netherlands, 1635–1636	250
Brazil, March 1636–January 1638	272
Epilogue	283

Appendix 1: Edited Sources on the Behaims   285

Appendix 2: Monetary Values (1550–1650)   286

Appendix 3: Altdorf School Ordinance   287

Appendix 4: Stephan Carl's Poem on the
    Occasion of Lucas Friederich Behaim's Birthday   288

Appendix 5: Genealogies of the Behaims   290

Appendix 6: Genealogical and Other Aids   294

PREFACE

❦ ❦ ❦ ❦ ❦ ❦ ❦ ❦ ❦ ❦ ❦ ❦ ❦ ❦ ❦ ❦ ❦ ❦

Children bring their parents joy and break their hearts in a thousand ways. I had not intended to delve so deeply into such an obvious truth when I began the research for this book. Nor had I intended to demonstrate it in the lives of teenagers and young adults. Having discovered a few handwritten notes by a six-year-old during an earlier study of a merchant from Nuremberg and his wife, I set out originally to find other examples of precocious expression by children in early modern Germany. Depending on the size of my find, my goal was to compile a small edition of letters by children. Knowing the riches of the family archives in Nuremberg's German National Museum, I naturally began there.

The museum houses the world's largest collection of German art and culture, and exhibits everything from ancient weaponry to modern toys. Like so much of the city of Nuremberg the museum is both old and new, with a medieval wall still standing at one end and a modern, postwar commercial metropolis at the other. The museum's center is a former Carthusian monastery and church dating to the fourteenth century, around which are spread 243,000 square feet of exhibition space. Among the museum's treasures is the first spherical representation of the earth (1491–92), the "globe apple" of Martin Behaim, a distant cousin of the boys who are the subjects of this book. (Behaim is thought by some historians to have helped Columbus chart his first voyage; his map of the world understates the distance between the Canaries and Cuba—where Behaim located Japan—by a factor of five.) There is also a library of 500,000 volumes devoted to German history and a properly spartan facility for visiting scholars, with an attached guest suite (at a mere eighteen Deutsche marks a day) for those who wish to immerse themselves in their research.

Because Nuremberg was one of early modern Europe's great merchant capitals, the city's archives have rich collections of family letters and papers. Among the richest is that of the Behaim family, which gave the city numerous political and cultural leaders. The name Behaim Family Archive may suggest to the reader a cavernous room, filled with moldy volumes, from which scholars emerge covered with cobwebs. Nothing could be less accurate: for the visiting scholar the Behaim Archive is in truth a large catalogue or repertorium, an immense but tidy prospectus of more than two centuries of Behaimiana consulted in a very modern reading room. When the scholar first sees the family letters and papers they arrive at his table in large, gray cardboard boxes escorted by middle-aged men in blue workcoats. Inside the boxes the materials are loosely placed together according to year in folders, some bound neatly with string. A box may contain a decade's correspondence or barely a year's. Archivists have already gone over the letters, as is clear from their markings in pencil in the corners of the letters confirming their dates. Sometimes they have hazarded to place undated letters in sequence on the basis of dates added by later hands, or according to their general content. Letters with no dating whatsoever end up at the back of a folder or box for the scholar to puzzle over.

Inside the museum I pored over the Behaim Repertorium and selected several examples more or less at random where the repertorium indicated that there was correspondence between children and parents. I then attempted to locate letters to traveling fathers, in the expectation of finding handwritten notes by small children that were sent along by the children's mothers. I cannot say that I had a single success in this undertaking. But the more I searched, the more impressed I was by the sheer volume of letters written by teenage and young adult males, particularly to widowed mothers and guardians. I soon learned that such correspondence stemmed from a common fact of burgher family life: by their early teens if not sooner, sons were routinely sent off to school, placed in foreign apprenticeships, or enlisted in service to Junkers or the military, where they prepared themselves for useful and rewarding work. The boys' absences easily extended into their twenties, for they often pursued more than one vocation before returning to positions near home. During this period of maturation and discovery, when most of their time was spent away from home, the youths remained in regular communication with their parents or guardians, on whom they continued to depend for money, advice, and, not least, contacts; hence, the enormous collections of letters.

In the end I did find the correspondence I had gone looking for. But it was by older children (though not necessarily less childish ones), and there was far more of it than I had expected. The result is this book, which deals with three Behaim boys from around the age of fifteen to around the age of twenty-five, with their emotional life, personal growth, and professional development. About one hundred and fifty years of the family's history are covered from the vantage point of their adolescent lives. Male members of the family became the focus of this book simply because, unlike their sisters, the boys traveled, and being away from home for long periods they left a detailed record of their experiences and thoughts in letters to home.

I have also intended to make a statement about the writing of history. Perhaps the major development in historiography over the last twenty years has been the widespread acceptance of historical subjects who are not literate, rich, or powerful, and of sources that are not written. Rituals and ceremonies, riots and trials, pilgrimages and inquisitions, clothing and gestures, Carnival and Lent—these are becoming the new "texts." Inspired by a desire to give ordinary life its due, a growing number of modern historians are attempting to hear in these sources the faint voices of Europe's masses. Historical records have revealed much about what ordinary people did and occasionally the very words of individuals are quoted or summarized by the lords and masters who exercise dominion over them. What is sadly lacking are the voices of the masses when they are not on a stage set by their betters or interrogated according to a script their betters have written. Historians simply cannot know directly why the masses did what they did and what went through their minds when they did it. Although their actions speak louder than words, they remain unexplained.

To be confronted by texts without words and by actions without motives understandably frustrates historians. Most often they seek to provide the missing human content with the assistance of the social sciences, deeply interpreting what few clues they have. Where contemporary mass experience falls short historians resort to their own experience or their reflections on it, supplemented by what modern science reveals about human behavior. This approach provides a ready and even beguiling access to the past, but the result could as often as not be described as deep speculation, and it also has an unfortunate side effect: the more they are studied and pondered in terms of present-day experience, the more the people of the past look and sound either like us or like primitives.

To shift from written text to textual events is to express doubt about the reliability of words and to declare one's faith in action; it also elevates the unconscious life over the conscious life. In the process it unleashes the subjectivity of modern historians and clears the way for all to render the past according to their own desires. If the only subjects who can speak authoritatively for the people of the past are deemed to be those who lack a voice that only modern historians can provide, then the past will in the end be whatever we historians say it is. Such an approach simply gives the present free rein over the past. And as any fair-minded observer of recent historiography will agree, few have been able to resist using the past to justify modern ideologies and social theories.

It is vital for historical study to have direct access to contemporary self-expression and analysis; otherwise historians will merely fashion and re-fashion the past according to current values and learn little that is new. What historians most need are deep sources. The aim of writing or reading about early modern Europe is not to prove or disprove the theories of some nineteenth-century psychologist or twentieth-century anthropologist; it is rather to obtain an understanding of what it meant to be a person in that age. The lessons of history can be learned only if we believe that the past can tell us something about humankind we do not already know.

What has traditionally set historians apart from all other commentators on the past is their conviction that the past has both the ability to elucidate itself and a right to do so. This has meant respecting the past and recognizing that it knows as much about human nature as we do. The trick has always been not to make the past more amenable to us in our terms, but to make ourselves more able to think in its terms. Historians who do their job well know how to vanish before their subjects. Their readers put down their books believing that they have gotten to know intimately not the mind of the historian but the people of another age, and that they have had their own values challenged in the process.

Because of the bias of much new history against literate people with means, there has been a tendency to lose sight of sources that best preserve the voice of the past. As historical subjects, voiceless people without means have admittedly proven more amenable to confirming the truths about human nature that modern historians hold to be self-evident. But having means and being literate do not necessarily preclude ordinary experience or make one incapable of exemplifying ordinary life. By the sixteenth century it is certainly common to find literate people from good families whose lives are ordinary to the point of impoverishment. And unlike the voiceless masses whose human experience and culture they share, these people are also able to speak for their age. They explain as well as act. They not only have experiences typical of their time but do so self-consciously. They enable the historian to interpret the past with evidence from contemporaries. As a result historical study becomes a genuine dialogue between past and present.

The teenagers and young adults of early modern Europe unveil a world of emotions and everyday life that until now has been virtually unknown. Despite the elaborate support systems arranged for them by their families, who were often prominent, once away from home these youths were very much on their own. Whether in apprenticeships, school, service to Junkers, or the military, they knew well the common man's life, some spending years in domestic servitude to foreign masters, while others experienced the poverty and misery of war. They had to negotiate their meals, lodging, and clothing, make friends, and win the confidence and respect of peers and masters. They also stole, lied, whored, drank, fought, and cheated. Constantly they confronted circumstances that tried their souls and threw them back on their own resources. Because they were young and dependent, they both wore their hearts on their sleeves and knew how to dissemble. They were at the same time spontaneous and calculating. Their own emotions and the values of the world around them remained at their fingertips. They felt more deeply and spoke more freely. The result, I hope the reader will agree, is a more profound revelation both of themselves and perhaps also of their culture than one finds in the contemporary adult world.

Of the 207 letters I have collected, all but three have been translated from manuscript and are printed here for the first time.[1] One who works with contemporary letters discovers quickly why they come into print so slowly. The most direct and intimate historical source, letters can also be the most elusive. Although they bring us as close as we can get to the past on its own terms, they often leave us with a sense of incompleteness. There are gaps in the collections, and individual letters can be undated, have pieces torn away, and have key words blurred beyond recognition. Once transcribed the letters may contain terms so individual or time-bound that their precise meaning is anyone's guess. And even when letters have been successfully transcribed and translated, they still convey the minds of people whose experience and culture are not our own.

Although the letters included here are not without such problems and

---

1. The three exceptions are letters 43–45 of Michael Behaim. Anton Ernstberger has summarized the highlights of Stephan Carl's correspondence in *Abenteurer des Dreissig-jährigen Krieges. Zur Kulturgeschichte der Zeit* (Erlangen, 1963).

have tested my agility, they are remarkably complete and provide full and continuous narratives. Where there are gaps in the stories I have attempted to fill them in with brief interludes or notes. And where a manuscript has been damaged I have sought to complete it on the basis of my best guess.

What we gain from these letters more than compensates for their occasional asymmetry and unruliness. As we see three young people grow and change over the years, we discover a largely unknown part of the emotional and vocational life of youth in early modern Europe. Each boy has a distinct personality, and we have feelings for him by story's end. We also behold the larger history of the boys' time as they live through and report it. The result is a fresh, contemporary perspective on a distant age and on what it meant then to be a teenager and young adult.

This would be a lesser book had it not been for the assistance of several friends, colleagues, and experts in German history. Matthias Senger and Gerald Strauss helped with difficult German passages, as James Hankins did with difficult Latin ones. Professor Hankins also rendered into English Stephan Carl's birthday poem for his brother Lucas Friederich. Anne Van Buren, Franklin Ford, and Thomas A. Brady, Jr., provided helpful information. On the other side of the Atlantic I received the friendly counsel of numerous scholars and archivists in Nuremberg: Frau Dr. Frhr. v. Andrian-Werburg of the German National Museum; Frau Dr. Schmidt-Fölkersamb, Dr. Karl Kohn, and Dr. Peter Fleischmann of the Staatsarchiv; and Professor Dr. Wolfgang Frhr. v. Stromer of the University of Nuremberg-Erlangen. He and his wife, Natalie, also shared with me the treasures of their home, the former Behaim residence at Burg Grünsberg. I owe a sizable debt to Vernon H. Nelson and Lothar Madeheim, archivists at the Moravian Archives in Bethlehem, Pa., who introduced me to the art and science of paleography.

As in all my work, I must give a most special thanks to my wife, Andrea, for her expert editorial judgment and other labors in bringing the manuscript to completion.

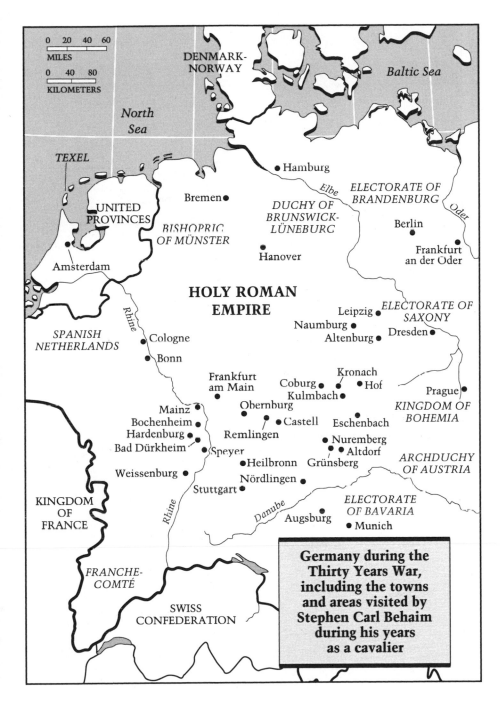

Germany

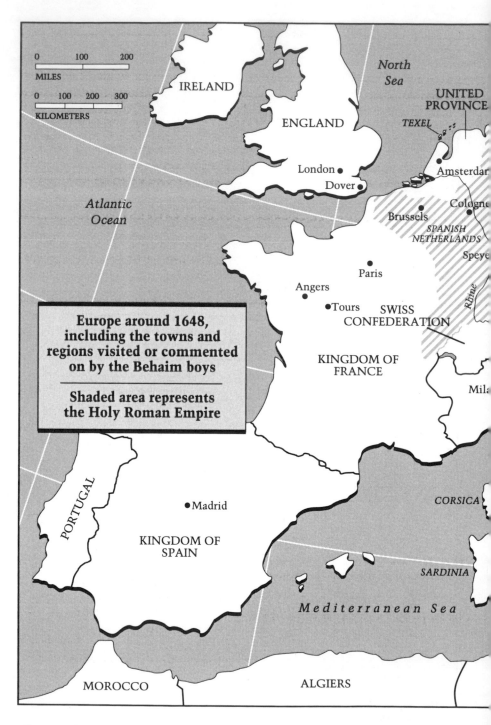

0   **100**   **200**

MILES

0   **100**   **200**   **300**

KILOMETERS

IRELAND

ENGLAND

North Sea

UNITED PROVINCE

TEXEL

London ●

Dover ●

Amsterdam

Cologne

Atlantic Ocean

Brussels ●

SPANISH NETHERLANDS

Speyer

Paris ●

Angers ●

● Tours

SWISS CONFEDERATION

Rhine

KINGDOM OF FRANCE

Milan

Europe around 1648, including the towns and regions visited or commented on by the Behaim boys

Shaded area represents the Holy Roman Empire

● Madrid

CORSICA

PORTUGAL

KINGDOM OF SPAIN

SARDINIA

Mediterranean Sea

MOROCCO

ALGIERS

Europe

Introduction

☙ ☙ ☙ ☙ ☙ ☙ ☙ ☙ ☙ ☙ ☙ ☙ ☙ ☙ ☙ ☙ ☙ ☙

This is the story of three boys: Michael, Friederich, and Stephan Carl. All were Behaims from Nuremberg, from two branches and three generations of that important family. Although they had distinct personalities and grew up to be very different, they had similar experiences in childhood. Each became fatherless at an early age; Michael (1510–69) when he was one, Friederich (1563–1613) at four, and Stephan Carl (1612–38) at eight. They were reared by their mothers, guardians, teachers, and the masters they served. Each left home at an early age to prepare a vocation—Michael at twelve for merchant apprenticeships in Milan and Breslau; Friederich at fourteen for school in Altdorf and Padua; and Stephan Carl at fifteen for school, the princely court, and the profession of arms.

Michael, maternally the poorest of the three, was in the end the most successful. He became an independent merchant by the time he reached his thirties. Friederich, the most secure, was also quite successful. He gained a village magistracy in his late twenties which he held for the rest of his life. Stephan Carl had every opportunity to succeed, but he was emotionally disturbed and failed utterly at everything he tried. Whereas Michael and Friederich returned home and raised large families, Stephan Carl died alone, disowned, halfway around the world.

During the sixteenth and seventeenth centuries members of the Behaim family held high political office and gained wealth as merchants. Although none of the three boys did as well, each could count the powerful and prominent in the city among his guardians, siblings, and relatives. During their lifetimes Nuremberg stood out among the great merchant capitals of Europe. For many people today Nuremberg first brings to mind Nazi crimes and war trials, a terrible modern legacy the city must carry into the future. But the Nuremberg of the sixteenth century and the early seventeenth was very different. The city was then admired as the Venice of the north, central Europe's gateway to the Adriatic and the Mediterranean. Its population grew during the sixteenth century from thirty thousand to forty thousand, and the city attracted many foreign merchants (eighteen firms from Italy alone). A diverse and industrious artisan community made up half of its inhabitants. On the tax rolls of 1568, 416 burgher or merchant families had property and money worth five thousand gulden or more; 240 families had wealth of ten thousand gulden or more. One of Nuremberg's citizens may have been Europe's richest man: the great merchant Bartholomäus Viatis (1538–1624) left behind an estate valued at 1,125,341 gulden. The immensity of such wealth may readily be appreciated by comparison with the average journeyman's pay in contemporary Nuremberg, which in 1597 was fifty-eight pfennigs a day, or around sixty gulden a year (and this represented a doubling of his salary since mid-century).[1]

The total wealth of Michael and Stephan Carl Behaim was around a thousand gulden, that of Friederich Behaim around two thousand. About half the wealth of each was in invested paternal inheritance, and half in shared family property. The boys had far more money on paper than ever in hand, and their wealth was always controlled by others. And because the boys were fatherless, their families spent more than they earned, so that each boy, including Friederich, grew up with a keen sense of impending economic difficulty. Michael lived as a member of the working class during much of his ten-year apprenticeship; Stephan Carl knew the life of a domestic servant and the squalor of the battlefield, and died virtually destitute.

Michael inherited from his father at least six hundred gulden and modest rent-producing property, most of which he shared with his older brother and sister. All his money and income however remained in the

---

1. Gustav Aubin, "Bartholomäus Viatis. Ein Nürnberger Grosskaufmann vor dem Dreissigjährigen Kriege," *Vierteljahrschrift für Sozial- und Wirtschaftsgeschichte* 33 (1940): 145–57; Rudolf Endres, "Zur Einwohnerzahl und Bevölkerungsstruktur Nürnbergs im 15./16. Jahrhundert," *Mitteilungen des Vereins für Geschichte der Stadt Nürnberg* (hereafter cited as MVGN), 57 (1970): 242–72, esp. 258.

The earliest depiction of the Behaim castle estate of Grünsberg. From an etching on a glass goblet by Johann Wolfgang Schmitt, 1676. Reproduced by permission of Professor Dr. Wolfgang Frhr. v. Stromer.

hands of guardians and relatives, who managed it for him with little consultation and, by modern standards, poor accounting of their stewardship. Throughout his apprenticeships Michael remained abjectly dependent on his foreign masters for virtually all his basic needs. He did have in his cousin Friederich VII Behaim (1491–1533) a wealthy, wise, and caring guardian, but one who was much distracted, both by his work and by seven children of his own. Michael's stepfather was a man of means in a position to assist him, but he had neither the legal responsibility to do so nor any liking for Michael, and the two were never close. When money did become an issue between them it was not Michael who approached his stepfather for assistance, but rather his mother who approached Michael on behalf of his stepfather, with whom she attempted to poach the children's paternal inheritance.

Friederich's economic circumstances are less clear, but they can be inferred from the circumstances of members of his family. Friederich VII, his grandfather and namesake (and Michael's guardian), had been a wealthy man. In 1529 he purchased the castle estate of Grünsberg in neighboring Altdorf for three thousand gulden. He died prematurely at the age of forty-two (in 1533), leaving seven underage children, among them four daughters. The household had so many dependent children, and so much went out and so little came in, that the estate of Friederich VII was rapidly depleted. In 1535 the children's guardians sold Grünsberg for 3,400 gulden.[2] The eldest son, Paul (1519–68), the younger Friederich's father and the one on whom the family's fortunes now hung, served an apprenticeship as a merchant in Italy before becoming in 1540 the agent in Antwerp for the Imhoff firm in Nuremberg, at a beginning salary of two hundred gulden a year. It was no small advantage to Paul that his mother was Clara Imhoff. The children also received generous assistance from their wealthy aunt Lucia Letscher, who left Paul a thousand gulden at her death in 1542, and lesser but still sizable sums to his brothers and sisters.[3]

On the death of his mother in 1548 Paul purchased the parental house in Nuremberg, valued at 2,500 gulden, for 2,000 gulden. The sum was

2. Matthias Thiel, "Archiv der Freiherren Stromer von Reichenbach auf Burg Grünsberg, Teil 1," *Bayerische Archivinventare* 33 (1972): 184, 192.
3. J. Kamann, "Aus dem Briefwechsel eines jungen Nürnberger Kaufmanns [Paul I Behaim] im 16. Jahrhundert," *Mitteilungen aus dem Germanischen Nationalmuseum*, vol. 2 (1894): 11–22.

divided among his siblings as their share in the property.[4] According to an itemized list of his household expenses, between August 1548 and August 1549 he spent 2,365 gulden on everything from food to taxes, including 570 gulden on his wedding to Barbara Kötzer in January 1549.[5] Clearly, within a decade Friederich's father had become a man of considerable wealth. But like his father, Paul Behaim died somewhat prematurely, at the age of forty-nine (in 1568). He left eight underage children, of whom four were daughters and the eldest child was only thirteen. And like his father's family, Paul Behaim's faced economic problems in spite of having a large estate. With their father's death they lost a steady income, and they had no wage earners ready to take his place. In addition to the household expenses loomed those for the boys' education. Although Friederich and his siblings never endured what a modern reader would call serious sacrifice, the specter of economic hardship always haunted Frau Behaim. She did not mean to exaggerate when in spring 1579, a decade after her husband's death, she urged Friederich to be thrifty with two gulden she was sending "because we do not have a lot [of money]."[6] Friederich was a fifteen-year-old schoolboy in nearby Altdorf at the time, and his board alone cost forty gulden a year; it would be many years before he would be self-sufficient. In an economizing measure two years earlier his brother Paul, a law student in Padua, had had his stipend reduced by his guardians from two hundred gulden a year to one hundred and fifty.[7]

Frau Behaim died on 31 December 1581, and during the following year the family estate was divided among the eight children. In November 1582 Magdalena, the eldest child and the family's bookkeeper, wrote to her brother Christoph, the second son, then twenty and employed in Augsburg, about his share. It came to 3,600 gulden, of which 1,567 gulden were in cash and the rest in property jointly owned by the children; this included the family house, gardens, and pasture, a mill, and household silver and furniture. Christoph also owed taxes and fees of ninety-five gulden on his property and seventy-five gulden on his money (about five and a half percent).[8]

4. J. Kamann, "Aus Nürnberger Haushaltungs- und Rechnungsbüchern, 1548–1568 (1576)," *MVGN* 7 (1888): 40.
5. Kamann, "Aus Nürnberger Haushaltungs- und Rechnungsbüchern," 39–65.
6. See letter 38 below.
7. W. Loose, "Deutsches Studentenleben in Padua 1575 bis 1578," *Beilage zur Schul- und Universitätsgeschichte* (Meissen, 1879), letter 24, pp. 29–30.
8. Magdalena to Christoph, 16 November 1582.

As befitted the eldest son, Paul II Behaim (1557–1621), Friederich's older brother and Stephan Carl's father, was given every advantage. Between the ages of fifteen and twenty-one he studied in Leipzig and Padua. At least two of his three marriages were to wealthy women. The first, Ursula Sitzinger, whom he married in 1583, may have had wealth of more than twenty thousand gulden.[9] Unlike his grandfather and father, Paul did not die young, and when he did die, at sixty-four (in 1621), his two eldest sons, Lucas Friederich and Paul III, were already well established. Of the ten children who survived him only four were minors, among them Stephan Carl. At his maturity in 1630 Stephan Carl had an interest-bearing inheritance of 1,560 gulden from his father, which dwindled to nine hundred gulden by 1632.[10] Well before Stephan Carl's death in 1638, the inheritance was fully depleted; hardly a gulden of it was lost because of circumstances Stephan Carl could not control.

This book is the story of the three boys' lives as teenagers and young adults. To contemporaries they were known as *Jünglinge*, youths between the ages of fifteen and twenty-five. Little is known about young people in early modern times, and even this is largely secondhand and somewhat speculative. Historians have attempted to recapture the experiences of young people through didactic literature, church catechisms, guild rules and minutes, autobiography (diaries, chronicles, housebooks), and artistic portrayals.[11] There is a more direct and reliable source, although not so easily accessible: the letters of the youths themselves.[12]

Mail was a precious commodity in early modern Europe. Although an "imperial" postal service existed, private couriers were far more reliable

---

9. Magdalena to Christoph, 12 January 1583.

10. Anton Ernstberger, *Abenteurer des Dreissigjährigen Krieges. Zur Kulturgeschichte der Zeit* (Erlangen, 1963), 65.

11. Kurt Wesoly, *Lehrlinge und Handwerksgesellen am Mittelrhein. Ihre soziale Lage und ihre Organization von 14. bis ins 17. Jahrhundert* (Frankfurt am Main, 1985); Wolfram Fischer, *Quellen zur Geschichte des deutschen Handwerks. Selbstzeugnisse seit der Reformationszeit* (Göttingen, 1957); Georg Steinhausen, *Der Kaufmann in der deutschen Vergangenheit* (Leipzig, 1899); Gerald Strauss, *Luther's House of Learning: Indoctrination of the Young in the German Reformation* (Baltimore, 1978); Steven Ozment, *When Fathers Ruled: Family Life in Reformation Europe* (Cambridge, Mass., 1983); Lawrence Stone, *The Family, Sex, and Marriage in England, 1500–1800* (New York, 1977); Simon Schama, *The Embarrassment of Riches: An Interpretation of Dutch Culture in the Golden Age* (New York, 1988).

12. For a brief bibliography of edited Behaim sources, including letters, see appendix 1.

and more often used. Carters delivered letters and packages daily between Nuremberg and Altdorf. One could always entrust mail to family
members, friends, and acquaintances who traveled back and forth across
central Europe on the business of Nuremberg firms. Even transatlantic
mail was reliably delivered, and considering the conditions within a reasonable time: a letter written by Stephan Carl from Recife, Brazil, on 3
May 1637 was received in Nuremberg on 14 October.

Occasionally, as with the three boys, letters to and from children are
of such great number, variety, and detail that it is possible to reconstruct
the children's lives and bring their age to life again. Such "deep sourcing"
obviates deep speculation and places at center stage the subjects of history
rather than the historian.

Each of the three boys is followed during his passage into adulthood:
Michael between the ages of twelve and twenty-four (from 1523 to 1534),
Friederich between fourteen and eighteen (from 1578 to 1582), and Stephan Carl between fifteen and twenty-five (from 1628 to 1637). Michael's
story exists only in monologue, for apparently no letters written to him
during his youth have survived. Friederich's story is told in dialogue with
his mother, by whom there remain thirty-eight letters written during
three and a half years of correspondence with her son. By contrast, many
people join Stephan Carl in telling his story, among them his mother, his
half-brother, guardians, teachers, lieutenants, colonels, middlemen, and
peers, all of whom leave letters either to Stephan Carl or about him.

Michael, the apprentice, was the youngest of three children. Unlike his
brother Stephan (1501–43), who was nine years older than he, and his
sister Margaretha (1506–1559), who was four years older, he never knew
his father. Also unlike them he remained distant from his mother, so
much so that he described himself as an orphan after her remarriage in
1518. His childhood experiences must have been anything but reassuring.
From the age of twelve, when he began his first apprenticeship in Italy,
he was virtually on his own. Money, success, and material security obsessed him. Few of his letters are without whining and complaint. He
seems to have kept almost entirely to himself, a reclusive, compulsive
worker. There is scant evidence of his ever having had close friends his
own age. Of the two people he describes as friends one is his second
cousin once removed, Paul Behaim, who was nine years his junior and
whom he watched over out of gratitude to the boy's father, Michael's
own guardian and mentor. The other "friend" was a sometime business
associate in Cracow who was slow to repay his debts. Michael's compa-

ratively early marriage to a woman from Breslau in 1533 further suggests an absence of male intimacy. And of course the marriage also had a materialistic aspect, for it accelerated and elevated his career.

Like most around him, Michael viewed youth as an impermanent and transitional state. Only the adult world fascinated and attracted him, for there alone could he gain the independence and privilege he so longed for. By contrast, Friederich and Stephan Carl made close and lasting friendships during their school days in Altdorf. Each also had a clear notion of the culture of youth and relished adolescence, Stephan Carl to the point where he resisted growing up. School was unlike the world of the merchant's apprentice, where masters were harsher authorities and peers more threatening competitors; like perhaps nowhere else at the time, school was a place where one's masters and peers might more easily be trusted and even loved.

Michael was haunted throughout his apprenticeship by a fear of being ill trained by his masters, and of reaching a dead end and being left a common household servant. Of the three youths he was both the most vulnerable and the quickest to stand his ground. Whether in legal conflict with his mother, in a struggle to hold his master to the conditions of his contract, or in choosing a wife, he acted as boldly as any modern youth. Yet despite his precocious adulthood, the boy in him was never far from the man.

Friederich was the boy most at peace with himself. The sixth of eight children, he did not see a brother or sister die until he was well into adulthood. At his birth he had five playful siblings, ranging in age from one to eight. He did lose his father when he was four and a half, but unlike Michael and Stephan Carl he never experienced estrangement from his mother, much less outright rejection by her.

Of Friederich's life we know directly only three and a half years when he attended school in Altdorf (three years) and Padua (half a year). His correspondence with his mother during this time provides a ground-level view of contemporary student life both outside the classroom and inside his heart and mind. The two wrote regularly to each other about the most basic things; spoons and forks, wash basins and tablecloths, candles and laundry sacks, paper, parchment, and quills. Frau Behaim can be tender and joke, turn philosophical, or curse and scold. Her advice is always practical and on occasion sage, as she counsels Friederich on food and drink, relationships and reputation, hygiene and health, and saving his soul and his money. She wanted especially for him to make the most of his school years and not to trifle. Always eager and trusting,

Friederich wrote to her about things a son could tell only a mother: scratchy laundry, the inferior food at school, his longing for cherries and special treats, his fondness for roses, and how he avoided the diseases of the bath. Both mother and son recognized these years as Friederich's growing years, physically as well as spiritually. The times could hardly hold forth a more normal and wholesome relationship between a parent and a child. Friederich's situation was probably as good as a burgher youth's could be in early modern Europe.

On the other hand, Stephan Carl began his life in competition with many siblings and in the presence of death. The first of Paul II Behaim's children by his third wife, Maria Magdalena Baier (married 1611, died 1641), he found himself in a family of nine half siblings, ranging in age from two to twenty-five. Of his five full siblings two died when he was four (his two-year-old brother Martin and his infant brother Johann), at six he lost still another brother in infancy, and his father died when he was eight. Although his mother outlived him, she virtually disowned Stephan Carl by his mid-teens.

Stephan Carl was by every contemporary measure a hellion and failed youth. Unable to complete his first year of studies at the Altdorf Academy, he was the first member of his distinguished family to fail. During his later service to a Junker his skills proved so rudimentary and erratic that his lord confined his duties to those of a domestic servant. His disobedience and ineptitude as a military courier landed him in prison. As a cavalier he was once wounded, twice captured, party to the death of a rival officer, and in the end a deserter. In summer 1635, at twenty-two, he made his way to Amsterdam, having resolved to seek passage to the West Indies and there begin a new life. But in the months before his departure his profligacy caused even him to take notice. Whereas Friederich considered the eighteen gulden he spent on excursions to celebrate his graduation "a lot of money" and apologized for this rare indulgence, Stephan Carl blithely ran up bills of a Reichsthaler a day during the six months he waited in Amsterdam,[13] or almost three hundred gulden all told. (A contemporary cleric with university training received a hundred gulden a year.) Stephan Carl's plans to make a fortune in Brazil also went awry. After running up more debts in the New Land with an unsuspecting fellow Nuremberger, he died a lowly musketeer at twenty-six.

Stephan Carl's family recognized early that he was incorrigible. After

13. A Reichsthaler was between one and a half and two gulden. See appendix 2 for a contemporary money table.

his departure from school at sixteen his half-brother and principal guardian, Lucas Friederich, recalled how Stephan Carl had been inclined from an early age to steal, and deemed him a bad seed. He concluded that what Stephan Carl needed most was a lord unafraid to beat and starve him out of his self-indulgence. Stephan Carl's mother was harsh in more subtle ways; she ceased to address him in her letters as "my dear son" and wrote his name on them in lowercase letters. His persistent profligacy, lying, unkept promises, and insincere apologies rendered all around him distrusting and cynical. Yet as hopeless as they believed him to be and as often as he bit the hands they extended to him, his guardians loyally endeavored almost to the end to find him a place where he might realize what promise he had and become self-sufficient.

That Stephan Carl was a young man out of control can be seen not only in his words and deeds, but even in his handwriting.[14] It is not that he wished to fail, for in his way he too wanted to be a success. He especially hoped to please his mother and regain her favor. And he was touchingly devoted to his friends at school, who enjoyed a true fellowship of scamps and whose company alone brightened his short life. But somewhere between his intentions, which may always have been uncertain at best, and reality, which never showed him much respect, he became badly lost.

14. See pp. 177, 202, and 257.

Michael V Behaim

🍎 🍎 🍎 🍎 🍎 🍎 🍎 🍎 🍎 🍎 🍎 🍎 🍎 🍎 🍎 🍎 🍎

One does not think of early modern Europe as a land of opportunity, particularly for the young. Nor does one readily associate with responsible parental stewardship its custom of sending children barely in their teens into apprenticeships or "service" outside their homes. Michael V Behaim's story both justifies and refutes these modern prejudices.

The parents and guardians of early modern Europe placed their children and wards in apprenticeships when they were anywhere from nine to sixteen years old. Merchant apprentices like Michael Behaim seemed to have started around twelve or fourteen, when they had attained good writing and accounting skills. Rarely did children end up in complete isolation with strangers. If they did not find a position with an immediate relative, friend of the family, or acquaintance, they lived and worked with someone who at least knew one of these. Parents and guardians did not make such arrangements casually and without references, and lines of communication, which could be intricate and difficult if a child were at a great distance, remained open and carefully maintained by all sides. This of course did not diminish a child's anguish at separation or guarantee him kind treatment from his new masters, but because apprenticeship was so normal and expected a part of growing up, children also undertook it with high expectation and a genuine sense of adventure.

For the children of poor families, the opportunities offered by service of this kind, however limited, were usually superior to those available at home. In this sense apprenticeship, even for the most lowly service, was almost always intended to better a child's prospects in the workaday world. For well-to-do boys in merchant apprenticeships, service prepared them

11

for a place in the family business or for their own business. They learned foreign languages and customs, mapped out trade routes, and made the acquaintance of the producers and middlemen who ran the markets. Contracts carefully specified each side's obligations. The master had not only to feed and clothe the apprentice, but also to tutor him in all facets of a craft or trade so that he might become proficient in it in a specified time. In return, apprentices paid varying fees for their maintenance and training and pledged the same obedience and loyalty to their masters as they extended to parents and guardians, an obligation reiterated in children's catechisms of the time. Merchant apprenticeships usually lasted for three years, but remained open-ended and could easily run for ten years or more and involve several different masters.

Michael lost his father in 1511, when he was a year old. One can only assume from Michael's descriptions of himself as an orphan that he was never close to his mother, who had two older children: a son, Stephan (born 1501), and a daughter, Margaretha (born 1506). After his father's death Michael may have lived from an early age with his uncle Michael IV Behaim, his chief guardian. When Michael IV died in August 1522 Michael's cousins became his new guardians: Gabriel Fütterer, a minor merchant in Nuremberg, and Friederich VII Behaim, an influential senator and Kriegsherr there. This made them the stewards of Michael's paternal inheritance until he came of age and his immediate contacts whenever he needed advice, money, or special assistance.[1]

Michael began his first apprenticeship at twelve in Milan. Arranged by his cousins Gabriel and Erasmus Fütterer, this lasted four and a half years. There is little information about this period of his life, although several

---

1. Fatherless children in Nuremberg had appointed guardians until they reached the age of fourteen (for sons) and twelve (for daughters), even when their mothers were living. At these canonical ages of maturity the guardians became "trustees" (curatores rather than tutores) until the children turned eighteen, at which time they might render them a final accounting of their stewardship and retire from service. But guardians continued to play a major advisory and supervisory role well into their wards' twenties: in fact Nuremberg's law at the time permitted parents to disinherit children who married without their consent ("hynter ine") when they were as old as twenty-five (for daughters) or thirty (for sons). See "Nürnberger Reformation (1479)," Quellen zur Neueren Privatrechtsgeschichte Deutschlands, ed. Wolfgang Kunkel et al. (Weimar, 1936), title 12, law 2, p. 7; title 18, law 6, p. 29.

letters survive. In summer 1528, at seventeen, he began a second apprenticeship in Breslau (now Wroclaw) that lasted until 1533. This period
was marked by a blossoming correspondence with his cousin Friederich,
who had long since become his confidant. In Breslau he had new masters:
Hans Stublinger, a merchant from Nuremberg with east European markets, and his junior partner, Hans Rappolt, a man in his late thirties who
directly oversaw Michael's chores and who, despite occasional lapses,
remained a respected mentor. Michael early recognized in him the secret
of Hans Stublinger's success. Stublinger, on the other hand, he came to
dismiss as an uncaring tutor and an incompetent model for his own
career.

The apprenticeship in Breslau was stormy, and throughout it Michael
had also to keep an eye on Nuremberg, where an inheritance was administered by various relatives in his absence. Not without reason did he
suspect that his mother and brother were intent on taking advantage of
him. His mother wrote to him only to send legal briefs, and his brother
Stephan collected rents from peasants on jointly owned land without
providing him any accounting, much less a share of the earnings. Two
hundred gulden of his money had been held since 1523 by the Fütterers,
and his cousin Jacob Groland, a member of Nuremberg's powerful privy
council, oversaw five hundred gulden in behalf of Michael and his sister.
Michael struggled with all these people at one time or another, and he
became in the process obsessed with identifying and protecting what was
his own.

This obsession grew from legitimate concern. When Michael entered
the apprenticeship in Breslau, his new master, Hans Stublinger, required
two hundred gulden, a fee Michael had hoped to pay from money recovered from Erasmus Fütterer. Without it he feared his apprenticeship
would end, along with his prospects of becoming a merchant. As the
youngest son of a deceased father, he seems to have been more vulnerable to such conditions than other merchant apprentices from Nuremberg. When Friederich's own eldest son, Paul, entered a three-year
apprenticeship in Cracow in 1533, the firm of Peter Antonio de Nobili
required no such fee of him, while promising board, clothing, and tutelage.[2]

2. J. Kamann, ed., "Aus Paulus Behaims I. Briefwechsel," *MVGN* 3 (1881): 76–77.

But the apprenticeship in Breslau also had its own special humiliations. Finding himself treated as a stranger and common servant, Michael chafed at a service that he believed ill prepared him to be a merchant. In his letters he pleads eloquently for "fairness and what is right." At one point he feels betrayed as much by the city as by his master and declares Breslau a mercantile backwater, the last place on earth for an ambitious young man to master the merchant's craft.

As Michael struggles with Stublinger for the right to buy his own clothes and dine at his master's table, he reveals himself both as a child at risk in a world of men and as a man precociously triumphant over childhood. He and Friederich recognized in apprenticeship the passage into manhood. It was a necessary artifice, more pleasant and rewarding to the old than to the young, but one from which all sides ultimately gained. Whenever the anxious and retreating youth in Michael asserted himself over the man he was being forced to become, Friederich found Michael's passage as frustrating as Michael did. Friederich exploded only once, in the months before his death in 1533, when Michael seemed to spurn his authority and friendship by entering a marriage in Breslau without at all consulting his relatives in Nuremberg. Although he boyishly apologized for his conduct, this decision, so freely taken, had enabled Michael at last to realize what he had long sought: to become "a man and his own man." Alone and in a strange land, he had not only arranged his own marriage but married into a prominent family as well.

Somewhat contrary to modern presuppositions about youth at this time, Michael was a teenager and young adult with far more ego than superego. He might pledge childlike loyalty to his masters, but he always expected to be treated like an adult in return. When Erasmus Fütterer dawdled with Michael's effects in Milan and kept his money, Michael hounded him through his cousin Friederich and in the end directly. When Hans Stublinger left him clothed like a clown and seated at the servants' table, Michael declared his apprenticeship null and void. He found himself alone in a world that required self-will and aggression for success, but that swiftly punished their expression in youth. To his good fortune, he always had a head as well as a chip on his shoulders. He survived the pitfalls of service while exploiting its legitimate opportunities. By contemporary standards he was a triumph of his culture; by modern standards he seems also to have triumphed over it.

Michael entered his first apprenticeship in late spring or early summer 1523, when he was about twelve. Only three letters survive from his four and a half years in Milan. As their salutations remind us, Michael wrote from a Catholic Italy to a still-Catholic Nuremberg. They also make clear that he is devout. But except for a description of the great plague of 1525, they say little about Milan or Michael's experiences there. Instead the letters reveal a youth far more concerned about what Nuremberg had in store for him later.

On 10 February 1518 Michael's mother married the Bohemian knight and imperial Schultheiss Hans von Obernitz.[3] From his first letter it is clear that Michael viewed the marriage as a threat to his livelihood. He foresaw new brothers and sisters displacing him and competing for the already waned affection of his mother. The apprenticeship in Milan also marked the beginning of intermittent litigation over the paternal inheritance with his mother and stepfather, some of it apparently frivolous.[4] Michael's interests had been guarded by his uncle Michael IV Behaim until his uncle died in August 1522. Because partible inheritance prevailed in much of Germany, particularly in Protestant lands, as a second son Michael could look forward to a real inheritance. But he feared that his mother, stepfather, and elder brother would act individually or in concert to deprive him in his absence of his fair share of the family's land and money. By the age of fourteen he already had an adult's awareness of the workaday world and experience of legal conflict.

1 ❦ Michael to Friederich, 1 February 1524

Praise be to God and Mary, 1 February, 1524, in Milan.

My friendly greeting and due, obedient, willing service. Dear, esteemed cousin, when things are going well for you and you are well and hardy, it is always a very great joy for me to hear it from someone. I, too, am well and hardy, praise and thanks be to God and his dear mother, Mary.

3. The *Reichsschultheiss* was a powerful magistrate who represented in the city's court the emperor's authority and interests in greater Nuremberg.
4. See n. 11.

Friederich VII Behaim (1491–1533). Reproduced by permission of the Staatsarchiv Nürnberg.

Dear, esteemed cousin, my dear cousin Gabriel Fütterer arrived here yesterday in good health, praise God, and he brought me a letter from you dated 2 January.[5] I have learned from it that our dear late uncle Michael Behaim,[6] who leaves behind the Lochnerin,[7] has appointed you and cousin Gabriel Fütterer to be my guardians. That is a great [relief] to me. If, as I hope, you now will protect what is mine and be my father, I in turn will act as befits a good son. You know well that I now have only the two of you [to protect] what is mine. It is lost if my mother has other children and holds them more dear than me.[8]

You write that Uncle Michael has made me an heir to his nontestamentary possessions,[9] but on condition |that I reach a certain age|. As you know, it is my hope, God willing, to conduct myself in such a way that you and all my family [shall someday] behold in me a gentleman. Of this you should have no doubt. May almighty God and his dear mother Mary grant me such grace that I too may become a man. I know nothing else to write to you at this time except that God continue to keep you [in good health]. Greet your wife, my dear cousin, and your children warmly for me. I rejoice to learn that all are well. Greet Aunt Michael and my mother, who is now away.[10]

Would you let me know how old I have to be [to receive the things Uncle Michael left me]? I believe he indicated an age. I sincerely ask you to let me know what it is. God bless. Dated as above.

> Michael Behaim, your willing and obedient servant and cousin always.

2 🐝 Michael to Friederich, 2 June 1524

Praise be to God and to Mary, 2 June, 1524, in Milan.
My friendly greeting and humble, willing service . . . Dear, esteemed

5. The name appears in the manuscripts in three forms; Fuetuer, Futterer, and Fuetterer, the last of which is the most common.
6. This is Michael IV Behaim (d. August 1522), a knight and official in Nuremberg. He had apparently become Michael's chief guardian after the death of Michael's father in 1511.
7. The wife of Michael IV was Catharina Lochner (d. 1527).
8. The reference is to his mother's marriage to Hans von Obernitz.
9. "Seiner unverschafften." This included such things as his uncle's sword.
10. Aunt Michael is the widow of Michael IV; Michael's mother may at this time have been in Bohemia visiting her husband's estate.

cousin, know that I have today received a letter from my mother, together with [a copy of] a petition she has filed with the city council.[11] I have read and considered it and I have nothing more to write about it except to ask you to request that she not pursue it any further, but simply abide by my late uncle's testament and instructions. I place all my trust and faith in you two in this matter[12] and I ask you very sincerely to protect what is mine. I in turn will act as befits a loyal cousin. I see clearly that my mother intends little good for me. But [if she will withdraw the petition], I will remember this good deed of hers when, with the help of God, I come of age.[13] Had she been my stepmother, I would not have expected such treatment from her! But she has done this not only to me, but also to my brother Stephan,[14] who has been a good and loyal [son] to his mother and has also wished to please his stepfather. In the end, he has become a stable groom and common servant, which I can well imagine to be the same fate they have in store for me. But surely they will fail now that you know my mind. If you will not take my mother's side in this and will protect what is mine as a true father, I will act toward you as befits a loyal son, and when almighty God helps me come of age, I will thankfully repay you as best I can.

Greet your wife, my dear cousin, and your children, and also Aunt Michael warmly for me. May God long keep you in good health. Dated as above.

Michael Behaim, your willing and obedient cousin and servant always

[P.S.] Make the best of this letter—written in haste.

3 ♥ Michael to Friederich, 14 March 1525

Praise be to God and Mary, 14 March, 1525, in Milan.

My friendly greeting and due, obedient, willing service . . . Dear, es-

11. "Eine supplication." The petition concerned the disposition of Michael's paternal inheritance, overseen by Michael IV Behaim before his death. The petition was evidently dismissed by the council on 8 May 1524, even before Michael received his copy of it. According to a *Ratsverlass* on that day, Hans von Obernitz and his wife were ordered "not to bother the council again on the matter of the late chief guardian Michael [IV] Behaim's testament." See entry no. 703.

12. He means Friederich and Gabriel Fütterer.

13. "Zu meinen tagen [kommen]," that is, "mundig werden." Michael promises generosity toward her when he has full control of his paternal inheritance.

14. Stephan, Michael's elder brother by nine years, died without children in 1543.

teemed cousin, I ask you not to be angry with me for not having written for so long. It has not been my fault. I would gladly have written to my dear relatives, but conditions here have made it impossible to do so until now. First, there has been a terrible plague throughout the land. More than a hundred thousand people have died, men, women, and children, as one may clearly see here in the city of Milan. Throughout I have been constantly at the side of my master. Two of his servant girls died, and he, his children, and his wife lay ill for a long time. But he has survived the plague.

You may well wonder how I survived. Indeed, everyone flees the city [in time of plague]. My dear cousin Erasmus Fütterer did much to help me. He would gladly have taken me out of the city, but he could not do so for many reasons. First, when the first servant girl died, I was confined to a house for forty days, which is the custom here [when one has been exposed to a plague victim]. Then, after I was released [from quarantine], he could not take me out of the city without my master's permission.[15] He also knew that I was in the plague area and that he could move neither backward nor forward [to me]. [It was] then [that] I vowed to make a pilgrimage to a place one calls Sancta Maria de Loreto in Italian, which is twenty-five Italian or five German miles from Rome. My master trades there. With all my heart, I believe it was first God and after [my vow] this very Sancta Maria de Loreto who protected me from the evil and illness of the plague, although I also believe a Virgin Mary is everywhere accessible to me [and not just in Loreto]. So far, I have not made the pilgrimage. But, God willing, I intend to do so; it has become the subject of all my prayers.

Dearest cousin, I sincerely ask you to talk with my dear cousin Gabriel Fütterer and ask him to write to his brother, my dear cousin Erasmus, and instruct him to provide me with a horse so that I may go with my master [to Loreto]. He plans to leave the first week of Easter. If I do not go with him now, I will have to go at another time. But this is the best time for me to go. I may then carry out my vow and see and learn something along the way about commerce, so that when I come home [to Nuremberg] I will be both a man and my own man.[16] Should I be abroad for four years and see no city but Milan, and learn nothing [more than what I can learn here], I will be a laughingstock [when I return].

15. The name of Michael's Italian master is never mentioned. There may have been several.
16. "Ein Mensch unnd recht mann auss mir werd."

I had much more to write, but time has been too short. I suspect you already know how the war has gone here.[17] So no more for now. May God long keep you in good health. Greet your wife, my dear cousin, and your two children, and all our good friends. Please let me know as soon as you can how I should plan. My master will be off the first week of Easter. God bless. Dated as above.

Michael Behaim, always your willing and obedient cousin

17. The reference is to Spanish, French, and papal forces warring within Italy.

In October 1527 Michael returned briefly to Nuremberg in transit to a new apprenticeship in Breslau, from which the bulk of his correspondence comes. And he was not long in Breslau before his masters sent him to Bohemia, where he arrived before the end of November. There he attempted to learn the language and customs, make contacts, and gain experience for the future. By his own later calculation he spent twenty-nine or thirty weeks there.

For Michael's training as a merchant's apprentice, Hans Stublinger had required a fee of two hundred gulden. During the months in Bohemia it remained unpaid; this caused Michael much distress, for he looked on service with Stublinger as a golden gate to the establishment of his own business later. The plan had been to pay the fee with the recovered earnest money given to Gabriel Fütterer at the outset of Michael's apprenticeship in Milan. Michael demanded from Erasmus Fütterer the residue of this sum plus a fair share of four years' earnings on it, after all legitimate expenditures on his behalf had been accounted for and deducted. For a youth like Michael, who was made anxious by a single lost gulden, Erasmus Fütterer's treatment of this money

as his own proved enormously disturbing.

On his return to Breslau in June 1528, Michael confronted another unexpected problem: his master neglected to provide him with needed clothing. The ensuing conflict with Stublinger over Michael's right to clothe himself became the great crisis of the apprenticeship in Breslau. Nothing else ever disturbed Michael so much or elicited more comment from him. For a youth at this time proper clothing was closely connected with proper treatment in all other respects. For Michael, the right to clothe himself as he pleased became the test of his master's devotion to him. He felt that being denied proper clothing not only caused him physical hardship and threatened him with serious illness, but also incapacitated him vocationally: he could not move about freely on the streets of Breslau because of his shame and embarrassment over the way he was dressed.

This confrontation with Stublinger occasioned both tantrums and eloquent defenses of personal liberty on Michael's part. It also left him forever cynical and unforgiving of his master. From then on he even doubted the goodwill of Hans Rappolt, who after Friederich was his trusted mentor.

The new apprenticeship entailed other humiliations. Michael had to dine at the common table and was subjected to the bullying of a tyrannical housekeeper. At one point he threatens to run away and go it on his own, supporting himself if necessary by the most punishing physical labor.

But Michael was temperamentally more given to using his own initiative than to self-pity. Although his masters held him in low esteem, he could point out other prominent people in Breslau who did not. At the same time as he shows Friederich his wounds, he delivers nonnegotiable demands to his masters.

4 ❦ Michael to Friederich, 8 October 1527

Praise be to God and to Mary, 8 October, 1527, in Nuremberg.

A reminder for my dear cousin, Herr Friederich Behaim.[18]

Dear, esteemed, gracious cousin, it is my sincere and humble request that after I have undertaken this journey [to Breslau], all my Nuremberg affairs henceforth be entrusted to your care. I have no doubts about this. In time, I will gratefully repay you and yours.

First, dear cousin, I sincerely ask you to collect as soon as possible the two hundred Rhenish gold gulden that Gabriel Fütterer has in his possession. Would you also deliver my letter to him?[19] And when my clothes arrive [from Milan], would you send them to me at the first opportunity?

Second, would you at your own discretion agree to settle [a few of my late] Aunt Michael's affairs,[20] and instruct the trustee of her estate to pay for several swords, a scabbard, and a sofa, all of which belonged to me and have since been sold [with her things]? And would you see if you can get anything from Sebald Pfintzing for the parrot?[21]

I also sincerely ask you to inquire with Herr Hirsfogel or Herr Her-

18. The letter is actually a note left behind for Friederich when Michael left Nuremberg for Breslau. He had lodged in Friederich's house while in transit from Milan.
19. The letter to Fütterer was left with the note.
20. She had died on 12 April 1527, and among the things sold from the house in the disposition of her estate were some of the "unverschafften" left Michael by his late uncle. See letter 1.
21. Pfintzing (1487–1543), a senator from Nuremberg and a property and tax authority, had apparently taken possession of a parrot belonging to Michael. See letter 39.

werter about the diamond Jörg Pock has shipped [to me],[22] or ask the apothecary by the Saubrück. His name is Jörg Sauerweit. He will be the first to know something about it.

Would you also instruct Jacob Groland to render an accounting [of the earnings on the money he holds] for my brother and me as soon as possible and to deliver my share to the pastor?[23] He should also provide you with annual reports on these [earnings]. I also ask that you implore Jacob Groland to sign over [to me] the three hundred and sixty gulden he holds as a [part of my] inheritance. I will write no more about this. You can handle these matters better than I. I leave them to you.

Would you also, as you see fit, sell all my old effects at the first opportunity? When almighty God helps me come of age, I will repay you. May God be with us all. Amen. Dated as above.

Michael Behaim, always your willing cousin.

5 🦋 Michael to Friederich, 22 October 1527

Praise be to God and Mary, 22 October, 1527, in Breslau.

My willing service. Dear, esteemed cousin, know that I arrived here safely yesterday, praise be to God. May God continue to grant good fortune and happiness.

I am here now with Hans Rappolt. Tomorrow he will send me with some carters to Cracow to the man who will be my master there. Herr Stublinger has already talked with him about my coming. But the rumor here is that plague is raging in Cracow. I have discussed this with Herr Rappolt. He says he will write to the master to whom I am being sent, and if there is a great plague in Cracow, he will order me to go somewhere else. I hope that is the case, because if there is plague in Cracow, I certainly am not going to stay there, as you also have commanded me. I also hope my [new] master is not one who would leave me in a place where there is plague.

Dear cousin, I wrote you a letter while I was en route here, and I hope that letter has reached you before this one. In it, I described how I had left an I.O.U. for one Rhenish gold gulden on the windowsill in the room

---

22. Pock is not further identified. The diamond was apparently lost at sea along with the ship that carried it. Michael frequently enquires about it.

23. Groland was Michael's powerful cousin. See the Introduction and letters 8, 14, 17, 19, and 29. The pastor in this instance served Michael as a trustworthy banker.

in your house where I slept. Please take it, and ask Hieronymus Fütterer to let you know when a man named Heinrich Widemann arrives in Nuremberg from Salzburg, and demand from him [Widemann] payment of the I.O.U.. It was to his son [Virgil] that I lent this money in Milan.

Further, would you also tell Jacob Groland or my brother to return to you the records of the late Michael Behaim, which I gave [Groland]? [When you get them] put them in my sealed trunks. Do not yield until he returns them to you. There are four or five books of them in red waxed packing cloth, which you have surely seen. Should these records be lost, I might be put at a disadvantage.

Since the messenger with whom I traveled here had no money, I bought him food and drink over the duration of the journey. So would you not give him any gratuity on my behalf [when he returns]? It is known that you give him something when he brings you a letter from me . . .

God bless. Greet your wife, my dear cousin, also my master and the entire household warmly for me.[24] Dated as above.

Michael Behaim, your willing cousin.

6 ❦ Michael to Friederich, 23 October 1527

Praise be to God and Mary, 1527, 23 October, in Breslau.

My willing service and every good wish. Dear, esteemed, gracious cousin, I am writing about a letter I received today from Milan. I must reply to it, and there is some urgency. It concerns Erasmus Fütterer. [While in Milan] I borrowed some money from an agent of Jacob Welser in order to expedite goods to the Fütterers. I sent the bill on to Erasmus Fütterer [with the instruction] that he pay either Welser or his Milan carter, neither of whom, I now learn from the letter, has yet received the money. I have also written Erasmus Fütterer a letter, which is enclosed. If he is in Nuremberg or soon shall be, so that you know for certain that he is no longer in Milan, then I ask you to hold on to the letter and deliver it to him when he arrives. If he is still in Milan, would you give the two [enclosed] letters—one for Fütterer, the other for Welser's agent—to either Hieronymus Jacob or Hieronymus Fütterer, who will surely know where to deliver them in Milan.

Know also, dear cousin, that I am still here [in Breslau]. Hans Rappolt wants me to remain here until St. Elisabeth's day [November 19]. The

---

24. The master is Hans Stublinger, then in his office at Nuremberg.

annual fair is now under way. Since many Poles and Bohemians are coming, we will find out if plague is still raging in Poland. If it is, Herr Rappolt
is going to place me with a Bohemian [master], so that I can learn the
language. It makes no difference to me where they send me. I will go
gladly. But I would prefer Bohemia to Poland. Germans almost outnum-
ber Poles in Cracow now, and it would not be possible for me to learn
Polish in the six months I am to be there. I will learn more if I am among
non-Germans. I will let you know where I will be living and working.

Would you greet my master, Hans Stublinger, and share with him the
contents of this letter, so that he knows how I am doing? I would gladly
have written to him now myself, but it has been only four days since my
last letter to him. I fear he might be annoyed to hear from me so often
when I still have nothing in particular to tell him about my work. Nonetheless, would you tell him on my behalf that if there is anything he
wants done and I can be of service, he need only let me know it and I
shall spare no effort.

Dear cousin, greet your wife, my dear cousin, and the entire household
for me, and be of one mind with me. In time I will repay you for everything with my humble service. May almighty God bless you. Dated as
above.

Michael Behaim, always your willing cousin.

7 🍎 Michael to Friederich, 6 January 1528

Praise be to our Lord Jesus Christ, in the year of salvation, 6 January,
1528, in Dobruska.[25]

My willing service. Dear, esteemed, gracious cousin, yesterday I received a letter from you, dated 23 November, 1527, that gladdened my
heart. You write that you have talked with Erasmus Fütterer about the
money and that he has promised to give it to you during the first week
of Lent.[26] At your instruction, I am including a letter to him urging him
to keep his word and to deliver the money to you on the promised date.
For should this two hundred gulden not become available to me, it will

25. This is a new, Protestant salutation. Dobruska is now in Czechoslovakia, just south
of Nachod.
26. This is a reference to the two hundred gulden mentioned above, which become a
frequent topic of Michael's letters.

mean the end of my service [with Stublinger].[27] I have stressed the urgency of the matter only because it is necessary to do so. I hope to God there will be no difficulty.

As for the money I owe [Fütterer], you may certainly tell him to give you an accounting, and please send me a copy. Instruct him to indicate item by item everything he has spent on me from the beginning, when I first went to Milan, until my departure [four years later]. I do not, however, agree to pay him for food and drink while I was in his house. And I do not believe that the late Michael Behaim ever gave him any money on my behalf that was to be his forevermore. As I calculate what I spent during the four and a half years in Milan, including what it cost my [Italian] master for board and clothes, the total comes to less than fifty Rhenish gulden. What was spent on me beyond this was for food and drink when I was his [Fütterer's] servant. Dear cousin, deal with him as you think best in this matter, just do not relent until you get the money from him . . .

You write that you have sent another letter to me by messenger. I have noted on your [present] letter that this letter has not yet come. I do not know why.

God bless. Greet your wife, children, and the entire household warmly for me. Whatever pleases and serves you, I am always prepared to do. Dated as above.

      Michael Behaim, your willing cousin.

[P.S.] Also greet warmly my master [Stublinger]. I could not write to him now as the time has been too short . . .

8 ❧ Michael to Friederich, 29 June 1528

Praise be always to God, 29 June, 1528, in Breslau.

My friendly, devoted service. Dear, esteemed cousin, on 25 June a letter from you reached me by way of my master, Herr Stublinger, and I have read it. I am, first of all, pleased that you have received both bill and payment from Barthol Haller and have given him a receipt.[28] But that Erasmus Fütterer got involved in the transaction pleases me not at all. I

---

27. Stublinger evidently threatened termination of the agreement if the fee were not quickly paid.

28. This is Bartholomäus Haller von Hallerstein (d. 1536), after 1529 the imperial Bann- and Stadtrichter in Nuremberg. The nature of the transaction is unclear, but obviously it concerned money or property belonging to Michael.

am truly annoyed, as I will write to him now and say, so that he rightly understands me. Would you also tell him face to face what I am writing here? I ask you sincerely to stop him when you hear that he is paying other people [my money]. By right, money held in trust shall be privileged.[29] Would you threaten him with that? Would you also tell my brother Stephan to keep after Jacob Groland until he also collects the hundred gulden of my sister's held by the above-mentioned Fütterer, so that we are not some day disadvantaged by [not having] it? I am also writing to Stephan about this. It will be my fifth or sixth letter to him, although he does not write me so much as a syllable in response. I cannot tell whether he still considers me to be his brother or not. Would you tell him that? But inasmuch as he has written to me in the past, I will continue to write to him.

My dear cousin, know that on 23 June I returned from Bohemia and began my service here in God's name. May almighty God grant me good fortune in this undertaking. Amen. While I was in Bohemia, I had to pay ten Bohemian groschen a week for room and board [that is] for food, drink, bed, laundry, and whatever else I needed. But I was with my first host for only three weeks and had to pay him no more than six groschen a week. Thereafter, I moved two miles away to a village because my boarding-house keeper had to go to Moravia, and there was no one in the house except his aged mother and a maid. I calculate that I have been in Bohemia for twenty-nine weeks. Nevertheless, I will converse here on occasion with a Bohemian, for it is not always possible for one to learn such a difficult language well in so short a time.

Dear cousin, I ask you for my sake to arrange with Herr Stublinger for me to buy my own clothes. When it is left to the masters to do so, they never provide one with everything one needs. You should not worry that I will buy expensive clothing for myself. I only want to be clothed as the other merchants' apprentices are. I am the only one here who must run to a master whenever I need a pair of shoes or a handkerchief or want to have my purse or my trousers mended. I do not like to do this, and it also makes no sense. Today one needs trousers, tomorrow a shirt or other things, and the masters do not always have the time to be dealing with such matters, so they become indignant when one asks for something two or three times. Also, I now have nothing worth wearing. I have not had a single article of clothing made for myself, not a pair of trousers or a jacket, absolutely nothing at all, since I moved here from Nuremberg.

29. "Rechtz nach solt pillich dass vormundgelt zuvor gen."

I am most in need of a coat, trousers, a jacket, and a cap. So, dear cousin, I ask you to write and instruct Herr Stublinger that I will henceforth clothe myself and that you will work out an arrangement with him on the clothes I buy.

My master has asked me to send his greetings to you and cousin[30] and to ask that you let him know at the earliest how things are going in his Nuremberg house. He would also like to know how things stand in Fischbach. I expect he will not soon return there. When you write to him about these matters, please also inform him that I will henceforth buy my own clothes . . .

I also left my notebook behind on the high shelf by the larder. In it is written the date I moved out of Milan and other information.[31]

Would you send me [my] small sheathed knife? The sheath has a silver chain, together with the knife. I need it here in the shop.

Would you tell [Er]asmus F[ütterer] to consider letting my clothes be sent to me with the goods of other merchants? I do believe one must wait a long time before he will let goods come from Italy.

God bless. Greet cousin for me. Make the best [of this letter], written in haste. I will have more to write you at another time.

Michael Behaim, your willing cousin.

9 ❦ Michael to Friederich, 31 August 1528

Praise be always to God, 31 August, 1528, in Breslau.

My devoted service, dear, esteemed, gracious cousin. In recent days a letter from you has reached me by way of little Michael, the messenger, who also delivered my rapier and notebook. I also happily learn from your letter that you, my dear cousin, and all of yours are well.

I have sent a letter to you by the above-mentioned messenger sincerely asking you as my dear, friendly cousin, to write to my master . . . and tell him to let me buy my own clothes.[32] I can see clearly how it is going to be for me, if it is left up to him to do so. Today I still must wear the old

---

30. "Dye muemen," that is, Friederich's wife, Michael's cousin. Mueme here connotes a close female relative, not Michael's aunt. Stublinger is now resident in Breslau.
31. Information pertaining to the case against Fütterer in the dispute over expenses.
32. The letter of 29 June, which Friederich either had not received or was not responding to because he disagreed with Michael at the time on the matter of buying his own clothes.

coat I brought with me from Nuremberg. Except for a pair of trousers and a jacket, he has permitted me to have no clothes made. Had my calves and thighs not begun to show through the old trousers I have worn since I arrived, I believe he would have left me to this day without a new pair. [As I now have only one pair of trousers], when I need to have them mended, I must now, if I may speak frankly, go about the streets bare-legged until they are sewn. I cannot and I will not tolerate the way I am being treated here. In Bohemia, I denied myself [everything]. I did not so much as have a vest made. All the time I was there I thought to myself that I would want for nothing, once I had joined Herr Stublinger [in Breslau]. Had I known then what awaited me here, I would have written you about it long ago, and I would not have pledged myself to him in the manner I have done. As you well know, I must give him so much money, twenty-five Rhenish gulden every year, and still he forces me to sit at the common table, where none of his previous apprentices ever had to eat, nor ever wanted to eat.

On the other hand, dear cousin, I do not want to withhold from you the obvious good opinion other friends and merchants here have of me. Since Hans Rappolt has gone to Frankfurt, and Herr Stublinger is in Liegnitz, I am here alone helping run the shop with another man who works for Hans Rappolt when he is away. As I have come to understand it, Herr Stublinger's business is one of barter and exchange.[33] Were it not for Hans Rappolt's skill in accounting, he might be described as a completely incompetent businessman. The two need one another. That is why I believe they will never break up. Hans Rappolt may only be Herr Stublinger's servant, but, believe me, as long as he lives, Herr Stublinger will never let him go. And this makes me worry that Hans Rappolt will not teach me all that he can. He is now almost forty years old and as he gets older, he will surely think about keeping his position. He surely knows that Hans Stublinger is not going to let him go, if there is no one who is qualified to take his place. So I worry that he will barely teach me all the things a merchant should know. I have been told this by others who know more about Herr Stublinger's business than I do.

So dear cousin, I ask you to consider my situation, for I am paying too much money to be treated as I am. And should I be taught nothing during the years I am here, it will truly do me great harm. I have learned about a servant of Herr Stublinger's, a man named Hans Klein, who was with Stublinger in Nuremberg and then here in Hans Rappolt's position before

33. "Tauschen und vertauschen."

Rappolt joined Stublinger. After Rappolt's arrival, Hans had to move [back] to Nuremberg with Stublinger and there became his household servant. Dear cousin, I worry that the same thing might happen to me. For I have been told that no servant of Stublinger's has advanced any higher in his business [than where he first began]. I can well believe that he has taken me for no other purpose than to run errands for him, sweep out the shop, care for Hans Rappolt's horse, clean his armor, and the like. So that I have enough to do in the shop throughout the day in winter, I must stoke the fire in Hans Rappolt's room. It is customary here for the house servant, not the maids, to tend the fire, so I do not resent having to do it. I want to do everything gladly, [but I do expect] to be instructed [in return]. So I will endure this for a year, but when the year is up, I want to be taken along to market where deals are made,[34] and to go to Frankfurt, as was discussed earlier, although not [yet] put into writing. Would you tell Herr Stublinger this when you talk with him? If I am [properly] instructed, I would hope to God in time to advance. But Herr Rappolt is such a strange man. He has not spoken a word to me now in two days. I hope you will know how to set everything right here. I ask only that you write Herr Stublinger at the earliest. If you do not want to write directly to him, then write [such a letter] to me. I will then let him read it [so that he knows that it] is also your wish that he allow me to clothe myself as I please.

I will tell you the reason why I want to clothe myself. First, when one here needs shoes, socks, caps, handkerchiefs, or money to pay the tailor for [mending] one's clothes or for other such little things, one must ask two or three times before they will give one anything, and I do not like to go through that. Then, if one tears his trousers, they do not permit them to be mended until one can no longer wear them. Then people here say that a person with such trousers is lazy and will not mend his own trousers and clothes. But should I try to do all this mending out of my own pocket, it would certainly be a goodly sum and the year would sooner come to an end.[35] But I will not do it. Might you see if you can withhold for my clothes the ten gulden I now have to give Herr Stublinger in addition to the two hundred gulden [apprentice fee]? If he does not agree, just stay after him, and he will come around. If not, then just do the best you can with him. But I expect him to permit it. There is truly no need to worry that I will clothe myself extravagantly. My only wish is

34. "Zu einem kauff . . . wo kauffschleg gemacht werden."
35. In other words, it is impossible.

that I not suffer want and have to go about in public wearing tattered clothes.

Dear cousin, you write that Erasmus Fütterer has not yet handed over the two hundred gulden you demanded he give you with interest. [You say that] he has answered that he will be shown to have little obligation to give me anything, as he will write to me himself and say, also that he will provide you an accounting. When he does so, please send it directly to me. And do have him write to me. I will certainly answer his statement that he now has little obligation to me. I would like to know if he can still find fools [such as I], who will be his servant, pay [their own] expenses, clothe themselves, give him wages, be a household servant, run errands for him on the street dressed in tattered clothes [and looking], if I may say so, like a pig, and he shall still say thereafter that one owes him money? You may certainly tell him that he does not find this written on his doctor's degree. Had he been all this time at the university studying [the matter], I expect he would [still] not be able to discover the money [he owes me] . . .

I have nothing more except to commend you to God's care. Greet your wife, my dear cousin, and all the servants, also Frau Albrecht Letscher and all good friends and relatives.[36] I am [still] very surprised that my brother Stephan has not written a syllable to me since I left Nuremberg. [Meanwhile], I have written him five or six letters. I cannot imagine why he does [not write]. Reproach him for it.

I ask you kindly to send me the small knife about which I wrote you before. It is in the trunk with the other weapons I [inherited] from [my] late [uncle] M[ichael] B[ehaim]. I truly need it here in the shop. Dated as above.

Michael Behaim, always your willing servant.

10 ❦ Michael to Friederich, 1 November 1528

Praise be always to God, 1 November, 1528, in the year of the Lord, in Breslau.

My humble and devoted service, dear, esteemed cousin. I recently sent a letter to you with Hans Stublinger. I hope it was safely delivered and without delay. . . . I am still awaiting your answer, and I ask you again to let me know something soon, for I cannot go on like this any longer. I

36. Frau Letscher is Friederich's sister, Lucia.

Letter from Michael to Friederich, 1 November 1528 (letter 10)

now appear in public dressed not as a merchant's apprentice, but as a beggar and a clown. Once again, I am awaiting the return of Hans Rappolt, for Herr Stublinger has promised that he will provide clothes for me as soon as he returns. He was just here for ten days, however, and my needs did not trouble him. He left me in the same condition I have been in since I moved here from Nuremberg. He is now back in Cracow and not expected to return for perhaps two or more weeks. So, again, I must make do for as long as he is away. I want you to know that the clothes that are now on my back are the clothes I brought with me [from Nuremberg]. Apart from these, I have only a pair of leather trousers and a barchent jacket from my master. Already the jacket is torn. Winter is approaching and I am beginning to freeze. I cannot tolerate the cold well, and there is not a day when I could not end up completely naked. But this will not happen as long as I have an alternative. Before I remain any longer with Herr Stublinger under such conditions, think well about the way I have been treated so far. I would rather do work that causes the blood to run from the nails of my hands and my feet and travel from place to place as a forgotten person, never again, life long, to return home, than to have a master who may clothe me [as he pleases] and make me feed where no apprentice of his has ever wanted to feed. I simply will not take it. If Herr Stublinger refuses to let me buy my own clothes, reproach him with all this. Ask him why he does not treat me like his other servants, whom he must pay. I will pass over the fact that I have to pay him wages.[37]

So at this hour, I will *revoke* my agreement with him, and it shall remain revoked so long as my grievances are not redressed. For how shall I ever learn anything and conduct any business with merchants, when I must go about dressed like a fool, which may please my master? God forbid that I should be silent about it and continue to waste my money on a useless [apprenticeship]. When I have served out my time here, I will be just as much an apprentice as when I first began. And in addition his business does not at all please me. Hans Rappolt himself tells me that his father has been a successful merchant and never served an apprentice-

37. Michael mentions three payments to Stublinger: the apprentice fee of two hundred gulden; ten gulden a year for board (which Michael wants returned to him to buy his own clothes); and an unspecified fee of twenty-five gulden a year, mentioned only once (letter 9). This was apparently a payment in lieu of the apprentice fee, still unpaid. It is not mentioned in Michael's summary of his contract with Stublinger. See letter 13.

ship. You may well know of such examples in Nuremberg. So I ask you
to talk to Herr Stublinger, but not to tolerate his arrogance, for the more
kind words he hears, the more justification he will have [in his own mind
for treating me as he does].

Make the best of this letter. I am turning to you in trust. Please take
what I have written to heart. You need not worry that I will be unable
to find a good master elsewhere, one whose business provides a more
useful apprenticeship than Herr Stublinger's. As I have written to you
before, should I find myself without a master, I am confident that, with
God's help and a little money, I can support myself honestly and honorably.

As far as I can judge from the time I have spent here observing and
learning as much as I could about my master's business, there is little
profit in it. But he has enough [inheritance] from his father [to keep it
going]. He makes a profit of eight to ten gulden per hundred, and that
gets him by. You may yourself have noticed that he is no great merchant,
nor does he let his business trouble him. He turns all his affairs over to
Hans Rappolt alone. I expect that Hans Rappolt will not stay with him
for long. I truly worry that he will one day simply leave the business
altogether[38] . . .

Greet my dear cousin, your wife, and the entire household. And would
you let me know if [Michael] promptly delivered my last letter to you?
God bless. Would you urge Erasmus Fütterer to write me and to send
his accounting [of expenditures]? Dated as above.

Michael Behaim, your willing cousin.

11   🐝   Michael to Friederich, undated fragment
[between 1 November and 10 December 1528][39]

Dear, esteemed, gracious cousin, I have this hour had a falling out with
my lord's [housekeeper]. There are many reasons for it, for which I am
not responsible. My lord, Hans Rappolt, is not here; he is away from

38. Earlier Michael was convinced that Rappolt neither would nor could leave Stublinger. See letter 9.
39. The German Museum has placed this fragment in the summer of 1532, but it better
fits the circumstances of late 1528. As the fragment makes clear, Stublinger has not yet
been paid the apprentice fee of two hundred gulden which he definitely had in hand
in 1532.

Breslau and I am not safe here with [his housekeeper]. He chased me with a knife. So I have found another place to stay until Hans Rappolt returns. But I fear that my masters will continue to treat me as they have in the past. If they do so, I will not stand still for it. I have told you this so that you will know not to give Herr Stublinger a single heller on my behalf until we have straightened things out.

Michael Behaim, always y[our] willing and o[bedient] cousin.

12 ❦ Michael to Friederich, 10 December 1528

Praise be always to God, 10 December, 1528, in Breslau.

My devoted service, dear, esteemed cousin. My letter is written in haste. I received your long letter the day before yesterday, together with Herr Fütterer's record [of expenditures]. In your letter you take exception on several counts, for the best, and I have made the best of your letter. It is not convenient to answer you now, for time will not permit it. But at the first opportunity, I will take up each of my demands again in the form I originally intended them and as I have written to Herr Fütterer about them. I think I have acted only after the most careful consideration. I have also recently sent you, unsealed, a letter for Hans Stublinger, which you should read, seal, and deliver to him. Therein you will perhaps have found all my demands [sufficiently discussed].

I am herewith writing to tell you again that I intend to clothe myself at my own expense and pleasure. You write that Herr Stublinger says again that he has instructed Herr Rappolt [etc.]. This is a very long-standing instruction, and what good has it ever done me? He gives you these good words in Nuremberg so that you will believe him [and drop the matter] . . .

I believe that as long as you are writing to me about these matters, I shall and must continue to suffer. And it is all because . . . you believe everything he says. But my Lord God knows how I have suffered since I moved here from Nuremberg and He knows that I have suffered enough. Although you do not believe me, I cannot go on. I must now leave the matter to God. Should I die today or tomorrow, I will in any case have suffered enough.

You also write that you have already deposited one hundred gulden with Herr Stublinger, when I have always asked you not to give him any money. He himself has meanwhile written to me (his letter is dated 20 November) to say that you have not given him a heller or a pfennig on my behalf as of the hour of his writing. So I do not know whether, over my sincere and oft-made plea, you have gone ahead and given him money or not. If you have done so, I am truly displeased. Since he has not kept our agreement for over a half year now, the agreement may properly be revoked, as it has been, just as my masters might also have revoked it, had I failed to please them. Since I have honestly maintained my part of the agreement . . . , I always expected you to believe me and come to my aid, not to be deceived by Stublinger's beautiful words.

Because I receive no relief . . . and the matter is not being resolved as I desire . . . , before I continue any longer with him under such circumstances, I will flee and no one will ever hear of me again, and I shall never my life long return to Nuremberg. Never did I think it would come to this. But it is clear to me that after I have served out my time and done all his bidding, he will not have paid me as much for my services during these years as I must pay him. So I prefer to do the best I can on my own and see if I can find other, good merchants to serve, wherever I must go to do so, and stop wasting my money here. Ask yourself, if you will, why trade here is no longer what it used to be. Also, it is not the custom here for a merchant's servant to pay his master a salary, whether he be small or large and can do nothing at all. It has never [before] been thought here that one should give money to masters, as I now do.[40] Here one does not [as elsewhere] take an apprentice from Nuremberg and send him to France or Italy at his master's expense to learn a language and leave him free in all things and give him responsibility for the accounts, the shop, and the merchandise, and take or send him back and forth to the fairs, where he can learn something and become somebody.[41]

Trade is now truly bad here and no longer what it was. I forget what I learned all my days in Italy and [the seven months] in Bohemia. I can now do just about as much as I could when I first arrived here. You may be asking yourself how much one can learn in a mere half-year. Had I been [in Bohemia] for a full year or for a year and a half, I could have learned the language well enough not to have forgotten it so easily.

Dear cousin, do not take my letter the wrong way. Consider what is

---

40. Michael must mean the ten gulden a year he contributes to his board and clothes and his having to pay his own expenses when he travels. See letter 13. A basic apprentice fee was not uncommon.
41. "Zu was komenn."

useful to me. I will answer your letter fully at the first opportunity. God bless. Greet all good friends and relations. Dated as above. Make the best of this; written in great haste.

Michael Behaim, your willing cousin.

13 ❦ Michael to Friederich, 3 December 1528

Dear, esteemed Herr Hans Rappolt.[42] You have asked to know how I want to conduct my apprenticeship. I pledged myself to Herr Stublinger in Nuremberg, and we have a written agreement in which all obligations are set forth, namely, that I shall render to Herr Stublinger two hundred Rhenish gulden, which he may use for his own profit. In addition, I shall give him ten Rhenish gulden each year for my board. Further, I shall be bound to him for three years, and beyond this I shall spend a half-year in Bohemia at my own expense, which has already occurred, as I have been there for thirty weeks. Moreover, Herr Hans Stublinger shall be obligated to provide all the clothes I need during these three years.

Since entering my service, I have been seated at the common table, where none of your apprentices has wanted to eat.[43] Surely you know how things are at that table, so I need not comment further. But so that you do not think that I am the only one who complains about such things, you may also ask the other servants about what passes over our table. And as so many of us sit there, the soup tureen is empty before one can wipe his mouth.

Since I shall be giving [Herr Stublinger] money for my clothes, I wish to clothe myself as I please. Now, as previously, I am in need of everything: shirts, a lined coat for winter, a plain one for summer, trousers, and a jacket, and a cap and shoes to go with them.

If it does not please my lords [to buy these clothes], then let me clothe myself at my own expense. According to the agreement I have signed, I willingly render two hundred gulden to my lords for their use.[44] But I want them to surrender to me the other ten gulden I shall be paying

42. Michael here shares with Friederich a copy of his letter to Rappolt and Stublinger in which he states his "final demands" to his lords.
43. Michael considers the servants to be of a lesser breed than the Behaims from Nuremberg. But see his later remarks to Paul Behaim in letter 45.
44. As of the writing of this letter this had not been paid to Stublinger.

them in addition. With that money I will clothe myself in all that I need at my own expense. It is well within your power to allow this.

But that I should now return to the house and eat with the household servants, and pay my money to do so, that I am no longer willing to do. That was not in the agreement we made in Nuremberg and it is contrary to it. If you want to enter a contract with Gregor Herberg for my board, you may do so, provided one does not also buy me a bed.[45] [For my part] I will neglect nothing, absolutely nothing, when I do my chores in the shop or in the office. When you see me doing something unreasonable, you may freely point it out to me. I will obey you at all times, and look on you as on my own father. And whenever I can be helpful to you, I am always willing to do so.

But I will not tolerate being struck or put in the stocks by Herr Nicklaus Utzman.[46] Recently, he threatened to strike me and twice he chased me down the hall. All the servants can attest to this. In addition, he threatened to have me locked with both legs in the stocks, and without consulting you about it. I will sweep out his room and stoke his fire, but should he have the power to do such things to me, then I will have become his servant [rather than yours].

There you have all my demands. If something is lacking, you may let me know. Do share all of this with Herr Stublinger. If these changes are not made, I will not remain with him any longer. But I will do what pleases and serves you. You should expect that from me at all times. Dated 3 December, 1528.

Michael Behaim, your willing servant

[P.S.] It is also my wish that what one here spends on me and lends me be repaid, and always with gratitude.

45. Michael apparently means to say that he is happy to remain in the new lodging he took during Rappolt's absence (see letter 11), while taking his board elsewhere. What he will not do under present circumstances is to have his room and board again with Rappolt and Stublinger.
46. The housekeeper who chased him with a knife. See letter 11.

Friederich was slow to comment on Michael's complaints about Stublinger, and when he did he took Stublinger's side, accusing Michael of presumption and impatience. Michael's impassioned rebuttal, eight manuscript pages long, portrays Friederich as both disloyal and naïve. How could he doubt his reasoned and persistent complaints? How could he fail to see through Stublinger?

Michael could never have been secure enough, and he now had many reasons to fret. In addition to the continuing conflict with his mother and stepfather, his relationship with his brother was also failing badly. Erasmus Fütterer continued more defiantly than ever to thwart his efforts to retrieve the residue of his Milan apprentice fee. Michael also sought in vain to find his sister a home in Nuremberg. Margaretha had not managed well with her stepfather, and at twenty-three she chose to leave her mother rather than move with her to Oscheling in Bohemia, her stepfather's home. She shared her unhappiness with Michael, as she sought his help in leaving the aristocracy and finding service in a burgher household in Nuremberg. Her stepfather might reasonably have expected her to be properly married by this time (twenty-three was the age at which women in Nuremberg could legally marry without permission from their parents), a concern Michael also shared. With Michael's assistance Margaretha finally came into Friederich's home, where she remained until her marriage in 1535 (at twenty-nine) to Joachim Camerarius.

Given these pressures, Friederich's siding with Stublinger proved to be the last straw. These same circumstances also help explain Michael's blundering with his cousin Jacob Groland,[47] who was among those assisting him in his efforts against Erasmus Fütterer. Groland also managed 360 gulden of Michael's inheritance. As early as October 1527 Michael had wanted Groland to sign an agreement that contained ironclad assurances regarding this money.[48] Perceiving both insult and aggravation for Groland in such a request, Friederich ignored it. But Michael persisted; by 1529 he was eighteen, the age at which a male in Nuremberg could legally in-

---

47. Groland's mother, like Michael's, was an Ortolph, although from a different branch of that family.
48. See letter 4.

herit, and he wanted to put his affairs in order.[49] He finally wrote directly to Groland, demanding that he sign an agreement setting limits on the share of earnings Groland could take for his own use as the trustee of five hundred gulden he administered for Michael and his sister (ostensibly Michael's 360 plus 140 of Margaretha's). The reaction to Michael's suggestion that his cousin Groland might be a greedy manager of his modest estate gave Michael a painful lesson in family relationships and trust.

14 🦚 Michael to Friederich, 7 January 1529

Praise be always to God, A.D. 1529, 7 January, in Breslau.

Sincere, devoted, and willing service, dear, esteemed, gracious cousin, and a good and happy new year to you, your dear wife, your children, and all members of your household. Your last letter, together with Herr Fütterer's accounting [of expenditures], arrived some time ago. I have been unable to answer it until now. Here are my views on the pressing matters.

First, you write me [only] after I have complained to you many times about the improper treatment I have received and still receive from my masters. Now that you have talked with Herr Stublinger about my complaints, I can see clearly from your letter how sweetly he has answered you, and led you to believe only the best about my situation here. You write that he was amazed that I had complained to you about him, especially after we had parted in Breslau in such great friendship, and he had promised me so many things upon Hans Rappolt's return from Frankfurt: a lined coat, a pair of trousers, a jacket, all to be newly made for me.

This is all true. He has promised me much upon Hans Rappolt's return. But if he really intended to have some clothes made for me, then after I am his servant and pledged to him, and he sees me with his own eyes suffering and in need, and I go and complain directly to him about it, and it is always his will to provide me with the clothes I need, then why has he not done so himself rather than order me to wait and delay further until Hans Rappolt returns? I have written to you and Herr Stublinger

49. Margaretha, who was older, had to wait until her marriage before she gained her inheritance, which Friederich continued to oversee for her, as he did also for Michael.

often enough about this. I thought the matter would by now long ago have been settled between you.

So although to this day I have received no clear answer and do not know where I stand, I have nonetheless gone ahead and ordered a pair of trousers and a jacket made for myself on credit. Whether I or my masters will pay for them, I really do not know. Now that it has become so terribly cold here, I also cannot manage any longer with my old coat, so this week I picked out fabric for a new coat and left it off with the tailor. The cold has already taken its toll on me. There are pussy boils all over my body and I can hardly walk or stand. To my great good fortune Hans Rappolt has gone off to Leipzig. Were he here, I do not know how I would cope with my painful chores. If my present condition persists, I believe I must die soon. But let God's will be done, for it must always be as He wills. Since no one will recognize my misery, there is nothing else for me to do.

Since you have been unable to get Herr Stublinger so much as to allow me to clothe myself at my own expense, so that I no longer suffer want and can begin to move about a bit in public again, I have written directly to him myself. He has given me no other answer than that he does not want me to go naked. At this point the Devil reminds me that I have also not gone naked until now, and yet I have suffered great cold and other miseries. No dog goes naked either. Herr Stublinger just wants to hide the fact that [to all intents and purposes] he already lets me go naked.

But enough has been said about this. I wrote you of my final demands in my last letter [which I sent] along with [my letter to] Hans Rappolt. I assume you have read that letter, which was sent unsealed, and that you have since delivered it to [Herr Stublinger]. Herr Rappolt has also sent him a [separate] note on which I have indicated everything I want.[50] If my grievances are not redressed as I desire, I will not remain any longer with Herr Stublinger. For I cannot bear it, although you write me that I should and must. I understand that there must be some suffering [in an apprenticeship], but even a donkey brays under too great a load. It is not true, as [Herr Stublinger] has said in urging you to write me, that I have fallen prey to some evil gossip mongers here. What really annoys him is that I am telling the truth. That is why he now accuses me of lying. I certainly

50. See letter 13, of which both Friederich and Rappolt received copies. As was customary with Michael's communications with his masters, Friederich read it first before it was sent on to Stublinger. Rappolt apparently sent still another summary of Michael's demands to Stublinger.

will respond to the hateful letter he has written me. Had I, God forbid, faithlessly sold all his goods or handled them improperly, what he now writes me might be fitting. Amazed by his letter, I let Hans Rappolt read it. He told me not to be troubled by it and to pay no attention to his lunatic mind, and otherwise to conduct myself honestly. But I will do so only if I am also treated honestly in return.

You write that you had not expected me to become so impatient and to want to fly before I had wings. You also point out that I have been here hardly half a year and that one will not always have the complaints one has at the beginning [of an apprenticeship]. Believe me, had I not thought the same thing myself and believed that with the passage of time I would receive better treatment than I got at the start, I would not have served a quarter-hour in my present position. I do not want everything simply given to me from the start. And even if I did, I realize that it would do me no good. I desire only one thing: fairness and what is right.[51] I know in your heart that you too want this for me and that my success pleases you. I fancy nothing for myself beyond what is right and fair. That you can see clearly in my letters.

You write that I might just as well have left you out [of this dispute]. Be assured, dear cousin, that had I known before what I know now, I would have bothered neither you nor my master with this apprentice-ship. But ask yourself this: if your own son were in some place paying his money for his maintenance, as I must pay my masters, and his board, bed, clothing, etc. were being provided [as poorly] as mine, and he wrote to you complaining about it, would you not go to his aid? This is all I am asking. I am turning to you as to my father, expecting every good thing from you and hoping for your assistance. In time I will be able to repay you and yours with my humble service. Someday, with God's help, you will see that all the promises I have made to you in Nuremberg and elsewhere are honestly kept. So I turn to you now in my need . . .

I see that the wine merchant has asked you for the ten gulden [I owe him] now that one of his daughters has gotten married. Would you try to have payment deferred until God helps me return to Nuremberg? If not, handle it as you see fit. It is, however, my will that the furrier, Conrad Sporl, the selfsame scoundrel, be given not a heller or a pfennig, regard-less of his reaction.

You also write that Martin Behaim is still owed fifty Rhenish gulden, a

51. "Dye billigkeyt/was Recht ist."

debt I am well aware of.[52] My friendly request is that you not mention this to many people so that he is not reminded of it. I hope in time to make a profit from this money, and I need it just as much as he does. I also know that you favor me before others [in this matter].

I also received with your letter Herr Fütterer's accounting [of expenditures] and have read it over carefully. I am herewith writing him my reaction. It is an accurate account, only I [still] refuse to pay the expenses he incurred while I lived in his [Nuremberg] house. You may certainly tell him that. He estimates that I was in his service no more than three months, but there was not one hour in those three months when I neglected any matter of his. I know well that I have served him diligently and maintained his merchandise and kept his goods as safe and secure as they would have been had he paid a servant a hundred gulden a year to do so. He emphatically reminds me of the friendship he and his parents showed me, and he says that I was a lot of trouble and work for them. He also claims to have lent me a lot of money without any interest and always to have given me my part of what was due him for my maintenance. With many other such sly phrases,[53] he makes me out to be a complete fool. I hope I know well how to answer him. But would you first send me right away another copy of his list of expenditures? I have misplaced mine and it is impossible to know if or when it will turn up again, although I still have the contents more or less in my head. I also ask you sincerely to give him no more money on my behalf than what he has actually paid out for clothing and for my master's boarding fee [in Milan]. I will not make good on a heller of the expenses he incurred while I was in his household, because during that time I was constantly at his service and had to do everything one told me to do, even though he had already arranged for me to enter the service of a new master in Milan and had shown me friendship. It stands [written in our agreement] that should he also one day have children, I will treat them as is fitting and proper, and that as I have fared at his hands, so they will fare at mine. You might remind him of this. If he does not respond fairly, deal with him as harshly as you can. It is not my will to have been his servant in

52. This is Michael's first cousin, Martin III Behaim, the son of Michael II, who was stationed at the Portuguese court. In 1519 he visited Nuremberg to honor his famous father, the creator of the "globe apple," the first spherical representation of the earth. What Michael owed him is unclear. The intrigue with Friederich to postpone payment is in any event revealing of their relationship.
53. "Docktorischen wortenn." A play on Fütterer's doctor's degree. See letter 9.

vain. Moreover, he should also have bought all my clothes with the money [we gave him]. Also, when I sometimes failed to please him or neglected some service of his, he always struck me for it. How dare he now say that I was not in his service! I expect you will know best how to deal with him.

Dear, esteemed cousin, you accuse me of having written Herr Fütterer a letter in which I attack you and which I should have sent directly to you. After you have written to him, I ask you to reread the copy of my letter to him, which you now have, and listen carefully to what it says.[54] It is true that I wrote [directly] to Fütterer. I meant to tell him that he should not have kept my two hundred gulden so long after we had given him notice and informed his brother of my great need of this money as I entered the service of my [new] master. Also, they promised to give us the money and the promise was not kept. This promise was also made to my master, as he required. I did not want Herr Fütterer to think that he could continue to withhold money from me, so I wrote to him that I wanted my money soon, that he plan to deliver it to you, and that he not stall any longer with talk. You yourself wrote me that you had demanded the money from him as soon as he arrived in Nuremberg, and that he had promised to give it to you on Laetare Sunday, only then to tell you when the time came that he did not have it. It was at this point that I decided to write to him directly and tell him that I did not need such [double] talk from him and that he would not find me still to be the fool he knew when I was with him in Milan. In short, I told him I wanted my money in my own hands and that I knew well enough myself how to put it to use. I also told him that I would not do as my brother, who all his life has passively followed [the advice of] his relatives, namely Michael Behaim,[55] Ulrich Fütterer, and Jacob Groland. You clearly see today what they have made of him as he loiters around Nuremberg. Had these relatives of ours, having seen correctly that he was not cut out for the university,[56] rather put him in a trade, had him learn a [foreign] language, and serve a master as I now do, thanks to you, then he would owe them lifelong gratitude. If, during his youth, he could have been

54. This letter is not extant.
55. Apparently Michael IV Behaim.
56. "Zu studieren." Stephan had apparently attended school unsuccessfully. See letter 19. Michael appears nonetheless to have resented the opportunity Stephan had and the obvious indulgence he enjoyed as the elder son.

placed in your hands rather than in theirs, as poor as I am, I would have pledged a hundred gulden to it. I know that my brother still can speak of you only with gratitude, never with complaint, and the same is true of me. I can say on his behalf that you have been a true friend to us all. I also know that had it not been for you, he would have loitered for a long time before anyone ever challenged him about it. For this, we can never repay you.

Dear, esteemed cousin, I ask you again, as friend and family, to read my letter to Herr Fütterer carefully and see in it the true text and original intention of my words. Do not let Dr. E[rasmus] Fütterer interpret my letter for you in any way he sees fit, for this time he has not given you a true version. Although he has studied for a long time and fancies he can do everything, he cannot any more than I. He has certainly failed with this text. Still, I would never have believed him capable of wanting to discredit me with you. Had I, God forbid, [turned against you] as he claims, I would then have placed all my trust in him, which I never in my life have done. I am truly pleased that he has let you read my entire letter so that you can draw your own conclusions about what I meant. Since, however, you have understood from him that I am demanding all that is mine from you, and [claiming] that I know [best] how to put it to use, you may well be wondering how I plan to proceed. I have often written to you that were I not with my present masters, I could, with a little money, support myself on my own until the Lord God helped me find something. When I wrote to Herr Fütterer and demanded what was mine, I meant the two hundred gulden he owes me and still must pay me. When [I say that] I know how to spend what is mine, I hope you will not reproach me for it. I admit that I overstated myself a bit in my letter to him, but I did so to make him a little more fearful about with-holding from me what is mine. Had I known that such [misunderstand-ing] would result [between us], I might have omitted several statements from the letter, namely that my relatives must give me what is mine when I want it, that I will not let myself be the fool my brother has been, etc.

You write that you also want me to have what is mine when I want it and that, God willing, you intend to give me a good accounting [of your stewardship] so that I will have no doubts about it. Truly you need not think that I have said or written this [to Herr Fütterer] out of anger [at you]. As mentioned above, I did it to pressure him to give me what is mine all the sooner. Had I not written so forcefully to him, I believe he still would not have written to me, nor have sent us the accounting [of his expenditures on my behalf]. I had previously written him more than ten politely worded letters without a single reply. But, believe me, I will never in my life forget this ploy to bring me into disfavor with you.

But enough of this. As for his accounting, everything is as he writes, only I refuse to pay the expenses [he incurred when I was in his house]. I also refuse to pay for the sequined jacket. I wore it perhaps six times, while he constantly had it on. Furthermore, he claims that the horse I rode to Milan sold for only nine Italian crowns there, when I know for a fact that it sold for ten. Also, when I left for Milan, I gave him two Nuremberg imperial gulden to keep for me, which I have never gotten back. He also lists a ducat that I [supposedly] received from the Welsers in Lugano, which is also not so, for I have borrowed no money from them. He cites eleven pounds, eleven shillings that I [supposedly] received in Feldkirchen from Jacob Pflom, which is, again, not true. Pflom did lend me one and a half gulden in Feldkirchen, but I repaid that loan to his wife in Nuremberg. Ambrosius Pizzo can attest to this. In sum, I received nothing more from him for my expenses after I moved from Milan to Nuremberg. I find in all no more than twenty-six pounds, thirteen shillings in Milan currency written down in my notebook. Apart from the aforementioned, I otherwise agree with his accounting of what has been spent on my behalf.

He also writes that he will calculate the profit he has made on my two hundred gulden for no more than three years. But this money was given to his brother over four years ago, and we are now in the fifth year. You will also know best how to deal with him in this matter.

I ask again that you have two letters written to Jörg Pock and sent to him by the first available messenger. There is a man here named Hans Holzbock. He will be coming to Nuremberg in about four weeks and, after Fastnacht, will be going on to Antwerp and then to Lisbon. You might seek him out when he arrives and write [to Pock] via him. I will also give him two letters. May almighty God make us strong in this.

I also ask you most sincerely to have Jacob Groland draw up an agreement, or some kind of formal assurance, regarding [the earnings on] the five hundred gulden he manages for me and my sister, stating that he may take no more than 5% in any one year [as his own profit]. If he wants to pay Mother a greater percentage [of the earnings], we have no objections. But inasmuch as we are all mortal, I want him, for my sake and for my sister's sake, to give us such assurance. What possible harm can such an agreement do? I asked you once before to approach him on this

matter, but I do not know whether you have done so or not. I have
encouraged my brother to look into these matters of mutual interest
while I am away from home, but I fear that he is so preoccupied that he
thinks neither of himself nor of me. I have also several times asked him
to send me the debenture regarding Poland, when he finds it.[57] While I
was in Nuremberg, he would not leave me in peace until I delivered to
him all [such legal] papers and letters, an entire trunk full. But now that
he has them, I believe he no longer thinks about these matters. Would
you have a talk with him? He has not written a syllable to me since I left
Nuremberg. I will also write Jacob Groland a note, but I ask you to implore him also. I expect he will do what I ask . . .

I also want to ask you sincerely to take my sister into your care so that
she might be honorably provided for. Would you do your best [to help
her]? She has just come from Mother and has been deprived of her noble
clothes.[58] She complained to me privately that it was not going well for
her at home. So would you look after her in her need? She is truly a good
person and very dear to me. I ask you very sincerely not to forsake her.
Perhaps you could talk with Frau Letscher or Frau Rotmund and see if
either might take her in for a while, at her own expense, if not otherwise.[59] My brother and I will promptly pay the cost from our own money
until one arranges an honorable companion for her[60] . . .

Do have a heart for us poor orphans, dear cousin, for truly we do not
know what shall become of us.

Greet your wife, my dear cousin, and all our good relations. Dated as
above.

Also, dear cousin, I am sending with this letter another for Herr Fütterer, which I would like for you to deliver to him personally. When he
opens it, ask him on the spot to show you the list of expenditures I have
enclosed indicating everything that was spent on me. Clearly you will

---

57. "Den schultbrief." This must be Michael's contract with Stublinger, or have something to do with it.
58. Margaretha, now twenty-three, had lived with her mother and noble stepfather, a
knight, in Nuremberg and Bohemia. She chose to leave her mother owing to unhappiness at home, most likely conflict with her stepfather. Because Nuremberg had strict
dress codes reflecting social class and encouraging social order, her decision also af-
fected how she dressed.
59. Frau Rotmund was Friederich's sister Catharina.
60. Marriage is meant, but this did not take place until 1535.

want to look it over carefully and make good only on what is found there. In brief, I do not agree to pay him any expenses [incurred when I was in his house].

Michael Behaim, your willing cousin.

15 ❦ Michael to Friederich, 11 February 1529

Praise be always to God, in the year of our Lord, 11 February, 1529, in Breslau.

My friendly and willing service, dear, esteemed cousin. I am writing only because a letter recently arrived from you and Herr Stublinger with the happy news of the resolution of our dispute. I can see clearly from your letter that you have made a very great effort on my behalf, some of which you might have spared yourself, had you said [earlier] that you would not permit me to be with Stublinger under such conditions. Then, he would have done all the things he should. But since the matter is now settled, I do thank you very sincerely for what you have done, and I hope now to be able to bear up here better than before. I will be as frugal and subdued as possible when I buy my clothes. My one request is that you have my effects, which should arrive from Milan in two leather trunks, sent on to me here at the first opportunity. Also, the coat I wore home to Nuremberg.

My master writes that I should ask you to give him now the two hundred gulden [he requires]. Would you please do so? He writes in the same paragraph that my three years of service with him shall commence only when you deposit this money with him. To my mind, it is not fair that the time I have served with him up to now is counted for nothing. Had he dealt honestly with me, that money would long ago have been in his possession, as I myself will now write to him and say. I do intend to do as he wishes, but I hope he will appreciate my side and not make so much out of such a small matter. If when my time with him is up, he should desire that I continue to serve him for an additional half year, I would not deny him. But that I should now be obligated to do so [in this way] is, to me, unfair. I recall nothing that I failed to do for him during this time.

May almighty God now grant both me and my masters a happy apprenticeship. Amen.

Since I moved here from Nuremberg, my masters have lent me cash to pay my boarding-house keeper in Bohemia and to take care of my other needs while I was there. I have received a total of seventeen gulden [with interest calculated] at fifteen batzen. Would you reimburse my masters that amount? Otherwise, I still owe the clothier, the tailor, and the cobbler. I have not yet gotten their bills nor have I paid them anything. But I will get a good, detailed accounting from each, for I know well what is and is not to my advantage when it comes to spending money.

Also, dear cousin, know that in recent days I have had exceedingly great pain from boils and have placed myself in the care of the surgeon. I have also had to take purgatives at the apothecary's. For these services, I will owe between one and four gulden. But I can do nothing [for myself] when [only] God is caring for me. Therefore, would you ask Stublinger to instruct Hans Rappolt to lend me money when I need it? Then I can get help for myself when I most require it. Believe me when I say that not a heller will be spent in vain or without gain. I have never in my life liked to waste money and, God willing, I do not intend to do so now. Surely you yourself know what it is like to be in need of something in a foreign land and have no one to turn to for it. So, dear cousin, do your best to persuade Herr Stublinger to instruct Hans Rappolt on my behalf, so that I am not left wanting. As you will see, I continue to conduct myself honestly and, God willing, I will learn in time how to increase what is mine.

Know also, dear cousin, that were I not in Herr Stublinger's service, I could gain another master if only I had four hundred gulden to present him as an investment. He would commit an additional one thousand gulden and take me with him on his journey to Milan and Venice. Although he has been there three times before, he cannot speak the language. So he would pay me an exceedingly good wage for my services. But I would have to commit myself to him for four years. His [Italian] trade is such that one can become acquainted with all kinds of silks, headwear, spices, etc. I might well learn something from him. But I have told him that I cannot promise anything until I have served out my time with my present masters. I share this information with good intentions. I know that this man likes me very much.

God bless. Greet your wife and children, etc. Dated as above.

Michael Behaim, y[our] w[illing] c[ousin].

16 ❦ Michael to Friederich, Reminiscere 1529[61]

Praise be always to God, in the year of our Lord, 1529, in Breslau.

My obedient and willing service, dear, esteemed cousin. I am writing to let you know that last week I borrowed ten gulden at sixteen batzen in your name from a merchant named Adrian Steinmayr. I urgently needed this money to pay the medical bills I ran up during my illness. Please do not be annoyed with me for doing so. Had Hans Rappolt not been away at the time, there would have been no need whatsoever to have borrowed this money. But when God suddenly afflicts me, there is nothing else I can do. I point this out only to justify my action.

In my last letter I asked you to deposit two hundred gulden as soon as possible with my master Herr Stublinger, as my agreement with him requires. If the full amount cannot or may not be covered by my own funds, would you kindly lend me the outstanding balance, so that the agreement with Herr Stublinger may be fulfilled? What you lend would be paid back over time from my [earnings] . . .

Dear cousin, [may I ask you again to] send at the first opportunity the things I left behind in Milan? If they still have not arrived, convey my astonishment to Herr Fütterer. He wrote me three months ago that they had reached Cleves. Were that true, they could by now have traveled a hundred times to Nuremberg, as the journey from Cleves is no longer a dangerous one. Should I have new clothes made [before these arrive], it would be a pure waste of money. Also let me know Herr Fütterer's reaction to my record [of his expenditures on my behalf] and whether he now intends to give me the money that is left over.[62] If he is ignoring this matter, please call his attention to it.

Nothing more for now. May God be with us all. Amen. Greet your wife, my dear cousin. Also, Frau Letscher and Frau Rotmund, all your children, and our good friends. Dated Reminiscere, as above. In great haste.

Michael Behaim, your willing cousin.

61. Reminiscere is the fifth Sunday before Easter. The letter was written between 12 and 29 February.
62. By Michael's accounting Herr Fütterer could not have spent on legitimate expenses much more than fifty of the two hundred gulden in question.

17 🐝 Michael to Friederich, 29 February 1529

Praise be always to God, in the year of our Lord, 29 February, 1529, in Breslau.

My friendly, devoted service, dear, esteemed, gracious cousin. It is always a very great joy for me to learn that you, your wife, and children are well. I, too, praise God, am in good health. For a while, I had truly feared I would become very ill, but, thank God, I now expect to be spared. But God's will shall be done.

I expect you have already sent Adrian Steinmayr the ten gulden I received from him during my illness. Know that Hans Rappolt has now gone off to Frankfurt, and I am here alone managing my master's business. God willing, the annual Breslau fair is set to begin here on Laetere Sunday. I intend to manage well and conduct myself honestly and apply myself diligently, so that someday I might be in a position to help us both. If only I could have gone with the others to the markets in Frankfurt and Leipzig. There I could have met people and gotten to know them. If I can see how they buy goods, then the next time I will have a good idea how to sell to them. I am still hoping that my masters will someday send me to the Frankfurt and Leipzig fairs. Dear cousin, would you, perhaps in six months or so, mention this to Herr Stublinger? Then I might learn about his business there . . .

God bless. Greet your wife, Frau Letscher, and the children warmly for me. Dated as above.

Michael Behaim, your willing cousin.

18 🐝 Michael to Friederich, 22 March 1529

Praise be always to God, A.D. 22 March, 1529, in Breslau.

Friendly and willing service, dear, esteemed cousin. On 15 March, I received your letter and one from Jacob Groland, in which he rages at me. He is angry because I wrote to him that he should make a formal agreement with us about the money he holds [in trust] for me and my siblings. I can see clearly that I have only deeply insulted him and that he has little sympathy for me. He calls me a fool and even demands that I come to Nuremberg and release him [from any further obligations on my behalf]. He writes that my brother is a hundred times more clever than I. I concede this. It is true that I am a prize fool and have no understanding.[63] I have written back to him that were I as old as my brother and had studied for a long time at the university, perhaps I too would be cleverer than I am,[64] as you can read for yourself in my letter to the aforementioned Groland, which I am enclosing unsealed. After you have read it, if you do not think it is too strong, please seal it and have it delivered to him. I do not answer half the charges he makes against me. I also want you to read the letter he has written to me. Had I murdered one of his children, his response to my letter would be appropriate. I have, in truth, written to him amicably and calmly. But enough of this. I ask only that you seal the letter and deliver it to him. He has written me expecting an answer.

I gather from you that my clothes still have not arrived [from Milan] . . . Herr Fütterer long ago told me they had already reached Cleves. Were that true, they could by now have made the journey to Nuremberg twenty times . . .[65]

Know, dear cousin, that on two successive evenings, March 16 and 17, around 5:00, a most terrifying sign has been seen by many people in the sky over Breslau. An enormous star appeared and near by it sat an old woman. A man, fully armored and carrying a bloody sword, then appeared and bowed down in great reverence to the star. Then he went over to the old woman and brutally struck her down. After this, the man went back to the star, bowed down again, and disappeared. This really happened; otherwise, I would not write you about it. Last week Duke Friederich of Liegnitz, our captain, sent a letter to Breslau telling of the appearance of a great multitude of armored soldiers bearing bloody swords in the sky over Liegnitz. What this portends one must leave to God.[66] But I thought it good to share it with you.

There is [otherwise] no special news here, except that they say the Turks are preparing a great offensive.[67] Many merchants have wanted to

---

63. These words have been underlined in the manuscript, evidently by Friederich.

64. Where Stephan was in school is unclear, but Michael's comments indicate that he was not a successful student. See letter 14. The comments also betray some envy and resentment on his part.

65. Earlier it was one hundred times! See letter 16.

66. It is unclear what was seen in the sky over Breslau and Liegnitz. Perhaps it was nothing more than a parhelion like that reported by Friederich VIII in 1580 (see p. 136), or possibly Halley's comet, which would have been due around 1529–30. Whatever the celestial phenomenon, people saw it as an apparition portending the Turkish destruction of western Europe.

67. Suleiman the Magnificent (1494–1566), sultan of Turkey, marched with an army of

move their wares out of harm's way, but his Royal Majesty, Ferdinand, has not allowed them to do so. He has ordered their shops locked with the goods inside. I will not comment on the reason, but you may readily discern it yourself.

Make the best of my letter. Let me know about my clothes without delay by the first available messenger. And send my coat as soon as possible. Greet warmly your wife and the children, and especially Frau Letscher ... God be with us all. Dated as above.

Michael Behaim, your willing cousin

19 ✿ Michael to Friederich, 25 March 1529

Dear esteemed cousin. I am writing in great haste to tell you that I have now written directly to Erasmus Fütterer about my clothes and expressed my amazement that they have been so long in transit and asked him to have them brought to Nuremberg at the earliest. I sincerely ask you to stay after him to get them to you soon so that I do not lose them altogether. Send them to me as soon as you can arrange it! Just demand angrily that he get them to Nuremberg at the very earliest! Is it not a disgrace that almost two years have passed since I departed Milan and my clothes are still not here? And we do not even know where they are! Would you tell Herr Fütterer to write me what he knows and to send the letter to me with the bearer of this note? Dated 25 March, 1529.

M. Behaim

20 ✿ Michael to Friederich, 15 October 1529

Friendly, devoted service always, dear, esteemed cousin. I am writing to you in great haste because I received letters from my sister and brother day before yesterday in which they write to me, as my brother and mother have done once before, to come immediately [to Nuremberg]. But they give no reason for this or say what I should do when I am there, only that you have instructed them to write this to me. Since I have not heard from you, I have no proper information. Also, I do not have my

---

24,000 men into Belgrade and Mohács in summer 1529, en route to the first siege of Vienna. From Michael's report it is clear that rumors of the offensive circulated as early as March and as far north as Breslau.

master's permission to be away, and I would never go anywhere without it. So I ask you to tell me if something is going on. Before any harm befalls me,[68] I would like to see if I can get permission from my master to be away, although it will not please me to have to interrupt the time I have promised him. So send me more information at the earliest opportunity.

My sister writes that I should tell you that the *Schultheiss* and my mother will soon be moving back to Bohemia. It is therefore my sincere request that you enquire again if someone there might keep the poor girl with them in Nuremberg,[69] while every effort is made to find her a good companion. I leave everything to your discretion, for I know you will handle the matter properly. We all remain in your debt. No more for now. God bless.

Dated in great haste. I will write again at the first opportunity.

M. Behaim, y[our] w[illing] c[ousin].

68. Michael seems to mean both harm at the hands of his mother and stepfather and harm to his career resulting from an abrupt interruption of his service to go to Nuremberg.

69. An effort to find a husband for Margaretha has been under way since January 1529. See letter 14, where Michael first raises the issue. The delay in finding proper quarters for her in Nuremberg probably resulted from overly optimistic expectations that she would readily marry.

The new year 1530 brought renewed conflict with Michael's mother. She wanted five hundred gulden from her first husband's estate to pay off some of her new husband's old debts. She claimed the money as her rightful, promised portion, agreed to in writing at the time of her marriage to Michael's father. But Michael's father had been dead for almost twenty years (since 1511) and his mother had married again in 1518. She offered to treat the money as a loan, repayable to the children on her death, if they would accede to her wish. At the same time she threatened a court suit and other reprisals if they did not. More out of fear than benevolence, Michael wanted to accommodate her. Friederich, however, was in the end not inclined to do so, and it was into his hands that the matter fell. After a year of litigation, both in the courts and before the city council, he secured for Michael and his siblings what by then had become 560 contested gulden.

In 1530 Michael also approached the end of his contract with Hans Stublinger. Although the earlier grievances over his personal treatment had been satisfactorily resolved, he believed now more than ever that service with Stublinger was a dead end and that Stublinger was a "pure villain." He worried whether he would ever be able to extricate himself from his relationship with Stublinger, for whom Michael's faithful and competent service remained a great bargain.

The Fütterers also reemerge at this time. Having pursued them for so long and in vain, Michael now hit on a scheme to retrieve his money from them indirectly; a victim of their deceit, he now entertained a little deceit of his own.

21 ❦ Michael to Friederich, 10 January 1530

Praise be always to God, in the year of our Lord, 10 January, in Breslau.

My devoted service and wish that almighty God grant us all a good and happy new year. Amen.

Dear, esteemed cousin, I am always happy to learn that you and yours are healthy and well. I, too, praise God, am in rather good health.

I have nothing special about which to write you except for two letters

I received on 3 January from my mother.[70] In one she fervently exhorts me to allow her to receive the five hundred gulden that my late father agreed in writing would be her marriage portion. She wants the money for her lord so that he may discharge a burdensome oath he made to Herr Kotzen at a time when he had a wife and children.[71] She writes that she will have her lord draw up an agreement, which she too will sign, providing for the sum of 500 Rhenish gulden to fall to her three children after her death. In brief, she is now generous enough, and she threatens us with the law if we resist her. Should it come to litigation, [she believes] that no law can deprive her of the five hundred gulden, because she has a written agreement in our late father's hand. So if we do not willingly agree, we will still be denied the five hundred gulden and more, etc.

I do not know how to answer her except to write that I know nothing about any power of mine to grant [money from Father's estate], and that I do not know to this day the status of our inheritance from Father. Also, I have no letter from either my brother or my sister indicating whether they want to allow this or have already indicated as much [to her]. So I am in no position to grant anything on their behalf. However, I indicated to her that I have given you the power to act on my behalf and that whatever you do with my knowledge and consent in matters such as this I will comply with. But let me say here that you should by no means grant this on my behalf, unless you think it is in my best interest to do so. As she indicates in her letter, a copy of which I enclose, she believes she can force payment from us by going to court. She cites the saying, "no law rules against a signed document,"[72] by which she means the agreement signed by our late father. Dear, esteemed cousin, so that we may never be placed at a disadvantage, I ask you very sincerely to read over the marriage agreement carefully (a copy of which she has also sent me), and see if you agree that the law, as she claims, is indisputably on her side. I have every faith in you.

70. The word "mother" is marked with a flag in the letter, and in the margin are written in Michael's hand the words, "die Ortolffin" (his mother's maiden name was Ortolph). Michael might have flagged her as "die Behaimin" (his late father's wife) or as "die Obernitzin" (the wife of the *Schultheiss*). His use of her maiden name suggests a rejection both of her and of her remarriage.
71. The "lord" is her present husband, Hans von Obernitz. The obligation is apparently a knightly service he had agreed to as a younger man and for which he continued to be responsible.
72. "Khein Recht spricht khein hanntschrifft ab."

I can see clearly from your letter of 5 January that my brother Stephan is trying by every means to realize his dream of not sharing the estate with me and other such fantasies.[73] It is your fault that he is so willful. I am also sorry to learn that no one on earth will take in the poor unfortunate maid Margaretha, my sister, and that our mother must rescue her. May God in heaven have mercy, and may you help her in her need. Amen . . .

[As for the two hundred gulden from Fütterer], it does not seem to me a good sign that neither he nor his brother has ever given us any earnings from this money since the day he received it from you. I can now appreciate the saying: "the slower a resolution, the greater the irritation." Thus, my sincere request that you emphatically demand from him now the earnings on the principal.[74]

As you point out, my desires and intentions in this matter are sufficiently known. I trust you to stand by me and protect what is mine.

I am unhappy to learn that Jörg Pock provides so little hope for the diamond and that you have sure information that the ship on which he placed it was lost [at sea]. I must now trust in God and leave all things to him, to rule over and command according to his divine will.

Dear, esteemed cousin, please receive this letter with favor and keep me in your care. I am eternally diligently devoted to your service. Greet your wife, my dear cousin, and all your children warmly for me. God bless. Dated as above.

Michael Behaim, a[lways] y[our] w[illing] c[ousin].

22 🦌 Michael to Friederich, 1 February 1530

Praise be always to God, in the year of the Lord, 1 February, 1530, from Breslau.

Friendly and devoted service always, dear, esteemed cousin. I wrote

73. It is unclear from the miswritten German manuscript whether Michael means that his brother does not want to share with him the fiefs they hold in common, or that he is seeking to share in those that belong solely to Michael, like the little garden fief discussed in letter 35. Either reading seems plausible.
74. The original expectation was that the Fütterers would support Michael from the earnings of the principal and then return to him the residue plus a share of the earnings after they had deducted their legitimate expenses.

you a short while ago[75] and I trust the letter has by now arrived. In it I pointed out to you all the letters my mother has written regarding the five hundred gulden. Just day before yesterday still another arrived with Focker's carter, a copy of which I enclose. Again you will see how she urges me to agree to give her the five hundred gulden now that my brother and sister have no objection. She still believes that if we do not give her the money willingly, we will have to do so against our will, and [she warns that] if the Schultheiss has to resort to the law to get it, he will not want to make any agreement [with us about repayment], so that we will receive not a heller or pfennig of it after our mother's death. She also indicates to me how you are to interpret her letter, namely, that she will have the Schultheiss make an agreement, secured by all his properties, providing that five hundred gulden fall to [us] three siblings after her death, and that we three shall be the first to be paid before all her other children which she has by then had with him.[76]

So this is the reason for my letter, dear, esteemed cousin. My sister has since written to say that she sought the advice of Christoph Kress, Barthol Haller, and others,[77] and that they have told her that if we go to court and Mother and the Schultheiss offer us a binding agreement that provides for the money's return after Mother's death, we cannot expect to force any further concessions from them. They also said that friendship is always better than enmity. So, esteemed cousin, seeing that it cannot be otherwise and that you yourself are of the opinion that we must give them the five hundred gulden, it is my sincere request that you have the letter of authorization[78] drawn up by a competent attorney. Just be very careful that there is nothing in the letter that might damage, obstruct, or otherwise put either me or my siblings at a disadvantage. You have my full authority to act [on my behalf] in this matter, as if it were your very own. I and my siblings will repay your efforts with especially diligent and humble service. God bless. Dated as above.

Michael Behaim, a[lways] y[our] w[illing] c[ousin].

---

75. Letter 21.
76. By this time Michael's mother would seem to be beyond her child-bearing years (she had married his father in 1500 and borne her first child in 1501). It is unclear how many children, if any, she had in fact had by her new husband until this point (1530).
77. Christoph Kress (d. 1535), a cousin, was among other things a Septemvir and Obrister Waagherr. He presented the Augsburg Confession to Charles V in 1530. On Barthol Haller see letter 8. These were very powerful and influential people.
78. "Vergewisung Brieff."

23 ❦ Michael to Friederich, undated fragment [after February 1530][79]

Dear, esteemed, gracious cousin, know that at this hour, when I should otherwise be taking our mail to the messenger, I have talked instead with Hans Rappolt and asked him why, after I had pledged myself to Herr Stublinger [with the understanding] that he would employ me regularly at the Frankfurt and Leipzig fairs, this has never been done, even though I have been in their service now for more than two years. I also asked him very politely if he might still send me to join Herr Stublinger at the Frankfurt fair, since he himself will not be going. He gave me a surprising answer: that inasmuch as living expenses there are too high now, he would under no circumstances consider sending me there and that it was sufficient that Stublinger be there. He then got up and left.

From this experience, I can well imagine your having a good talk with Herr Stublinger about such a move for me, only then to have Herr Rappolt refuse to let me go because he requires my services here. I worry that nothing will ever come of my [desire to] move to Frankfurt or Leipzig as long as I am with them. Rather, I will have to remain here, a common servant, sitting in the shop, sweeping, fetching beer and wine, and otherwise doing common menial work, although such things are not in my agreement with Herr Stublinger. Had I wanted to perform such services, I need not have entered an apprenticeship and squandered my money in the process. Herr Stublinger is a pure villain.[80] I can readily imagine him saying to you about easy money: "if one seeks it, one might find it somewhere[81] . . ."

Dated in great haste.

    M. Behaim, y[our] w[illing] c[ousin].

---

79. This belongs with letter 24 (2 September 1530), in which the issue of going to the fairs at Frankfurt and Leipzig remains prominent, and in which Michael says he has been with Stublinger for "three years," obviously counting his thirty weeks in Bohemia as part of these. He had returned from Bohemia to Breslau on 23 June 1528. If one counts from the latter date, he would have been with Stublinger for a little more than two years. In the present letter he says that it has been "more than two years" since his service with Stublinger began. This would place the letter in early 1530, probably late February or early March, as Michael looked to the spring fairs. In letter 24 he discusses the fall fairs, and writes that because plague is raging in both Frankfurt and Leipzig he is not pressing his lords to send him to them.

80. "Es ist Eytel puebery mit dem Stublinger."

81. This is apparently a quotation from a conversation Friederich had with Stublinger.

24 ❦ Michael to Friederich, 2 September 1530

Praise be always to God, in the year of our Lord, 2 September, 1530, in Breslau.

My devoted service always. Know dear, esteemed, gracious cousin that your 18 August letter arrived safely on 31 August and I have read it. What concerns me at this time is that my masters have [again] not sent me to Frankfurt or Leipzig [for the fall fairs]. I am not saying much to them about it, because plague now rages in both places, and I can well imagine that business will be bad this year at the Frankfurt fair. So had I already moved there, I might have met few customers and learned nothing at all. Nonetheless, if Herr Stublinger had wanted to keep his part of the agreement with me, he should reasonably have employed me in these places long ago, as he led me to believe he would do when I first "pledged myself to him." As you write, he is truly a foolish fellow.[82] Here also one has no respect for him whatsoever. As in Nuremberg, no one will have anything to do with him.

Dear, esteemed, gracious cousin, you indicate that you believe that Herr Stublinger has not sent me to the fairs during these three years because he may think that he will not have me with him beyond my promised time of service. I have not at all asked him about this. Should he now offer me a large salary to continue with him in my present capacity, I would carefully consider it, but I do not know whether I would accept, because I know now that continued association with him is not in my best interest.

I will share a confidence with you. I notice that over time Herr Stublinger let Hans Rappolt travel [and learn all about his business]. I also know, praise God, that Herr Rappolt wishes only good for me. Often he has generously offered to assist me. He has now told me that when my years with Stublinger are up, I should leave without any further ado. He presented the matter in such a way that I could see clearly what was in my best interest. Still, it is hard to believe that [Herr Stublinger] will let me go.

Otherwise, I have been approached by two important men here, each of whom runs a very successful business. One has asked me if I would like to continue to work in Breslau when my time with Herr Stublinger is up. They want to retain me now, if I like the idea of working for them.

---

82. Friederich now shares Michael's assessment of his apprenticeship in Breslau.

They have even offered to secure my future services with a nice advance. But I have not wanted to tell them anything at all at this point.

Therefore, d[ear], e[steemed], g[racious] cousin, my hope is in God, and God willing, there will be no emergency if I am not in someone's service. I will have masters enough, and in time I will also serve you and yours to your profit. God bless. Dated as above.

M[ichael] B[ehaim], y[our] w[illing] c[ousin].

25 ❦ Michael to Friederich, undated fragment [before 16 October 1531]

Dear, esteemed, gracious cousin. I thank you profusely for your good will toward us and your untiring efforts on our behalf. When we can and may, my brother, sister, and I will repay you and yours. You faithfully took up our cause when we were poor orphans and now you have won a decision in court that will be difficult for us to repay, although I understand that our mother has appealed [the decision] to the city council.[83] I hope she will not be able to gain anything there. So I ask you again to do your best for us in this matter, which I entrust to you as if it were your own. I hope to almighty God it will cause us no further trouble.

My siblings and I remain devoted to serving you and yours always. You have only to command us. Dated in letter.[84]

Michael Behaim, y[our] w[illing] c[ousin].

26 ❦ Michael to Friederich, 16 October 1531

My devoted service. Know dear, esteemed Herr cousin that I am by God's grace well and hardy. I am always pleased to hear the same about you and all of yours.

My letter is not about anything in particular, only I do not want to withhold from you that in recent days I have received two letters from my mother. In both she asks me for God's sake to depart immediately

83. This letter belongs with letter 26. The dispute was last referred to in February 1530 (letter 22). Friederich has won the case in court ("vor der Statgericht"), but still must contest his mother's appeal to the council ("fur einem E. Rath").
84. The comment makes clear that this self-contained note is really a fragment of a larger letter.

[for Nuremberg]. Each letter, to be brief, fills almost an entire sheet and says the same thing. I was moved to answer the second letter as soon as I had read it. I told her that my masters would not permit me to put a boot outside the door so abruptly, also that it would be improper for me to leave on such short notice because they have asked me to remain until we have closed out the accounts of the [recent] trading. I also received a letter from my brother with the news, now confirmed by Hans Stublinger, that you have won the decision on the five hundred gulden for us three siblings before the city council. (For this, we can never repay you, although, for my part, I intend to make every possible effort to do so, because gratitude is not enough.) I can only conclude [from these two communications] that Mother may again be looking greedily on my future and that she and the Schultheiss want to design a new financial stratagem to take advantage of us three (or, at least, of me). Hence, I ask you sincerely for your honest opinion of what I should do. I hope to be done with the accounts in four or five weeks at the longest. Do you think I should then come to Nuremberg? Let me know your mind by the first available messenger. I will abide by your letter. May God be with us all. Dated in haste as above.

Michael Behaim, y[our] d[evoted] cousin.

[P.S.] Apart from these two letters, my mother and I have not written a word to each other in two years.[85] Since I do not intend to agree that the Schultheiss be given this money on the terms he has proposed, I wonder how we can again reach any agreement with one another on this matter. People are beginning to get angry with me again, just as before.

27 ❦ Michael to Friederich, 5 November 1531

Praise be always to God, in the year of our Lord, 5 November, 1531, in Breslau.

My devoted service, dear, esteemed, gracious Herr cousin. I am always happy to hear of your health and well-being. I, too, praise God, am in good health.

I am writing to you because I have learned from a trustworthy good friend that Erasmus Fütterer has a paid debt here of between fifty-six and

---

85. The last mention of the matter to Friederich was made on 1 February 1530, when Michael, believing he had no alternative, instructed Friederich to comply with his mother's demands.

sixty gulden that is being held for him by a local burgher named Jacob Soner. With the help of Dr. Ribisch, Soner collected this money from a Bohemian lord, who incurred the debt long ago in Milan with the late Gabriel Fütterer. I can at this point only conclude that Erasmus Fütterer fully intends to delay payment indefinitely of what he owes me. It perhaps pains him to contemplate ever having to pay me this money. So one must see if it can perhaps be gotten from him in a similar [indirect] way [similar to the one Soner used to collect his money]. If you think it worth a try, you might indicate such to him. Tell him to write and instruct Jacob Soner to deliver the above-mentioned sum, whatever it turns out to be, to my masters here.[86] Soner has also told me that E[rasmus] Fütterer still does not know that he has received this money from the Bohemian lord. So you might approach him in a roundabout way,[87] [that is, tell him] that you have learned from me that the Bohemian lord [who owes him money] is now willing to pay him [indirectly, through Soner] and that when he does, he then write Soner as described above, so that the money may promptly be given to me here. Otherwise, I fear that I will get my money from him only ever so slowly. Let me know what you think about this as soon as possible.

I would like to leave here soon. If only I could be finished with my masters! One now worries about plague in Breslau. It is already breaking out nearby. Within the last four days or so a councilman named Stephan Joppener, two of his servant girls, two of his daughters, and a small child of his died, and I have just this hour learned that his wife also lies ill. May God protect us from such pestilence. You might write to Herr Stublinger or Herr Rappolt and urge them on my behalf to send me away at the first opportunity and not detain me here any longer. But do so only in your own name. I do not want them to know that I wrote to you about this.

May God's grace be with us all. Dated as above, in great haste.

Y[our] w[illing] c[ousin] Michael Behaim.

---

86. Because the sum in question is between fifty-six and sixty gulden, Michael now seems willing to settle for a great deal less than what he had earlier believed to be due him. Indeed Michael has almost reversed the proportions, for he had made Fütterer's legitimate expenditures out to be no more than fifty of the two hundred gulden in question (letter 7), not to mention any accrued interest over the eight years the money has been in his hands.

87. "Mit frembder Red ann Inn khomenn."

By spring 1532 Michael had served out his contract with Stublinger, and then some. But as he had feared, he remained in Stublinger's employ, strung along by the special pleading and moral suasion to which he was so susceptible. Reluctantly detained, he inched determinedly toward the day when he might honorably and amicably walk away. At the same time as he contemplated departing Breslau, he also began to lay a foundation for his own business there. To this end he twice planned to visit Nuremberg in late spring or early summer, to lay claim there to his share of the family estate, which amounted to at least six hundred gulden. But he was prevented from doing so, first by his brother's departure to his stepfather's home in Bohemia and then by serious personal injury. He was also hobbled emotionally by Turkish aggression in Hungary and Austria, which he saw as the beginning of the end of Western civilization.

The growing rift between Michael's masters, and Stublinger's failing health, finally provided the opportunity to leave. Michael set a departure date in the first week of August, gave Hans Rappolt his notice, and bought a horse. When he finally left Breslau he was still not completely out of Stublinger's service. But after settling some business for his master en route, he arrived as Friederich's guest in Nuremberg, probably in early September, and at last began to put his affairs in order. At twenty-three he lacked not only direct control over what he owned but even a proper idea of what he owned. He also remained dependent on third parties for ending his rift with his brother over the division of their income from peasant rents.

Michael did not long mull over his future in Nuremberg. He had decided to start his own business, to trade among Breslau, Liegnitz, and Nuremberg. Already before leaving Breslau he had made financial commitments for the coming fall fair in Frankfurt that again sent him in quest of the elusive debt owed by Fütterer.

Between August 1532 and February 1533 when he was traveling and tending to personal business, Michael fell completely silent. When he wrote again to Friederich, he was in Liegnitz bringing the books up to date for a dying Hans Stublinger, his last service for his former master. Later he went back and forth between Nuremberg and Breslau. He was also beginning to repay some of his debt to Friederich, as well as grooming a future business associate, by helping Friederich's son Paul, an unhappy novice apprentice in Cracow, explore a possible new position.

28   Michael to Friederich, 1 April 1532

Praise be always to God, in the year of our Lord, 1 April, 1532, in Breslau.

My devoted service, dear, esteemed, gracious Herr cousin. I have written you two letters since my departure,[88] one just to inform you of my arrival here, which I sent with the Nuremberg messenger Theumel, the second with a local messenger, Bastian, in which I enclosed your house key. I have been carrying the key with me all this time and had forgotten to return it until now. I hope you have received both letters and the key by now.

Know dear, esteemed, Herr cousin that my masters met here during the recent fair and took much private counsel together. I have been able to learn that Herr Stublinger was confronted on several matters. In my opinion, it is hard to believe that they will remain together any longer. The closing-out of accounts has [accordingly] been delayed until between now and Pentecost. They have asked me to stay until the accounts are done [saying that] I have been their best worker for so long and have pleased everyone throughout my apprenticeship. I have told them that it will not be possible for me to remain here so long without harming my own interests and that I had to be in Nuremberg over Easter to deal with my brother on the matter of the fiefs, which now greatly preoccupies me. I urged them to think about my own well-being. In sum, I have discussed the matter with them as thoroughly as I thought appropriate. I do believe it will be necessary [for me to stay until the accounts are closed]. No one asked whether I have already spent my whole life with them doing this. But it is now out of my hands. At one point, Herr Stublinger gave me this answer: "Dear Michael, I will myself write your cousin [Friederich] and tell him that you cannot leave at this time because our business needs you. So join with us, if we can once again ask you to do so, so that we are not shorthanded." I had to agree to do so for propriety's sake, while hoping that it shall not mean my personal loss. Should Herr Stublinger write you such a letter as he proposes, would

88. Michael has been in Nuremberg since his last letter (5 November 1531).

you write him an answer that supports me and discusses the matter thoroughly, so that one here finds my arguments [for departing] all the more legitimate?

In the meantime, I am hoping to almighty God to get some good advice on my own career. As soon as I am free of my masters I am coming [to Nuremberg]. You might set aside a day to consider what you want to do with cousin Paul.[89] If you are still willing for him to come to [to Poland], I might try to find him a position, for it is my hope that he may be as well provided for here as he is at home until, with God's help, I am established [in my own business]. But I have no doubt that it will be [a] difficult [time for him]. May almighty God choose to rid this land of war and pestilence.

Dear, esteemed, gracious cousin, it is my sincere desire and request that you do well [by me] while I am here. What cash I have of my own is now scattered among people [in Nuremberg]. You could, with the best decorum, pull it all together. It makes no difference in the end whether it is a heavy or a light package, just so that the total amount is great enough that when I want to undertake something in God's name, I will have the funds to do it. Also, tell Jacob Groland and my brother, Stephan Behaim, to bring their records up to date, because, God willing, I intend to be in Nuremberg shortly before or after Pentecost and take charge of all my affairs, so that I may know exactly what is mine (even though it is, no doubt, little). In short, I am planning to order my affairs and thereafter to entrust them to God's almighty hand. May he grant me good fortune. Amen.

As for Erasmus Fütterer, by no means let up on him until he hands over the money, whether this happens graciously or not. I just will not have this on my mind any longer . . .

I commend you to the grace of almighty God. Greet [your] wife, [my] cousin, and the children, and all the household. Let Paul answer the enclosed letter to Daniel Schelling. Dated as above.

Michael Behaim, y[our] w[illing] c[ousin].

29 ☙ Michael to Friederich, 8 April 1532

Praise be always to God, in the year of our Lord, 8 April, 1532, in Breslau.

My devoted service, dear, esteemed, gracious Herr cousin. Your letter

89. Friederich's eldest son.

of 20 March arrived safely from Nuremberg on 2 April . . . As you indicate, my brother, Stephan Behaim, has now moved to Oscheling with Mother. May I have the patience to wait until his return, when, with God's help, I may then come home and put a little order in my affairs, as I previously announced I would do. My wish now is that you not let [Stephan] take advantage of me. Write him a little note indicating my concern. If he has some of my money with him and is keeping it from me, you might tell him that I will need that money in the future and to keep it intact. I still believe that above and beyond the principal sum of six hundred gulden, I will also need money for provisions, a horse, my expenses, perhaps also for freight, and for the many emergencies that suddenly arise . . . I will not call your attention to it again. I know that if you could pull a lot [of money] together for me, you would not fail to do so . . .

Know also, dear Herr cousin, that I would gladly have sent you the smoked carp long ago. The problem has been that throughout the season when one buys carp, I have been overwhelmed by my masters' business. We have all been bunched together here every day since the fair's end, closing out accounts, so that I have not been able to find the time to ride out and make a proper selection. Now that the work is tapering off a bit, one can no longer get carp of quality, because fish generally are spawning now and the carp lose their scales and are no good. In addition, I did not arrive here until Laetere Sunday, and since then only one wagon has departed Breslau for Nuremberg. So even if I had managed to buy the carp, I still would not have been able to send them to you. So please do not think that I have simply been negligent. I have truly thought about it often, and I would like to have done it for you as soon as I arrived. But I have just never had the time. So I fear that we can only queue up until the next fish harvest. Then, God willing, I will provide you with enough good smoked carp for an entire year.

Enclosed is a letter to Baptista de Franckfurt which I took from a messenger. I expect his wife had written it thinking she could still catch him here. He has, however, been gone for three days. Would you deliver it to him with my compliments and explain to him that I took it from the messenger as a friendly service to him?[90] I would like to write him myself, but I have no time now. God be with us all. Written in a very great hurry. Dated as above.

Michael Behaim, y[our] w[illing] c[ousin].

---

90. Michael does not want Baptista to think he has invaded his privacy, for spouses were very sensitive about the confidentiality of their letters.

30 ❦ Michael to Friederich, 21 May 1532

Praise be always to God, in the year of the Lord, 21 May, 1532, in Breslau.

My devoted service, dear, esteemed, gracious Herr cousin. The accident that befell me by God's decree and about which I wrote you in my last letter through a third party has prevented me from coming to Nuremberg as I had planned. But, praise God, I am now much better. Only my right hand remains incapacitated. I hope to almighty God that it is not permanently injured. It is, however, keeping me here for the present, and I fear I will have to sit out the market on John the Baptist's Day [June 24]. But as soon as I am able, I will make ready to leave and, God willing, settle my affairs here once and for all. I thank almighty God that I have such gracious masters, especially in Hans Rappolt and Georg Sibmer.[91] You have heard me say this many times before, and I repeat it now so that you will not be worried about me. I can well imagine that my accident has given you a shock. I had not myself believed that God would be so gracious to me in my recovery.

May almighty God bless and keep you. Greet [your] wife, [my] cousin, and the household for me. Dated as above.

Michael Behaim, y[our] w[illing] c[ousin].

31 ❦ Michael to Friederich, fragment, 10 July 1532

Praise be always to God, A.D. 1532, 10 July, in Breslau.

My willing service always. Dear, esteemed, gracious Herr cousin, know that I have loaded a barrel I had specially made with my effects and bearing my mark and sent it to you with the carter, Heinz Hasloch. I trust it will reach you in good order. You will also know it by the invoice. Please keep it at your house until I arrive.

Rappolt and I alone managed the recent John [the Baptist's Day] fair. Herr Stublinger has lain ill with a high fever in Liegnitz now for four weeks. This has made it impossible for my two masters to reach any decision on the business they have in common. Two days ago Herr Rappolt returned to the lead mines in Poland, twenty-four miles away. We had a heated discussion before his departure and I made it clear to him that I will not be detained here any longer. He pleaded with me to remain

91. Unclear who Sibmer is; perhaps a new boarding-house keeper.

only for the two weeks he will be away, [saying that] we would then settle our affairs and that I could truly look on my release as imminent. Still, I fear an unhappy surprise,[92] because he and Stublinger are presently fighting and cannot agree with one another. But with God's help, I will be honorably discharged and, God willing, they shall not [again] extend my time. You need not worry about this. Although I must remain here somewhat longer, God willing, it will do me no harm.

I also expect to have to conduct some business for Rappolt at the upcoming Frankfurt [fall] fair. So if God does help me reach Nuremberg, I will have plenty of writing to do . . .

My sister indicates in her last letter that I should let you know who Herr Baptista does business with here. I have so far been unable to find anyone who knows. I observe that he has a trusted associate, who occasionally checks out materials for him here. He sends him samples, for example, and asks him whether he can buy them for him. The man's name is Hieronymus Grau and he works for Herr Merten Bruchman in Frankfurt a[n der] O[der]. He is very busy here. He always stays in his room. He has an office in the house where Baptista stays when he is here. He takes his meals there also. The Grander of Augsburg have their office and shop in the same house. Baptista has traded with no one here [yet] . . .

32 🐝 Michael to Friederich, 14 July 1532

Praise be always to God, A.D. 1532, 14 July, in Breslau.

My willing service. Dear, esteemed, gracious Herr cousin, I trust my most recent letter has reached you safely by a Liegnitz messenger. Hans Rappolt still has not returned [from Poland], so my arrival [in Nuremberg] is delayed. I will, of course, leave as soon as I can. Looking ahead, let me sincerely ask you again to pursue Herr Fütterer. If that money is not available, my plans will fare badly and great shame will befall me. I hope to God there will be no problem if only you earnestly pursue him, because being nice to him will not help. [To remind you of] this is one reason for my letter.

The other is to report the news received here last night from Herr Friederich Schilling in Cracow. He has reliably learned that the Weida has attempted to bring the Cossacks and the Siebenbürger totally under his

92. "Die Sach wirdt ein hundt habenn wollen."

control,[93] so that he might dominate the entire region.[94] But the majority [of the people] would not acquiesce. So the Turks gave the Weida 30,000 men to take the land by force. When the Cossacks saw this [great army], they joined with those from Herm[an]stadt. A great multitude of people then gathered in Siebenbürgen to oppose the Weida, and they defeated the 30,000 men on the Turkish and Weida's side, slaying them all. God grant that this report is true! There is no word yet about the Meissener Minekiwitz,[95] in case you have heard it said that he was definitely killed. A Pole named Lasko, who several times performed brilliantly on the Turkish side, barely escaped with his life, only one of three to survive.[96] Here one believes [this report]; [the victory] has been attributed to [divine] mercy.

Yesterday we received news from our merchants in Hungary that on John the Baptist's Day the Turkish emperor personally arrived in war-ready Weissenburg with a very great army.[97] [Reportedly] he swore to his God on his sword that he would not leave the Roman Empire until he had conquered it. One can well imagine such an intention, but God will thwart it. In brief, people everywhere are writing and talking about this powerful Turkish offensive, yet neither here nor in the Empire does one see how we can escape it, and little help or resistance is forthcoming. Perhaps God will now blind the German nation and leave it to such punishment [as Turkish domination]. We must all pray to God for mercy. Otherwise, there will be no way out.

I have been burdened with the task of sending several additional letters, which are enclosed. Please have one of your servants deliver them to the proper parties and do not trouble yourself with them.

May almighty God be merciful to us all. Dated, as above, in haste.

Michael Behaim, c[ousin].

33 ❦ Michael to Friederich, 27 July 1532

Praise be always to God, A.D. 27 July, 1532, in Breslau.

My devoted service always. Dear, esteemed, gracious Herr cousin, I am

93. The Wayda, or Weida (leader), is the Magyar John Zapolya.
94. The events recounted here are occurring in Transylvania, now in central Rumania.
95. It is unclear who this is.
96. Michael may be receiving reports of the battle at the fortress Güns. See n. 101.
97. This clearly is only a rumor rife in Hungary. Letter 33, which also reports the Turk to be in "war-ready Weissenburg," alleges that the Turkish emperor died in battle at Mohács (ostensibly Suleiman is meant). In Western imagination this would have been a fitting vengeance for the death there in 1526 of King Louis. See n. 100.

especially pleased to hear of your health and well-being. Know that I, too, praise God, am in good health.

Dear Herr cousin, Rappolt returned from the lead mines only two hours ago, and I have had a frank discussion with him. I told him, in brief, that I will not be detained here any longer. While he was away, I bought a horse and I have set a firm [departure] date. In approximately eight to ten days, I will, in God's name, ride away from here. But I fear that my journey to Nuremberg must be almost a hundred miles long because I still have to transact business for my masters en route in Chemnitz, after going first to Liegnitz. And I will not be able to tarry long in Nuremberg, because I have also promised to represent them at the Frankfurt fair. For me, there is nothing more difficult than traveling alone over such a long distance. May almighty God give me good fortune. Amen . . .

I will not hide from you my fear that the two hundred gulden my masters hold here will be difficult to get before Stublinger returns to Nuremberg.[98] He lies ill in Liegnitz and is now very weak. So my masters have not been inclined to end their wrong [in my regard]. In brief, I must for the present play a waiting game. Although their promises remain unkept, I will not give in, and I do know well enough how to deal with them. You need not worry that I will absolve them [of their promises]. This is where the matter presently stands.

There is plenty of news here, which I believe it good to share with you. A list arrived yesterday of those killed thirteen days ago at Mohacs, twenty-four miles away,[99] and among them was the Turkish emperor. King Louis of fond memory also died there.[100] When he [the Turkish emperor] arrived there, it was written and said that he should be three times better equipped with every weapon and stronger than before, for it has now been three years since he threatened Vienna.[101] Here we all

98. The reference is to Michael's apprentice fee, paid more than four years earlier. See letter 13. Like Fütterer's fee the two hundred gulden were apparently given for purposes of investment, with the expectation that the principal or at least a sizable portion of it would be returned at the end of the apprenticeship.

99. Away from where is not clear; surely not Breslau, which was not within twenty-four German miles (120 English miles) of Mohács. Michael may mean Güns. See n. 101.

100. During a more famous battle there in 1526, Louis II Jagellon, the young king of Hungary, died during a cavalry charge on 29 August.

101. Vienna was first besieged by Suleiman between mid-September and mid-October 1529. Another major offensive, launched in 1532, faltered after a three-week battle at

assumed that he had perished long ago. He wanted first to besiege Vienna. May almighty God have mercy on our own. Amen. One still detects little resistance here.

I have just this hour learned from a respected and trustworthy Frankfurter that Bishop von der Neis wrote to the city council [of Frankfurt] about the reception the Turk gave the imperial messenger in war-ready Weissenburg. He [the Turkish leader] first heard the messenger out and accepted a gift from him. Then he gave him a gift in return. He then had both gifts placed before the messenger and ordered them to be hacked to pieces before his eyes. This is a great tyranny.

Make the best of this letter. May almighty God protect you. Dated in haste, as above.

Michael Behaim, y[our] w[illing] c[ousin].

34 ❦ Michael to Friederich, 16 February 1533

Praise be always to God, in the year of our Lord, 16 February, in Liegnitz.

My devoted service always. Dear, esteemed, gracious Herr cousin, know that I am, praise God, well and hardy. I have been to Cracow with Paul [Behaim] and back again. But I have had so much work to do on Herr Stublinger's records [of his dealings] with Herr Rappolt. I have now spent a good week in Liegnitz with Frau Stublinger's father running figures day and night, and we are still not at the end.[102] I fear that Rappolt and Stublinger will not be able to separate amicably. I have had both to threaten and to plead with old Heyder to get his assistance and advice.[103] To be spared him would be dearer to me than the gift of a hundred gulden. But I do everything for reputation's sake in the hope that I shall not thereafter be harmed by it. This time is no exception.

---

the fortress Güns, sixty (English) miles south of Vienna. See Dorothy M. Vaughan, *Europe and the Turk: A Pattern of Alliances, 1350–1700* (Liverpool, 1954), 115–18.

102. Stublinger, who has been gravely ill, is now dying in Liegnitz. (He was dead five months later, for on 25 July Michael wrote to Nuremberg for a copy of his testament.) In anticipation of Stublinger's death Michael assisted in the division of the business between Stublinger and Rappolt. That he had to rely heavily on Frau Stublinger's father for information about their long relationship indicates that Stublinger was very ill indeed.

103. This could only be Frau Stublinger's father.

When I left Breslau to come here, I asked Hans Rappolt to direct any messenger bound for Nuremberg this way, as I have a letter for you from your son [Paul]. That he has now done, and he also sent me a letter from Paul from Cracow. I enclose it for you so that you may see that he is still well. I have a great deal to write you, but time will not indulge me. The messenger has indicated that I can hold him up for no more than a quarter-hour, as he must quickly be gone. I plan to ride to Breslau day after tomorrow, God willing. From there I will bring you up to date on everything with the first available messenger.

For now, know that, praise God, a good beginning has been made. I faithfully followed your instruction in Paul's regard and introduced him to a gentleman here on one of his good days. May God grant him luck. I spoke personally with Herr Boner,[104] who has now also spoken with Paul. And I have further recommended Paul to many esteemed gentlemen here. In sum, there is no need for you to worry about him; he is as well cared for here as he is when he is at home.

Make the best of this letter. I cannot hold the messenger any longer. I will write you all the news with the next available messenger. Herr Heyder, his wife, and Frau Stublinger send sincere greetings to you and your wife, etc. Greet [your wife, my] cousin also on my behalf. Dated in very great haste, as above.

Michael Behaim, y[our] w[illing] c[ousin].

[P.S.] Tell Gabriel Imhoff[105] that I have designated someone to buy five hundred firm Schonburg quinces for me in Lublin,[106] sixty miles beyond Cracow.[107] [The shipment] will not reach me in Breslau until Laetere Sunday. I hope to receive something good. I will send it out [to Nuremberg] as soon as I can. I will also write to [Imhoff] about it myself with the next available messenger. Do indicate to him and his wife my willing service, etc. It is impossible for me to write to him at this time. Also I have not had a Nuremberg messenger until now.

---

104. Paul was very unhappy in Cracow and Boner was a prospective new master.
105. Gabriel the younger (1498–1578), who had married Helena Welser in 1522.
106. "500 quitt forder schonburgh." It might also be read as "500 guett forder schonburgh," making even more of a mystery out of schonburgh.
107. Again, it is unclear how Michael figures mileage. Lublin is thirty German miles or 150 English miles northeast of Cracow. Michael was obviously thinking of distance actually traveled, not of distance measured as the crow flies.

35 ❦ Michael to Friederich, 30 April 1533

Praise be always to God, A.D. 1533, 30 April, in Nuremberg.

Dear, esteemed, gracious Herr cousin. I have asked you to sell my 3 gulden annuity[108] together with the hens I receive annually in rent from the garden in front of the outer Runner's Gate. Here again, in writing, is my final request and judgment that you sell the same as soon as possible and for as much as you can get. For, as you know, I have purchased two pieces of crimson[109] from Hans von Plo[b]en on [the assumption that I will have] this money.[110] The total sum is eighty-five gulden, eight schillings at fifteen batzen [interest]. He has treated the sale as a cash purchase, but friendship requires that the money be delivered to him within four to six weeks at the latest. I have emphatically promised and assured him that you will send him the money on my behalf without fail. So, dear Herr cousin, make every effort to sell the fief[111] for whatever in God's name it is worth, so that faith is kept with [Herr von Ploben]. After careful consideration, I have concluded that using the money [in this way] will be more profitable to me than letting it lie there in rents.

As I told you, I could not reach agreement with my brother on [the division of our income from] the peasants. So I herewith empower you and Jacob Groland to act on my behalf in this matter, so that my brother does not continue to collect money on my behalf. Whatever you [two] think is best in this matter shall also please me. Herr Letscher told me he would also be happy to assist. In sum, you will know how to handle the entire matter properly.

May almighty God keep you. Time has run out on me. Dated in great haste.

Y[our] w[illing] cousin, Michael Behaim.

---

108. "3 gulden werung."

109. "Purpianische tuch," the rich cloth worn by kings and popes.

110. Von Ploben was a rich and influential merchant in Nuremberg whose family originally came from Plauen in Saxony.

111. "Das zinslein": his right to income, produce, and fowl from the garden.

In mid-February 1533, during Carnival, Michael exchanged private vows with Margaretha Emmerich, a woman from Breslau of some substance. He describes the marriage as "born of God." Neither Friederich nor any other relative from Nuremberg had direct knowledge beforehand of the betrothal, although Friederich claims to have heard from others about the courtship. By contrast, Margaretha's family seems to have been involved in the original decision. Michael made a point of stressing her family's enthusiastic support of the marriage when he finally announced it to Friederich.

As Michael had expected, the reaction in Nuremberg was completely sour. Not one of his relatives attended the formal public ceremony on 15 June. Friederich himself responded with sarcasm and disbelief, clearly hurt that he had been left out of such an important decision by Michael, whom he had advised for so long on so many matters. In his apology Michael expressed regret for his behavior, but he also blamed it on the irresistible providence of God. To reassure Friederich he emphasized the prominence of Margaretha's family and his own good fortune in becoming a part of it. Although Michael clearly loved and admired his new bride, he knew that knowledge of her substance rather than of his affection for her would most likely heal Friederich's wounded heart. Margaretha's family was in a position to help Michael establish a trading business in Breslau. It is inconceivable that his new in-laws did not see in Michael a man with a future.

36 ❦ Michael to Friederich, 22 May 1533

Praise be always to God, A.D. 1533, 22 May, in Breslau ... Dear, esteemed, gracious Herr cousin, I cannot in all good conscience withhold from you any longer the news that almighty God, my heavenly father, has graciously bestowed upon me a good, respectable girl, whom I have my life long done nothing to deserve, nor can I do so now. She is, as I desire, at one and the same time both a good person in her own right and the child of respected and important people here. She also has a good livelihood and a considerable inheritance awaiting her when her mother dies. And she has her own town and country houses. I cannot thank almighty God enough for bestowing such good fortune on me. I never thought I should marry into such a considerable family here in

Breslau. But do not take my word for it. Inquire among her family's relatives in Nuremberg, and discover for yourself whether I have spoken correctly or not. You may, for example, get good information about her family from Herr Sebald Pfintzing and Daniel [Schelling], etc. Her [late] father was Hans Emmerich, her mother a Horneck, the sister of Bartholomaeus Horneck. The Hornecks practically run the city council. I point this out only so that you will not think that I have perhaps secretly done something wrong. In sum, I have told you only half the story.

Do not hold it against me that I did not first seek your advice in this matter. There are many reasons why I did not, and the distance between Breslau and Nuremberg is so great. May almighty God grant us good fortune and success. Amen.

D[ear], e[steemed] Herr cousin, I herewith invite you, [your wife, my] cousin, and all your household to my wedding. And would you not let the effort involved deter you from honoring all our relatives and friends with an invitation on my behalf so that no one is overlooked and angry with me, especially [people like] Albrecht Letscher and his wife, Joachim Rotmund and his, etc., in short, all who you think should be honored with an invitation? Should I write personally to each one, it would be too many letters; and I cannot do it at this time, because the messenger has just given notice at vespers that he must be off early in the morning with the opening of the gate.

I have worried that few of my relatives and friends will come to honor me at my wedding, even if the date is set well in the future. So, in God's name, my bride's family and I have decided to hold the wedding approximately five or six days before John the Baptist's Day [24 June]. Hence, you and all good friends who want to come do not have much time to prepare. [Those who do] will be shown every honor here.

Dear Herr cousin ... I ask you by no means to delay in selling my [garden] fief and satisfying von Ploben. Again I ask you not to dawdle with this, but to do it immediately. More is at stake in this for me than you may realize. At another time, I will give you all the details. Time is too short to do so now.

May the Lord God keep you in his grace. Dated as above.

Michael Behaim, y[our] w[illing] c[ousin].

[P.S.] It goes well with Paul in Cracow. I succeeded yesterday in getting Herr Boner's letter for him. I will send you his coat of arms with the first messenger.[112]

---

112. Boner's coat of arms is in the Behaim Archive. It was sent to Friederich so that he might better acquaint himself with the man Paul might serve. See letter 38.

37 🦔 Michael to Friederich, 1533, fragment [before Michael's wedding day]

Dear, esteemed, gracious Herr cousin. I have indicated to Hans Heugel,[113] his brothers, and family your goodwill and your wish to be at their service, both for the sake of your son Paul and for good old family's sake, in deference to their Nuremberg ancestry.[114] They thank you very much for your graciousness even though they have not met you. Because I have become their close relative by marriage,[115] I have been their guest and they have promised me good hunting on their lands. They are giving me all the game they catch for my wedding day, which will mean at least the two stags presently in their nets and whatever else God provides [between now and then].

They have also asked me to ask a favor of you. It is that you trace the Nuremberg Heugels' ancestors and their marriages as far back as they can be found and identified, whether it be only one, two, three, or four coats of arms. The Heugels know nothing about their Nuremberg ancestors. Do not mind the cost; no expense is too great for them in this matter. I ask you to undertake this task as diligently as possible, as a gesture of friendship to my new in-laws. They can gratefully repay your efforts. Written in great haste in order to catch the messenger.

Michael Beham

38 🦔 Michael to Friederich, 26 June 1533

Praise be always to God, 1533, 26 June, in Breslau.

My friendly, willing service always. Dear, esteemed, gracious Herr cousin, know that I am, praise God, well and prospering in the honorable and divine estate of marriage. I hope that you and all members of our family are also well.

On 14 June, I received by way of Hans Heugel, my brother-in-law, both

113. One of Michael's new in-laws in Breslau.
114. Paul was still seeking a new position, and the Heugels were well connected.
115. A marriage (heyrat) preceded a wedding (hochzeyt). The wedding, usually in a church, was a publication of vows that the couple had already made, either in the presence of family and friends, or, as Michael and Margaretha apparently did, in the presence only of God.

your answer and my sister's to my friendly letter [about my marriage].[116] I am too busy now to answer you because the annual fair is upon us. So I must postpone writing until another time. But you have misconstrued my letter when you say that I slander my own name of Behaim. I must respond to this and explain exactly what I meant with the next available messenger.

I have this hour received a letter from Paul in Cracow . . . He also sent me [Herr Boner's] coat of arms, here enclosed, as I asked him to do at your command so that you could see it. You may expect a longer letter from me next time.

My bride asks that you greet warmly all the appropriate people there on our behalf. God bless. Dated as above, in haste.

Michael Behaim, y[our] w[illing] c[ousin].

39 ❦ Michael to Friederich, 25 July 1533

Praise be always to God, A.D. 1533, 25 July, in Breslau.

My sincere, willing service. Dear, esteemed, gracious Herr cousin, it gladdens my heart to learn that you and all our family are in good health. My wife and I, praise God, are still very well . . . I have been unable until now to answer the letter you wrote me after my marriage. Here follows as much as it seems necessary to me to defend my honor.

First, you divulge that you had good knowledge of all my doings already before my letter and that you knew that I had married into a respected family, although not into royalty.[117] [You also say] that you had not expected me to succumb to love and, especially considering how rich I am, to settle for such a modest meal.[118] [You are also unhappy because] after all you have done for me, I departed Nuremberg without confiding in you and even flatly denied the marriage. From all this, you [say you] now might conclude that my heart and my tongue have been far apart from each other.

Unfortunately, all that you say is true. I too would have been happier had you been informed from the beginning. I will try to explain why

---

116. Letter 36.
117. "Zu einer Erbarnn freundtschafft, aber doch nicht zu furstenn."
118. "Weyl sich ein zimliche narung zu meinem Reychtum ubel reympt." This is surely intended to be sarcastic.

things have happened the way they did. I ask you to hear me out with an open mind.

Our finding each other was a very rare event, and there is much to write about it. But, in brief, I can only look on it this way: she caught my eye and I caught hers, and we were joined together by God, because He had ordained that it happen this way by his divine will.[119] I thank Him for having given me a good, respectable girl, whom none of my family need be ashamed of. To speak frankly, God might have punished me with a loose whore with lots of money who is the talk of the town.

My wife and I hope now that it is God's divine plan to give us good fortune and success so that we may live together comfortably within the estate of marriage as our ancestors have done. We are prepared to make the necessary sacrifices so that some day we may have more than we now have. There is a saying: "when two poor people have become rich or two rich people poor, it is by the grace of God." But, lest I sin, I have not complained in the past about my poverty. I thank God that I am neither the poorest nor the richest of men . . .

I admit, d[ear], e[steemed] Herr cousin that I was wrong to think that I should not share my plans with you or seek your advice before the event, as would have been reasonable. The thought did occur to me. Many times I convinced myself completely that I should do so and I often started out for your room. Very often at the market and on the street or when we walked together in the private garden, I wanted to share with you something of the matter as it then stood. But I had such great fear of your angry reaction. You had preached so many good sermons to me on taking a wife that I never could in the end reveal it to you. Yet in my heart, I still thought, "O, God, had I only spoken up!" Then, perhaps, I might have thought more about my plans. But it had by then already happened, at Fastnacht, when I returned from Cracow after taking Paul back.[120] You shall not understand it, but, God as my witness, I do now regret it, and the thoughts I had about it at the time when I was with you were painful enough. The marriage cannot now be undone;

119. "Das sie mir unnd ich Ir ersehenn unnd also von got zusammen gefuegt seindt/ weyl ers dann der gestalt nach seinem gotlichenn willenn verordnet." Michael defends a clandestine marriage, which was opposed especially by Protestant authorities but also by Catholic authorities. There were four months between the private betrothal (early February) and the public ceremony (mid-June).

120. This must have been in early February, before he departed for Liegnitz. See letter 34.

it is something born of God. May He now give us good fortune and success. Amen.

You also accuse me of despising [the name of] Behaim and believe that you have never in your life heard anyone shame the Behaims the way I have done by saying that I never imagined I would gain a wife here from such a family. D[ear] Herr cousin, please remember that to my masters here I have always been a broomsweep and house servant, as I have often indicated to you before [when I complained about] the extraordinary chores they have made me perform. And all the while I was losing my own money and getting nothing in return. No one here ever recognized me as a Behaim from Nuremberg. So you must understand that under these circumstances I could not imagine getting a wife from such a [prominent] family. I hope I have insulted neither myself nor any other Behaim by having done so, even though I have not married into royalty.

That among all my relatives you found none who wanted to come to my wedding, I blame on the great distance [between Nuremberg and Breslau]. I did honor them with an invitation, for which they do not consider me good enough to thank. They have replied belatedly through my sister. This I blame on their well-demonstrated friendship, which, during my days away from you, I have discovered to be not worth a heller. Since leaving, I have enjoyed the friendship of none of them, save for one, possibly two, dinner invitations, not much more, extended to me "out of friendship."[121]

But d[ear] Herr cousin, I can never repay the good deeds and friendship you and your children have always shown me and my siblings. It is true that your efforts on our behalf have always been great. You have always meant us well and shown us every loyalty. I herewith acknowledge in writing that you have done more for me than all my relatives. In time you will most certainly be repaid for it. For now, I can only make promises. I ask you again not to despair of me altogether, for I am today expecting as much favor from you as ever.

I must show you my good and true intentions by providing at least a rough sketch of what my wife brings to me [in the marriage], so that you may readily see that she has also gotten her equal here in me. First, I have already received 800 Rhenish gulden in cash. I also have at least an estimate of my share of the property, which I hold jointly with my two sisters-in-law. When my mother-in-law dies, there is 1600 Hungarian gold

---

121. The words "schadenn halbenn" (out of shame) are stricken, and over them are written the words "freundtschafft halbenn."

gulden in dowried property. That is an ample 2400 Rhenish gulden. Also, I am receiving free food and drink for a year and a day after the wedding from my mother-in-law, along with the services of a maid and a servant. Thereafter, I am promised free lodging in half of the house. So far I am pleased, and I get along with my mother-in-law. However, a year and a day after the wedding, I must begin to maintain the house myself. May eternal God grant me good fortune to that end. Amen.

My mother-in-law also provides me with all necessary household furnishings, bedsteads and quilts for me and my servants, chests, wardrobes, and whatever belongs in a room—tables, chairs, pewter settings, linens, etc. Also the jewelry, clothing, and accessories it is fitting to give with a daughter.

So I have had a stately wedding and for a long time there have been more formalities than I desire, prolonged by the family of the bride. In sum, all this shows you their good and true feelings [about the marriage]. If you doubt my word on this, just ask around.

God willing, I am planning a business which will allow me to trade with Liegnitz and Nuremberg, while maintaining my markets here in Breslau. This will also prepare the way for an eventual market in Poland, which I find an appealing prospect, if almighty God grants good fortune.

D[ear], e[steemed] Herr cousin, since I am contemplating trading more in conjunction than in competition with Nuremberg,[122] and wish to do so successfully, would you ask Peter Antonio if I might be his agent here, as Hans Heugel [is for others]?[123] If he does not want to do this, you might propose the following arrangement. If he will supply me with a wide range of silks of his own choosing, which I can retail to other buyers, I will provide him a good accounting of what I am able to sell each year and have the remainder delivered wherever he wants it to go. In return, I ask only for a fair share of the profits. I hope to be able to sell such goods here profitably over a good part of the year.

D[ear], e[steemed] Herr cousin, I ask you to devote all possible attention to this matter. I look on it as a deed for your son as well as for myself, so that the Behaims might also become merchants [in Breslau]. Think it over carefully, and if [my plan] pleases you, do your best to move the arrangements forward without delay. We can have a trial run for a year

---

122. "Furderlich unnd nicht hinderlich zu Nuremberg."
123. Peter Antonio de Nobili was an old business associate of Friederich with a warehouse in Nuremberg. Friederich's son Paul later worked in his firm in Cracow. See p. 83.

or two, during which either party may at any time withdraw if he becomes displeased. I intend to be a completely different kind of agent than Hans Heugel. Although he has never had to sell a heller's worth of merchandise for Peter Antonio here, he does trade regularly in fish (herring, etc.) with Frankfurt an der Oder [as an agent for others].

Herewith, d[ear], e[steemed] Herr cousin, you have a full account of my plans and activities. I also ask you [still again] not to let the effort involved discourage you from reaching the best possible agreement you can between my brother and me with [regard to] our peasants. I also want you to do your best to arrange for my brother to pay me annual installments on two of his notes [which I hold], one for one hundred thirty-three gulden, the other for forty-three gulden, one pound, sixteen pfennigs, a total of one hundred seventy-six gulden, one pound, sixteen pfennigs, at eight pounds, twelve pfennigs [interest]. I give you my full and complete authority to settle this matter on my behalf. Whatever you work out shall also please me. I have long awaited a letter from you saying the matter has been settled, as you and Herr [Albrecht] Letscher promised it would be. I can well imagine that no one except my brother has prevented this from happening. I have also written an encouraging letter to Herr Letscher. I ask you now to try again with him to resolve this matter at the earliest. If it cannot be settled without me, just make sure that my brother takes no more than what is due him from the peasants and that my share is safely handed over to you. If you would rather not be bothered with it, instruct young L[inhardt] Münsterer to hold my share.[124]

D[ear], e[steemed], gracious Herr cousin. This letter comes to you with every good intention. Please accept it as such. Do let me know how the two matters stand, namely, with Peter Antonio and with my brother. Greet [your] wife, [my] cousin, and all your children. May the Lord God be a gracious father to us all.

Y[our] w[illing] cousin.

[P.S.] Hans Rappolt has several times asked me, first, to tell you that he is at your service, and he has further inquired if you can help him get a copy of Herr Stublinger's [last will and] testament. He will gladly pay whatever it costs and you may send it to him here. He also wants it sent as soon as possible. Whenever an opportunity arises to repay you and yours for this favor, he will always do so.

Michael Behaim.

---

124. It was Münsterer, obviously a trusted friend, who later informed Michael of Friederich's death. See letter 40.

Paul Behaim was Friederich's eldest son and the one on whom the family pinned its hopes. On New Year's Day 1533 Friederich had met with two great merchants, the Nuremberger Andreas Imhoff, Paul's maternal uncle, and the Italian Peter Antonio de Nobili. Together they signed a contract enrolling Paul, fourteen years old, in a three-year apprenticeship (his first) under the tutelage of a family friend in Peter Antonio's firm in Cracow. Paul later returned to Nuremberg to take a position in the firm of his relatives, the Imhoffs.

When Paul left Nuremberg for Cracow on 2 January, Michael escorted him. Finding himself in the role of a mentor must have pleased Michael, and he no doubt had much to tell Paul about the life that lay ahead. During Paul's first year the two visited each other in Breslau and Cracow, as Michael exercised fraternal oversight and care.

First apprenticeships were predictably difficult, and Paul's proved to be particularly so. A proud and moody youth accustomed to privilege, he did not endear himself to his foreign masters nor even to Michael, whose marriage he resented and ridiculed. Nine months into his service his father died (September 1533), leaving his mother with six children in addition to Paul, five of them girls and five under twelve years of age. The family's future now depended urgently on Paul's success.

Michael broke the news of Friederich's death to Paul. By modern standards he did so crudely, first scolding Paul for apparent rudeness to a business associate in Cracow, Bernhard Gaysler, whom Michael had asked to give Paul money when he needed it. But death was painfully routine in these times, and Paul now needed more than ever to keep his eyes fixed solely on the future. As Michael also makes clear, he too was grief-stricken by Friederich's death, and was struggling valiantly to look beyond it.

40 ❦ Michael to Paul Behaim, October 1533

Praise be always to God, A.D. 1533, October,[125] in Breslau.

125. No day is given, but it was received in Cracow on 28 October. From the contents

My friendly and devoted service always. Know, dear cousin Paul, that I returned safely on 16 [October], praise and thanks be to almighty God. Amen.

I have discovered that in my absence Hans Heugel delivered a letter from you to my servant, dated 25 September, in which I happily learn of your health. Please thank your master, M[onsieu]r Antonio, very much for the greeting he sends me through you, and greet him warmly on my behalf. Also let him know that I am completely at his service.[126]

What you have written in response to my last letter, I will pass over for now.[127] You *do* have in me a true cousin, and you really should never think otherwise. I will do for your mother, you, and all your siblings all the good I possibly can. You may count on my being faithful.

You indicate that Bernhard Gaysler answered your request for his promissory note with harsh words and also contradicted you by denying he had ever seen Franz Behl.[128] This surprises me, for it is not like him. I must believe that you addressed him rudely, for he is always a fine, reasonable fellow with everyone. I have often admonished you to treat people decently.[129] With the best intentions and for your own good, I again in friendship ask you to do so. It just will not do for you to exalt yourself above your own kind and to treat someone who is your equal as less than yourself.[130] People are not impressed by that, especially in a foreign land. By birth, I too am of noble origin, yet from time to time I must eat with many a gentleman who would perhaps not have been good enough to serve my late father. Dear cousin, I want to share with you in friendship this lesson I have learned and I hope it is one you will accept in good will. All my life I have heard the saying, "kind words break no teeth."

---

it becomes clear that the letter was written after 17 October. This letter and the two that follow are in J. Kamann, "Aus Paulus Behaims I Briefwechsel," *MVGN* 3 (1881): 105–10, 117–20.

126. Michael hoped to become his agent in Breslau. See letter 39.

127. The letter must have contained criticism of Michael's marriage, which Michael here chooses to put off until a later date. On 26 November he wrote to Paul asking him to cease his "much useless talk about my wife," and assured him that although married he could "still ... be useful to people." Kamann, "Aus Paulus Behaims I Briefwechsel," 111.

128. Paul had attempted to collect money that Gaysler owed to Michael.

129. "Mit ydermann fein glimpffig seyst."

130. Paul was at the time also trying to get a copy of the Behaim coat of arms, no doubt to impress upon his hosts his importance. See letter 42.

Still, it surprises me not a little that Bernhard Gaysler should complain about making a note for what he owes me. I will certainly write to him about it now that you have told me of his harsh words. But that you now believe that you cannot expect anything good from my good friend [Gaysler], I also plead innocence. I cannot always know how it is in a person's heart. When someone gives me good words, I expect it to be as he says. I had asked him, on my behalf, to let you come to him when you are in need and not to allow you to go wanting. Often plain fellows [like Gaysler] will be as much help to one as great lords, whom one, out of fear, may not always dare approach.

Kind, dear cousin, know that as I approached Leipzig, I ran into Hans von Ploben and other Nuremberg [merchants] who were there on business. I learned from them that Nuremberg is in the grip of a great plague and that more than a third of the city has fled, especially the patricians. Of their number none remain except the seven senior councilmen.[131] Also, no one can remember when so many artisans fled the city in time of plague. May God have mercy on us!

I ask you not to be frightened when I now tell you bluntly that almighty and eternal God has called your father, my dear cousin and the best friend I and my siblings have had on earth, out of this valley of tears and into eternal life. Young Lienhard Münsterer wrote to me in Leipzig that he died on 25 September. May God be gracious and merciful to him and to all souls who believe in Christ. Amen. I understand, however, that he did not die from the plague. As you know well, he has lain ill for a long time.[132]

Do not resist the will of almighty God in this. Leave it to His divine grace, and bear in mind that we all must die and that nothing can prevent it. I wrote to your mother from Leipzig, but I cannot know whether she is still in Nuremberg or has gone to Grünsberg.[133] I hope each day to hear from my sister. May almighty God bless and keep you. Dated as above.

Michael Behaim, your willing cousin.

[P.S.] I cannot write any more [about your father] because of my great

---

131. "Die 7 alten herrn" or *septem viri*, the most powerful of the forty-two members of the Small Council.

132. On 26 November Michael wrote that according to Paul's mother, his father had died of poisoning: "man hab ims zwtrinckenn geben." Kamann, "Aus Paulus Behaims I Briefwechsel," 111. The reference is to the cumulative effect of the medicinal "poisons" given to treat his illness, not to a foul deed.

133. Grünsberg was Friederich's little castle estate in nearby Altdorf, purchased in 1529.

grief. Whenever I think of him, I must cry. Gladly would I now have ridden all the way from Leipzig to Nuremberg, but because of the plague there, I have given it up. God willing, I hope to go as soon as it stops, perhaps by Lent.[134]

Dear cousin Paul, I have this hour received a letter from you, dated 5 October, and with it your letter to Albrecht Letscher. I will send it on to him with the next messenger. Although Dr. Scheurl rode from here on 17 October, I think he is going to join his wife in Amberg, where he has fled the plague.[135] I have also just received the two promissory notes in a letter from Bernhard Gaysler; tell him that I read his letter with pleasure.[136]

Would you deliver the enclosed letter to Stanislaus Romer, and tell him that it has been delivered to me by our host in Bautzen, Hans Koch.

As I was sealing this letter, a messenger arrived from Nuremberg with a letter from my brother, who writes that your mother and all the children, also my sister, are well and hardy in Grünsberg.

M. Behaim.

41 ❦ Margaretha Behaim to Paul, 28 October 1533

My most sincere greeting and every good wish . . . I expect it is now known to you that we have lost your dear father . . .to whom the Lord God is disposed to be gracious and merciful—of this we should have no doubt whatsoever, for he is, as God wills, a child of eternal life. So, dear cousin, I ask you most sincerely to leave the matter to the Lord God, for we can bring nothing back by crying. If crying helped, I would cry day and night, for I know that I have lost in him not a cousin, but a dear father, for he treated me as a father does [his child]. Alas, we must now surrender ourselves to almighty God, for this is his divine will and we must submit to it. Although it hurts, God will have it so. Believe me, hardly anything worse has ever happened or could happen to me my life long. Dear cousin, give yourself entirely to God, commend yourself to

134. Michael evidently expected the plague to continue for three or four months.
135. Michael apparently contemplated trying to catch Scheurl and give him the letter to Letscher, which would indicate that the present letter was written not long after the seventeenth.
136. Gaysler had evidently decided to do business directly with Michael rather than with the apparently petulant Paul.

his divine grace and mercy, leave all that you do to him, and trust in him completely with all your heart. He will not forsake you and yours. You have a devout mother and many good friends, and in Andreas Imhoff I see not only a friend, but also a father. He is at all times and in all matters devoted to Mother.[137] So write to him and thank him for all his efforts and ask him to take you into his care. Let him know that you trust him. Commend yourself and all your siblings to him as to a dear father. [Tell him] that you shall always be willing to serve him as far as possible in your humble position, and that you want always to heed him and to please him. And [assure him] that what it is not possible for you and your siblings to repay him, you will ask the Lord God to give him a thousand-fold.

If you have the time, write also to the Letschers and to your grand-mother. I have no doubt that you know what to do. You should also expect every favor from me and my brother Michael. When you need something of mine, only let me know . . . I am certain that the same is true of my brother.

Dear cousin, be mindful of your duty and do what pleases your master and your Mother, and the Lord God will never forsake you, that you will see. Have a little patience [with your apprenticeship]. Soon you will have put a year or three behind you, and then things will be better for you.

When you have the time, write to me again. Klara, Apollonia, Hans, Lucia, and Katharina all send warm greetings,[138] as does the maid. Herr Rotmund and she are in Altdorf.[139] God bless. Written in Grünsberg, on Simon and Judah's Day [28 October], 1533.

Margret Behaim, your willing cousin.

42 ❦ Michael to Paul, 18 January 1534

Praise be always to God, A.D. 1534, 18 January, in Breslau.
My friendly, willing service and wish for a good and happy new year.

---

137. Margaretha here refers to Paul's mother as if she were her own, offering further commentary on her and Michael's alienation from their mother and their closeness to Friederich's family. Andreas Imhoff became the guardian to Paul and his siblings.
138. Paul's siblings.
139. The reference is to Katharina Behaim, Friederich's sister and the wife of Herr Rotmund.

The Behaim coat of arms with a phoenix affixed. Reproduced by permission of the Staatsarchiv Nürnberg.

Dear little cousin,[140] my last letter went out to you on 26 November, 1533, with Simon Weuer, Herr Bartol Focker's servant. With it I sent you a bundle of letters. They came to me here in Breslau on 15 November from Nuremberg with a letter from your mother. Since then I have received two letters from you, dated 6 and 14 December in Cracow and delivered to me by Hans Heugel on 16 and 21 December. I have read both carefully, and I am answering them as far as it seems to me to be necessary.

I am happy to learn of your health. Although trustworthy people here have reported to me disparaging remarks that you have made about my marriage, since you deny having made such remarks and call all these people liars and do not even want to know their names, I will drop the matter. But I want to ask you most sincerely not to make such comments again in the future. Just devote yourself to serving your master and do not concern yourself with my marriage, tobogganing, or other activities. If I had wanted advice in the matter [of my marriage], I think I would have sought it from your late father, who was an understanding man. Although you did not say so, it has long been clear to me from your letters that you thought you should have been consulted [about my marriage]. At the time I looked on you as still young and too inexperienced to advise me in such matters, and hence I did not turn to you. Furthermore, I have had none of my relatives suggest that I should never have proceeded as I did.[141] Since the matter could not have been otherwise than it was, I have entrusted it to God. I ask that you also try not to make light of it.

As you desire to know about my life here, I will tell you. You have heard that I am racing toboggans. It is an activity I pursue in moderation. Because there is otherwise not much fun in this land, I need this as a seasonal recreation. I am also attending to my little business, which involves many quality goods from Nuremberg and Leipzig. I will confide in you that I am hoping that my brothers-in-law, the Hornecks, will take me into their firm. They do more than 20,000 gulden in trade between here and Antwerp, Nuremberg, and Leipzig at every fair. They have always had their own warehouse in Antwerp. Franz Schleicher was previously their Nuremberg agent. Although we do not yet have an agreement, I hope to almighty God that one will soon be reached. I will let you know

140. "Liebes vetterlein." Paul would turn fifteen on 25 January. He is here being put in his place by Michael, who was annoyed by his criticism of his marriage.
141. As Paul has evidently done in the letter to which Michael here replies.

when we do. So now you know my plans. But would you keep them to yourself and not tell anyone about them until it happens?

Dear cousin, I ask you most sincerely to be a devoted, honorable, and conscientious worker for your master. Do not be proud or arrogant and spurn the extra little tasks as being beneath you. When your time is up and you are a little older, you will be relieved of such chores. I have now served foreign masters for eleven, going on twelve, years, and I have always had to stoke the fire, sweep [the office], and fetch wine and beer [for older workers]. And when, at last, my promised time was up, I still had to do so. In addition, I have always had to pay my own money [to be an apprentice] and was unable to earn anything for myself. And, as you know, I have all this time been away [from Nuremberg] and without my parents. Nowhere have I felt at home. In foreign lands I have been more often at the mercy of undisciplined fools than of honest men. Although I too am a Behaim from Nuremberg, my family and coat of arms have been of no help to me. I tell you this so that you will not presume on the same, for people truly attach no significance to such things. Today it is no different in Nuremberg than elsewhere in the world: one who has money advances, while one who has nothing gets little in addition. People observe that one has nothing; they do not ask who one is. And therein lies the problem. I tell you on my truest word of honor that had the Lord God not provided for my marriage, I would not know where to turn now that your father has died. He was the best friend I and my siblings have had on earth. May the eternal Father now repay him with every good thing eternal life has to offer. Amen.

You have asked about the bird we Behaims have on our coat of arms. It is a phoenix. Such a bird no longer exists. There is a complicated story behind it, which I cannot go into here. I once wrote your late father and also asked him so sincerely to send me a painted coat of arms. He wrote back such a chapter to me, accusing me of such great pride. I could not begin to write you all that he said. He did not believe that I should be concerned that my coat of arms was lost. As he did not expect me to be riding in a tournament, he did not think that I would be needing it. Rather I should be applying myself to what my master commanded me to do. In short, [he scolded me] for caring so much about something that I should never have desired in the first place. Nevertheless, I subsequently wrote to my brother and got it from him, as I recall. When I read your letter, my wife was present, and she asked that I send it now to you. You will find it here enclosed. With great effort I can still have it painted on paper here in Breslau. But truly, were it gilded a hundred times, you still should have it, and with it everything that is dear to you.

Dear cousin, just be useful, honest, humble, willing, and helpful to everyone. Then you will succeed and be held in favor by all. I hope almighty God will help us Behaims create a business,[142] so that we, too, may in time rise [in the world]. Please accept my letter as intending only good, for I have truly written it from my heart.

My wife sends her sincere greeting. May the lord God bless you. Greet both your lords for me warmly, particularly Herr Antonio. Dated as above.

Michael Behaim, y[our] w[illing] cousin.

[P.S.] Enclosed is the letter from your mother. The letters you sent me have been sent on [to Nuremberg] with a sure messenger. You may be assured that they will be safely delivered to your mother. Would you personally deliver the enclosed letter to Bernhard Gaysler? If he is not there, keep it until he returns. But be sure he gets it as soon as he arrives. He is in Bartol Focker's service.

142. "In ain handel helffen."

❦ EPILOGUE

Michael survived both family conflict and foreign apprenticeship to return to Nuremberg an experienced merchant, with markets in Breslau and Cracow. He and Margaretha arrived in September 1540 with their four-year-old son Michael VI, their second child. Anna, their first, had died in Breslau in February. They had eight more children in Nuremberg, six of whom outlived them.

A few surviving letters from 1540 suggest a reconciliation between Michael and his mother after the death of his stepfather in 1539.[143] In early August he and his family visited her in Oscheling. Michael went on alone to Nuremberg to ready their house; he had hoped to occupy one on Dyliggasse (now Theresienstrasse). Although arrangements progressed so far that he had stocked the cellar with beer and wine, the deal fell through in the end. By November he and his family had settled into a house only a few steps from the Behaim family house on the corner of Zistelgasse, now Albrecht-Dürerstrasse 4. Michael happily reports to Paul, then in Antwerp working for the Imhoffs, how he and his wife were shown every honor and friendship by Paul's mother and Aunt Letscher, who presented them with invitations and gifts. There was also a gift of silver from the Imhoffs, as Michael's Nuremberg relatives now belatedly blessed his marriage. Unfailingly enterprising, Michael also asked Paul to enquire whether there might be a firm in Antwerp interested in making him its agent in Nuremberg.

In the end Michael succeeded against the odds and beyond his own expectations. Having fought failure and defeat for so many years, it is unlikely that he ever stopped looking over his shoulder. But he was also no longer the anxious boy he was in Milan. By his mid-twenties he was secure enough to be altruistic and even magnanimous. He showed this in his relationship with Paul Behaim, to whom he remained a patient friend, just as he had frequently promised his beloved cousin Friederich he would be.

143. J. Kamann, ed., "Aus dem Briefwechsel eines jungen Nürnberger Kaufmanns," 17–18.

Friederich VIII Behaim

❦ ❦ ❦ ❦ ❦ ❦ ❦ ❦ ❦ ❦ ❦ ❦ ❦ ❦ ❦ ❦ ❦ ❦

Friederich VIII Behaim (1563–1613) was Paul Behaim's third son, named after his grandfather Friederich VII. Michael must surely have known him during the six years their lives overlapped in Nuremberg before Michael's death in 1569. One can picture Michael, now mellow and secure, telling young Friederich stories about his grandfather's many kindnesses to him when he was a boy. But how different were the temperaments and experience of the two as youths. In contrast to Michael's boyhood world, Friederich's was secure and enriching, and he loved life.

In 1578, at the age of fourteen, Friederich enrolled in the Altdorf Academy nearby. The new school had been established only recently (1575) as a regional high school (*Landesschule*) for greater Nuremberg. Although its status was elevated to that of an academy in 1578 by Emperor Rudolf II, it did not become a full-fledged university until 1622. As an academy, it was about halfway between a public school (*Gymnasium*) and a university proper and could confer only bachelor's and master of philosophy degrees. There students perfected their Latin, broadened their humanistic learning, and as they advanced attended public lectures in the basic university subjects (the arts, philosophy, theology, medicine, and law). Academy programs varied widely across Germany in the number of required classes (from as few as four to as many as ten) and in the time spent in each (from as little as it took to demonstrate mastery of a subject to two full years). Altdorf had four classes and moved students along at their own pace.[1]

1. Georg Mertz, *Das Schulwesen der deutschen Reformation im 16. Jahrhundert* (Heidelberg, 1902), 190. On the conditions of Altdorf's development see W. v. Stromer, "Wirtschaft, Gesellschaft und Kultur des Reichsstadt Nürnberg

As a beginning student, Friederich lived in the college under the care of Herr and Frau Oertel, who also provided students with board and other services. Herr Oertel was the school's *Oeconomus*, or chief steward, with special responsibility for the twelve indigent youths charitably supported by the school. As Friederich quickly discovered, his was not a kitchen for boys with aristocratic tastes. For Friederich's schooling Frau Behaim paid around sixty gulden annually: ten to twelve gulden a quarter for board, plus another five gulden for Friederich's room in the college (less than half that for the room he took in the city with two classmates in spring 1580). The average journeyman's annual wage in Nuremberg industries was forty gulden.[2] Friederich's schooling was a sizable expenditure for his family, fully the equivalent of the cost of a modern college education.

A widow since 1568, Friederich's mother had eight children between the age of thirteen and the age of twenty-three, when Friederich began school in Altdorf. Five of them lived at home with her. Her eldest son, Paul, studied in Leipzig and Padua and gained a position at the imperial court in Prague in 1579. In 1576 her second son, Christoph, then fourteen, had been apprenticed to an official in Regensburg. Friederich's school years were hard times for this family that had been accustomed to a lot. When in 1582 his elder sister Magdalena defended her engagement to Balthasar Baumgartner, Jr., a man of means about whom her brother Christoph had doubts, she vividly recalled the spectacle of their mother "always spending, while taking nothing in."[3]

Away from home for the first time, Friederich was as anxious as any modern freshman. Although Altdorf was no great distance from Nuremberg (only twenty-six kilometers), he might just as well have been in Utrecht. In addition to peer approval and academic success, he fretted

---

vom 1580 als Ausgang und Umfeld den Universitätgründung in Altdorf," *Jahrbuch für Frankische Landesgeschichte* 41 (1981): 155–64. The "General Rules" of Altdorf's founding ordinance convey something of the school atmosphere, particularly the commitment to protect and educate the young. See appendix 1.

2. Rudolf Endres, "Zur Einwohnerzahl und Bevölkerungsstruktur Nürnbergs im 15/16. Jahrhundert," *MVGN* 57 (1970): 258.

3. See Steven Ozment, *Magdalena and Balthasar: An Intimate Portrait of Life in 16th-Century Europe* (New York, 1986), 34–35.

over his room, meals, laundry, books, clothes, health, and the mails. His mother both consoled and scolded him, alternately smothering him with maternal instruction and demanding that he take firmer control of his own life. Her letters are a how-to manual for the sixteenth-century collegian, as she counsels or cautions him on his dealings with boarding-house keepers, physicians, roommates, stokers, maids, and even prostitutes. From dress to medicine to firewood to food, from money to travel to study to drink, no aspect of his life went unsupervised.

By every measure Friederich was a docile and obedient youth. Not until summer 1580, when he was seventeen and beginning his last year in Altdorf, did he have a serious confrontation with his mother. This was a particularly stressful time for them both. Friederich had long suffered from recurrent eye infections, which he sometimes describes as inflammation (*flus*), sometimes as a film or blemish over one of his eyes (*fel*). An eye affliction of the time known as *fel* left its victim blind. What Friederich describes sounds like a ferocious sty. His problem worsened in summer 1580, and desperate for a cure he became the patient of a high-priced eye surgeon in Altdorf whom his mother considered a charlatan. Frau Behaim was herself distressed at the time by her own financial problems, and she also suspected that heavy drinking might be inflaming Friederich's eyes. (Depending on whom one believes, Friederich's daily consumption of beer may have quadrupled since his freshman year.) His mother's reluctance to pay his surgeon, who had some stature in Altdorf, caused a public scandal, which a plenary session of the faculty and Friederich's own special pleading finally resolved. But his mother did not find his behavior courageous or smart during the episode.

Frau Behaim had good reason to worry about Friederich's health and welfare. Nuremberg had already endured terrible plagues since his birth. In 1570 sixteen hundred children died of smallpox, and between 1573 and 1576 sixty-five hundred children and adults fell victim to plague and dysentery.[4] By modern standards medical science was still primitive. Physicians explained disease in terms of the buildup of foul matter in the body, which upset the body's humors (blood, phlegm, choler, and bile) and weakened its resistance to infection. Prevention consisted mainly of avoiding the sick and the places they frequented, like the public baths. It

4. Endres, "Zur Einwohnerzahl," 205.

was believed that breathing the same air as the afflicted or even having their odors cross one's body could cause infection in time of plague. In their official proclamations physicians in Nuremberg urged people to practice personal hygiene and sobriety. They also recommended regular purging with water, by forced drinking and sweating (hot baths), and the use of laxatives. For many, Friederich and his mother among them, the surest means of prevention was regular bleeding. This involved opening veins in different parts of the body with special lancets or applying heated glass suction cups to scarified tissue. Bleeding was thought to remove accumulated foul matter from the body and thus to restore humoral balance. Contemporary almanacs, informed by both the Gospel and the zodiac, indicated with a small symbol of a lancet the most auspicious days of the month for bleeding. Physicians in Nuremberg recommended this preventive measure twice a year, in spring and autumn. As the letters make clear, Friederich faithfully met his bleeding dates.

Friederich concluded his studies in Altdorf in June 1581. He then spent perhaps two years in Italy, where, like his brother Paul before him, he studied law in Padua before returning home. He eventually became a *Pfleger* in the nearby villages of Gräfenberg and Hiltpoltstein north of Nuremberg, a kind of town manager with both judicial and police powers.

Friederich's three-and-a-half-year correspondence with his mother ended with her death on 31 December 1581, two days after Friederich's eighteenth birthday. That so many of her letters survive makes the correspondence particularly interesting. As a rule, letters coming into Nuremberg from children were kept far more often than those going out to them from parents and guardians. Unless the adults were meticulous in preserving copies of their correspondence their letters usually vanished at their destination. Because so many of Frau Behaim's letters have survived, their correspondence records the relationship between a mother and her son as well as the trials of a maturing youth.

🐝 ALTDORF, 1578–1581

1 🐝 Mother to Friederich, 2 August 1578

Dear son Friederich. With the carter I am sending you three more shirts in an old sack. They may still be a bit damp, so you should hang them over a window for a little while when the sun is out.⁵ I am also sending you a satin cap, two spoons, and a small fork. There is also half a Rhenish gulden you must pay to matriculate.⁶ In addition, I am sending you a gulden which I still owe your hostess. Please present it to her. And I am sending two hand towels. You need not return the sack. Although it is filthy, you may use it to put your dirty wash in. When it wears out, let me know, and someone will send you another. Nothing more. God bless. 2 August, 1578.

[unsigned]⁷

2 🐝 Friederich to Mother, 5 August 1578

Kind, dear Mother. I am letting you know that I received the letter and the money yesterday, also a sack containing the cap, the two spoons, and the small fork, three shirts, which were already completely dry, and two hand towels. Would you also let me know where I should have my wash done? And send me a signet. I also want Paul to buy the *Orationes Demosthenis Olynthiacae*, have it bound, and send it to me.⁸ I need it in my second class.⁹ No more. God bless. 5 August, 1578.

Y[our] L[oving] S[on],
Friederich Behaim

---

5. Frau Behaim had evidently rushed to get them on the departing mail cart.

6. The school ordinance required children with means to pay a matriculation fee of one-half gulden; it waived the fee for the poor. Mertz, *Das Schulwesen*, 594. See also letter 4.

7. Unsigned letters may be drafts; clean copies were mailed. In this way copies of correspondence were preserved.

8. Paul II Behaim was Friederich's eldest brother.

9. According to Johann Sturm's *Schulplan* for Strasbourg (1538), students read Demosthenes' *Orations* at the age of ten or eleven, a couple of years earlier than the age at which Friederich is reading it. Mertz, *Das Schulwesen*, 148.

3 ❧ Mother to Friederich, 8 August 1578

Dear son Friederich. I have gotten your letter from the carter and learned of your need of a book. Paul has asked around and there are two versions available. One looks like Hebrew to me and costs seven *Zwelfer* unbound;[10] another costs seventeen *Zwelfer*, also unbound, but it has the Greek and the Latin side by side. Let me know which you need.

As I read further, you also ask about laundry. I have spoken with Frau Oertel, who tells me that there is a woman there who washes for the counts and takes dirty laundry. But at eight pfennig a shirt it is too much, and [she charges] more for linen and the like. Therefore, Frau Oertel says that if I want, she will also do your wash for you, since she otherwise only washes twice [a week]. So leave your laundry with her and I will give her some money for it.

The Oertels have indicated that when a student wants a drink at the afternoon snack or at dinnertime, it is provided from Herr Oertel's cellar in either [a full] measure, at four pfennigs, or a half measure, at two.[11] So pay him immediately for what you need, and write down in your account book what you put into the money box.

I also asked them about a surgeon, and they indicated their willingness to direct you to the man who opens veins at the bath, if you will tell them when your time to be bled comes.[12] So you may do so when it is time. And do go bathe every month when it suits you best.

No more for now. God bless. 8 August, 1578.

      [unsigned]

4 ❧ Friederich to Mother, 11 August 1578

Filial love and devotion, dear Mother. When you and the others are well and hardy, I rejoice to hear it. Know that I, too, am still in good health.

Dear Mother, you write in your last letter about the availability of a Hebrew book. But I have not asked you for a Hebrew book. You have

10. A *Zwelfer* or *Zwolfer*, was a twelve-pfennig piece.

11. "Die mas . . . ein seidla." A "seidla" was a little more than a pint, a "mas" a little more than a quart.

12. Regular bleeding was taken very seriously within the Behaim family. On the subject see Ozment, *Magdalena and Balthasar*, 119–20.

misunderstood me. I have written you about a Greek book, and I prefer the one with the Latin and Greek side by side, because [Demosthenes] is much harder to understand than other Greek books.

Regarding the [extra] beers I drink in the evening, I am deferring payment, as are the others here, per Herr Oertel's command. But I make a note of everything. Should I pay for it now, I would not have much money left. For at Herr Oertel's instruction, I have had to serve the twelve orphans and my table companions around fifteen full measures.[13] That is already sixty pfennigs. And I have also spent three pounds on my own needs,[14] namely, thirty pfennigs to Pulmair for an inscription,[15] thirty-six to Kerba for a tankard, and I am having a storage box[16] made for twenty-eight pfennigs.

May I ask your advice about a key to my room? My roommates go to Pestner's to eat, and they return very late, so I always have to wait an hour or two. [This is the policy with keys.] When the time comes for me to vacate the room and make way for another, I must sell the key to the person who is moving in. [The problem is] that for three years, since the founding of the college, no more than three students have been in the room, so that I [the fourth] can buy no key from another.

Would you send me a signet? I can hardly manage [without one].

Nothing more except greetings to the entire household, especially to Ketterla[17] for her shilling, and to Ela[18] who cried for me when she left [Altdorf]. God bless. 11 August, in Altdorf.

> Y[our] L[oving] S[on]
> Friederich Behaim.

5 🐝 Friederich to Mother, 14 August 1578

Kind, dear Mother. I am writing to let you know that Matthias Löffelholz has taken his son from the pastor's home and now wants to put

---

13. "Den 12 Kaben" (Knaben). The twelve *alumnos*, or orphans, were charitably supported in the college. Mertz, *Das Schulwesen*, 596–97. On Friederich's buying beer for them see letter 14. As *Oeconomus* of the college Herr Oertel had responsibility for them. See n. 64.

14. A pound was thirty pfennigs.

15. The school charged matriculating students with means a minimum of thirty pfennigs for each additional inscription into their records. Mertz, *Das Schulwesen*, 596–97.

16. "Repositorium."

17. His sister Catherina, who is eighteen.

18. Short for Helena. A household servant. See letter 36.

Altdorf in the mid-seventeenth century, by Matthias Merian, Topographia Franconiae
d.i. Beschreibung u. Eigentliche Contrafactur der Vornembsten Stätte u.
Plätze des Frankenlandes (1648; new edition, Kassel, Bärenreiter Verlag, 1962),
p. 20. The college where Friederich lived during his first years in the academy is clearly
marked (C). Like the other students, Friederich took his meals in private homes, first with
the Oertels, then with the Gruners. Reproduced by permission of Bärenreiter Verlag.

him in the room where I am.[19] So either I must move out or someone must perhaps talk with Herr Löffelholz about this. I know that you will not want to trouble him. Nevertheless, we, namely Herr Oertel and Herr Sigel,[20] have discussed it, and we discovered that there are several noblemen, among them a von Gich and a von Ceib,[21] who want to move out [of the college]. We have also spoken with the Inspector,[22] who advised us to talk first with Herr [Hieronymus] Baumgartner and [find out] if he is in favor of it.[23] I wanted to let you know about this, for I only learned of it myself at sundown [today] 14 August. Otherwise, I would have written a more careful letter than the one I am writing now by candlelight. Either Herr Sigel or Paul must talk with Herr Baumgartner. The two noblemen [in question] are not now here, so it is still uncertain whether they will [in fact] move out once they arrive. Meanwhile, Herr Oertel wants to put me in a room in his other house until I find a place to stay.[24] Nevertheless, I want you to let me know soon what Herr Baumgartner says, so that I will be sure of my situation. Löffelholz's son will want to move in next week. His secretary has been here today to inspect [the room] and make arrangements for his meals.

Nothing more for now, except my greetings to all the household and to Martin,[25] and to all who have worked on my shirts. God bless. In haste. I have no more time. 14 August, at 1:00 A.M. by the great clock, 1578.

> Y[our] L[oving] S[on]
> Friederich Behaim.

19. Matthias Löffelholz of Colberg (1533–79) was alter Burgermeister after 1578. His son (1563–1605) was Friederich's age.

20. Also "Sigelt." A school authority. See letter 9.

21. A von Gich enrolled in both 1575 and 1578, Friederich's year. Elias von Steinmeyer, Die Matrikel der Universität Altdorf, vol. 2 (Würzburg, 1912), 229. There is no Ceib or C. eib in the Altdorf matriculation lists, so who this second youth is remains unclear.

22. The "Inspektore," or examiner, was traditionally an older student responsible for the students' moral behavior and studies ("inspector morum et studiorum"). Here he also monitored the students' living conditions, particularly their treatment in boarding houses. See letter 12.

23. Hieronymus Baumgartner, son of the late Bürgermeister Hieronymus (d. 1565), had helped establish the Altdorf school and was its first curator. Baumgartner's daughter Rosina became the second wife of Friederich's brother Paul in 1591.

24. As the Oeconomus of the college Herr Oertel placed students in the official boarding houses.

25. Martin was an occasional household worker with tailoring skills. See letters 9, 10, and 12.

6 ❦ Mother to Friederich, 16 August 1578

Dear son Friederich. I have your letter with the news of Löffelholz's planned change [of residence]. You must make room for him, as we indicated we would. Paul is not here now, but in Würzburg on business of the estate.[26] If something does not detain him, he will be back on Monday, and I will then send him out [to Altdorf] to see that the best arrangement is made for you. Should Löffelholz meanwhile want to move in within a day or two, you might ask him to delay because of the double ride.[27] If it cannot be done, then, for your sake and for mine, do ask Herr Oertel for assistance. He once left you with Herr Plunter in [   ] house.

The bedclothes are taking a while to make [   ]; one day, two helped.

Herr Held[28] has talked with Herr Baumgartner [about the planned changes in lodging]. He says it would be best, and each student would learn the most, if he could be where his tutor is. Therefore, the matter must be taken up with Herr Zan to see if it can be so arranged.[29] If nothing can be worked out, then you must ask the Oertels to help you for a while until something comes vacant.

I am herewith sending the signet with this letter. Nothing more for now. Greet Herr Oertel and his wife for me. 16 August 1578.

        Mrs. Paul Behaim

7 ❦ Friederich to Mother, 11 September 1578

Filial love and devotion, dear Mother. When you are well and hardy, I rejoice to hear it. Know that I am still in good health. May almighty God continue to keep us both in such good health. Amen.

Dear Mother, I have recently written you about a book one calls *Orationes Demosthenis Olynthiacae*. I also gave Paul, who was recently here, in-

---

26. "Der leen halb."

27. That is, Friederich would have to return home without immediate alternative lodging.

28. This is Friederich's uncle Sigmund Held, who with Jacob Imhoff became Friederich's guardian after Friederich's mother died in 1581. See letters 99 and 100. Held was the *Losungsschreiber*, or secretary to the tax board. He was married to Juliana Römer, Friederich's maternal aunt.

29. Herr Zan is Friederich's preceptor. See letters 16 and 17.

structions about it. You have not yet sent it to me. I need this book every day, so please send it to me at the earliest via Kolb.[30]

I also ask you to send me a blood-letting lancet, so that I can be bled. The other students have their own special lancets. It is dangerous to let oneself be cut with the [common knives at the baths] used to bleed the peasants and everyone else.

I know nothing more to write at this time. Greet the household for me and all our good friends. 11 September, 1578.

> Y[our] L[oving] S[on]
> Friederich Behaim

8 ❦ Mother to Friederich, 12 September 1578

Dear son Friederich. With this letter I am sending you the two books and some pears from the garden. Eat the pears in moderation so that you do not get sick. There is also a pair of ball candles for when you need them and a pair of horns so you can extinguish candles without breaking them. Thirdly, as I last time sent you [large] candles and a pewter lamp for small ones, buy yourself a few small candles and use them when you are not reading and writing so that the large candles may be saved for studying.

I have no other news except that we have lost two aunts this week, godmother Rietter and Doctor Christoph's widow. God bless. 12 September, 1578.

> Mrs. Paul Behaim

9 ❦ Friederich to Mother, 25 September 1578

Kind, dear Mother. Know that the nobleman who lived in my room has taken all his things away, including a tablecloth that was his and had covered the table where I work. So would you please send me another? The table is badly soiled and a disgrace when people enter the room. Also, if you have a good pewter pitcher, please send it along with a basin, for I have none in my room.

Herr Sigel has indicated to me that the Masters will bring several poor

---

30. Kolb, the carter, made daily runs between Nuremberg and Altdorf.

burgher children out to the college,[31] and several here who will not be approved by Herr Baumgartner must move out. For this reason, he wants to know whether Paul has spoken with Herr Baumgartner about me, as he said here [he would do], so that I too must not move. The others will leave on All Saints. Would you let me know about this at the earliest?

Otherwise, I have nothing to write at this time. Greetings to the household and to Martin. Tell him to visit me again before winter. 25 September, 1578.

> Y[our] L[oving] S[on]
> Friederich Behaim

10 & Mother to Friederich, 27 September 1578

My greetings and best wishes, dear son Friederich. I have received your letter and requests, and I am herewith sending you an old tablecloth. Although it is not fine and pretty, it must still absorb a student's ink and be of use to you. Since it has been dirty for a long time, you may want to have it washed out a bit. I did not have time to air it. I am also sending a hand basin and a pitcher.

Paul has gone to Prague with Joachim King to find himself a master there.[32] Otherwise, I have no further news, except that Martin has no desire to travel at this time. So long as the days remain long and there is life in us, [Jacob] Schleicher and his wife will come out to visit you once [   ].[33]

Greet Herr Oertel and his wife. Greetings to you from the household. God bless. 27 September, 1578.

> Magdalena Paulus Behaim.

[P.S.] Keep the pitcher clean. Always ask Oertel's maids to scrub it out when they clean. Take it down to them and fetch it when they finish with it, or have one of your companions who washes up with you do so, so that its cleaning is not a lot of trouble for the maids. Otherwise, they will find it a wearisome task [and neglect it].

31. Apparently these are some of the twelve orphans mentioned in letter 4.
32. That is, a position for Paul. See letter 16.
33. The Schleichers were relatives and friends. See letter 55. Because it is late September, the days are beginning to shorten.

Letter from Mother to Friederich, 27 September 1578 (letter 10)

11 ❦ Friederich to Mother, 13 October 1578

Filial love and devotion, dear Mother. When you are well and hardy, it gives me great joy to hear it. I am also still in good health.

Dear Mother, know that although the first quarter is not yet over, I have been unable to get by on the gulden you gave me for [my personal use], and I have spent an additional half-gulden. I would still like to make do on a gulden per quarter in the future, but I need many things for which I must spend money. So I ask you to send me as much as you will, and I will use it [accordingly] for my needs.

Also, my everyday trousers are full of holes and hardly worth patching; I can barely cover my rear,[34] although the stockings are still good. Winter is almost here, so I still need a [new] lined coat. All I have is the woven Arlas, which is also full of holes. So would you have my buckram smock lined as you think best? I have not worn it more than twice.

Oertel's cooking declines daily. Seldom if ever do I enjoy a meal, for the food he is serving now is thoroughly unclean, especially the meat, which is spoiled. Also, my throat is so swollen that I can barely swallow. I need some warm mead for it.

Nothing more for now. I would like to have written you sooner, but

34. "Ich kaum das gesess bedecken kan." On "Gesess" see n.73.

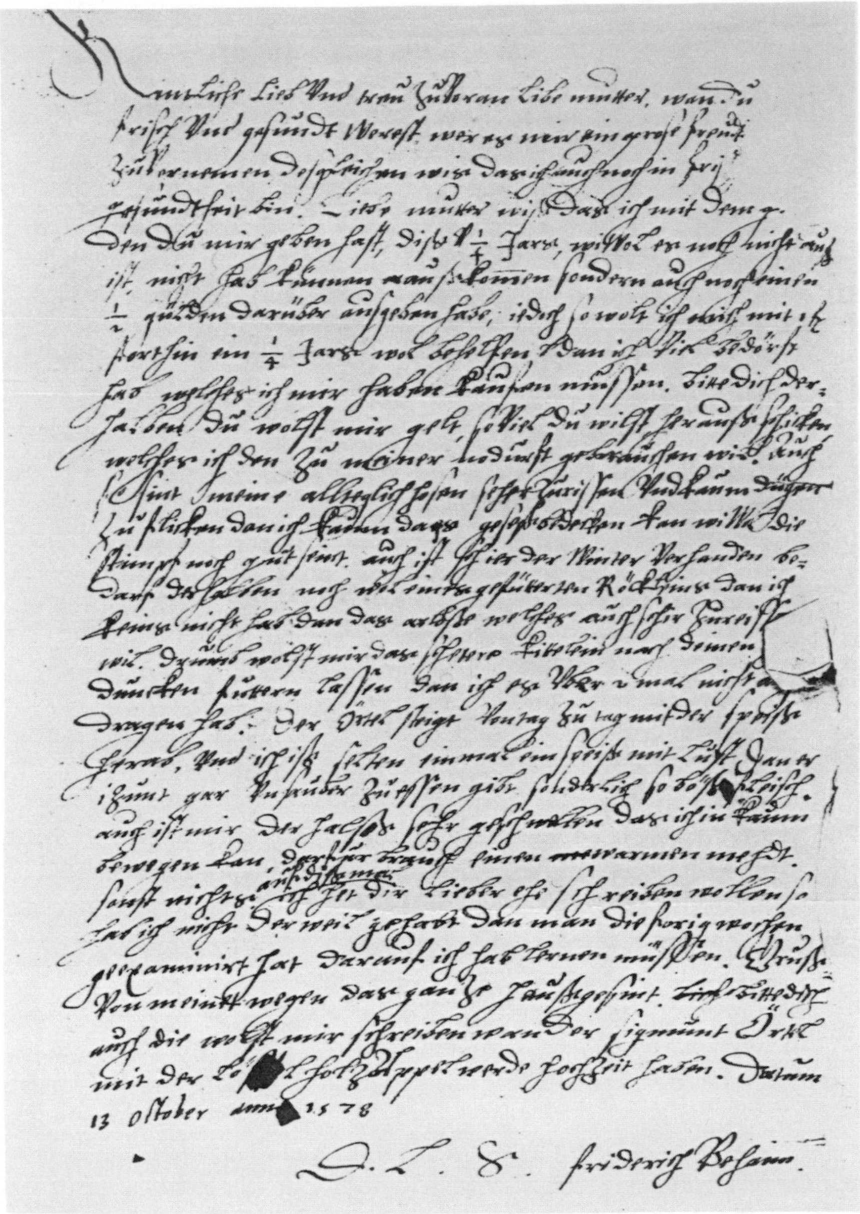

Letter from Friederich to Mother, 13 October 1578 (letter 11)

I have not had the time because exams were held last week and I had to study.

Greet all the household for me. Please write me when Sigmund Oertel and Appolonia Löffelholz are getting married.³⁵ 13 October, 1578.

> Y[our] L[oving] S[on]
> Friederich Behaim.

12 ❦ Mother to Friederich, 14 October 1578

Dear son Friederich. I have your letter and news of your health. I and all in the household here are also in rather good health, praise God. May God continue to give us his grace. Amen.

You write that you have been unable to get by on the money [I gave you]. I will let it pass this quarter, but see that you do manage on it in the future. Enclosed is another gulden.

As for your clothes, I do not have Martin here with me now (we are quarreling), but he has begun work on your clothes. He has made stockings for your holiday trousers, which I am sending you with this letter. Since your everyday trousers are so bad, wear these leather holiday trousers for now until a new pair of everyday woolen ones can be made and sent to you, which I will do as soon as I can. Send me your old trousers in the sack I sent the pitcher in. As for the smock you think should be lined, I worry that the skirt may be too short and that it will not keep you warm. You can certainly wear it for another summer, if it is not too small for you then and the weather not too warm. Just keep it clean and brushed. I will have a new coat made for you at the earliest.

You also write about your board. You must be patient for a while. You may not at the outset lodge a complaint against [Herr Oertel], especially while you are sitting at his table. [Only] he may speak out who eats his food and is also an authority in the house. So it would be better if the Inspector, who is there for a reason, reports it.

Will you once tell me who your table companions are? Also, let me know by All Saints what you have spent on beer and what you owe the tailor, so that I know how much to send you for the quarter.

As for your throat, there is nothing you can take for it but warm mead. Gargle often with it and keep your head warm. Put a muffler or scarf

---

35. On these two see Georg Steinhausen, ed., *Briefwechsel Balthasar Paumgartners des Jüngeren mit seiner gatten Magdelena geb. Beheim (1582–1598)* (Tübingen, 1895), 71, 150.

around your neck and wear your night coat when you are in your room. Avoid cold drinks and sit perhaps for a while by the fire. And do not forget to be bled on time.

When you need paper, let me know. Paul has gotten a supply, for which I paid one and a half gulden. I have not yet heard when the Oertels' wedding is planned. When I find out I will let you know. Jobst Tetzel is the bridegroom of Maria Gralat.

I am sending some cleaning flakes for your leather pants. After you have worn them three times, put some on the knees. Since Martin is not around, I will have your old coat patched up and sent to you with the next carter [so that you can wear it] until a new one is made. Send me the two sacks with the next carter. You will find the gulden in the trouser foot that is tied with a string.[36]

Nothing more for now. God bless. 14 October, 1578.

    Mrs. Paul Behaim.

13 ❧ Friederich to Mother, 16 October 1578

Filial love and devotion, dear Mother. Know that I have received the money and the sack with my trousers. As you write that I should let you know who my table companions are, there are six. Hans Kersin, who is Herr Zisselgassen's [step]son; Johannes Schmidt, from Fürth; the third is named Christoph Keferlein, who was once Herr [Hieronymus] Baumgartner's servant; a fourth from Bavaria; the fifth, with the name of Peter Kögel, who has been one of the twelve orphans; the Inspector; and myself.

I am sending the two sacks back with Kolb along with a letter that belongs to Jacob Schleicher.

Otherwise, nothing more for now. God bless. Greet all the household for me. When I have the time, I will write to each of them. 16 October, 1578.

    Y[our] L[oving] S[on]
    Friederich Behaim

---

36. Stockings were attached to the pant legs, hence a "trouser foot."

14 ❦ Friederich to Mother, 30 October 1578

Filial love and devotion, dear Mother. When you are well and hardy, it is a great joy for me. Know that I, too, am still in good health. May almighty God continue to give his grace to both of us. Amen.

Dear Mother, I know from your last letter that I should write you today, 31 October, and report what I owe Herr Oertel for beer and laundry. It comes to one gulden, two pounds, three pfennigs. But know that I drink no more than a half-measure of beer, occasionally a full, each day. In addition, I must, as I am committed to do, buy some beer for the twelve orphans. As for the laundry, Frau Oertel charges so much for my wash and will do a shirt for no less than eight pfennigs because she claims that she must wash everything with soap. So I would like to know what kind and how much soap one must have for my shirts. You will surely know this. She also leaves my laundry very scratchy. Had I known that, I would have taken my laundry to the woman who washes for the Polish counts and barons. If you like, I will try to find someone else to do my laundry for one and a half or two gulden a year. I also owe the tailor twenty-four pfennigs, which I am carrying over to next quarter.

I am now in need of books. Since Paul is now here [in Altdorf], would you ask Jacob Schleicher to fetch the books on the enclosed list from Paul's library, and would you then send them to me with the next mail? I [also] need a pair of slippers. Would you have a pair made for me?

I have heard here that old Herr Sebald Haller has died, but I do not know for sure.[37]

Nothing more, except greetings to all the household and to all our good friends. 30 October, 1578.

> Y[our] L[oving] S[on]
> Friederich Behaim

15 ❦ Mother to Friederich, undated

Dear son Friederich. I have received your letter about the laundry and read that we still owe Herr Oertel one gulden, two pounds for laundry and beer beyond your board. Know that Herr Oertel has just been here

---

37. Sebald Haller (b.1502, d. 26 October 1578) was one of Nuremberg's most famous citizens. He held many powerful positions, among them those of secretary to Emperor Charles V, alter Burgermeister of Nuremberg, and Septemvir.

with me and I gave him ten gulden. If there is now another quarter-gulden due him, I will pay that too.[38] As for your laundry, you may do as you please with it, send it out [weekly] or contract [for the entire quarter]; it is up to you.

I am herewith sending you the coat and another pair of trousers, which you can wear on holidays or workdays. I only had eight laces at home for you. [I am] also [sending] the books now. No more. In haste.

I indicated to Herr Oertel that I would send him six chickens, should you two be eating together, but the gamekeeper has not yet brought them to me. I expected him yesterday, but he did not come. When you write again, send back the sack.

[unsigned]

16 ❦ Mother to Friederich, 7 November 1578

Dear son Friederich. Since my last letter, I have just been too busy to write or send you anything. So I am herewith sending you three gulden out of which you may pay Herr Zan for the tutorial and Herr Oertel the quarter-gulden still owed him for laundry and beer. Meanwhile, Herr Oertel received ten gulden from me—the quarter-gulden belongs to the past rent—which will be due him for this quarter.

You write that often you do not drink all of your beer at meals, but only a little of it.[39] Whenever you find that you have a swallow or more left over, take it with you [to your room] in your small mug, so that your tankard stays behind and is no trouble. You wrote me earlier that one keeps track of how much beer you take and writes it all down.

You can certainly have a basket woven for yourself at the cooper's and write or carve your name on it.

As for your laundry, you can either keep looking [for someone else to do it], or continue this winter [with Frau Oertel].

The gamekeeper still has not brought the chickens.

38. Friederich's mother has calculated ten gulden for board and an additional gulden, two pounds for beer and laundry, minus the one gulden Friederich has directly paid Herr Oertel from the money she sends him. This leaves about a quarter-gulden (ein ortt), or two pounds.
39. This letter is not extant. Although Friederich has written before about several of the topics here mentioned by his mother, this is the first reference to a problem with leftover beer and to his need of a basket.

I notice that you will have some money left over for emergencies.

Paul is now with a master named Andreas Gail, who is a doctor of law and imperial counsellor and warden.[40]

I have no more news. Keep the three-quarter-gulden you will have left over[41] and use it to buy wood for your fireplace when you need it. God bless. 7 November, 1578.

> Mrs. Paul Behaim.

[P.S.] Just as I was about to seal the letter, the gamekeeper arrived with the chickens. I am sending you half a dozen. Present them to Herr Oertel and eat them with him. The maid also put in some special treats for you.[42]

17 ❦ Friederich to Mother, 9 November 1578

Filial love and devotion, dear Mother . . .

Dear Mother, I have received the three gulden and given two to Herr Zan for the tutorial and likewise Herr Oertel what I owe him. I also presented him with the chickens. And I have received the groceries. I sincerely thank you. With this letter, I am returning the sack.

I know nothing else to write you, except to thank everyone who helped or advised on the food. And greet everyone for me.

I have no good quills. Otherwise, I would have written you a better letter.

The trousers you sent are completely too small. At the first opportunity I must have the tailor let them out. God bless. 9 November, 1578.

> Y[our] L[oving] S[on]
> Friederich Behaim.

18 ❦ Friederich to Mother, 20 November 1578

Filial love and devotion, dear Mother . . .

Dear Mother, as I wrote you in my last letter I need a pair of slippers.[43]

40. Paul joined Gail in Prague in October.
41. That is, after paying Herr Zan two gulden for tutorial and Herr Oertel a quarter-gulden still owed for beer and laundry.
42. "Ein Spitzwerk." Most likely cooked meat for the celebration of Martinmas, although the term can also mean fancy pastry.
43. Friederich first asked for slippers in his letter of 30 October (letter 14). Because there is no mention of them in his letter of 9 November, there must be a lost letter sent after 9 November.

So that you do not forget about them, I want to remind you. Also, be very sure to have them made large enough, for I have grown since [coming to Altdorf]. Would you also send me paper and parchment?

Otherwise, I have nothing special to write to you, except that Erasmus Göringer, the son of the former city secretary here and the brother of Georg Göringer, who was once a guest of [Sigmund] Held, has married a chaplain's widow in Hersbrück.

Otherwise, I have nothing more at this time except greetings to all the household and to all our good friends. 20 November, 1578.

> Y[our] L[oving] S[on]
> Friederich Behaim.

19 ❦ Friederich to Mother, 27 November 1578

Filial love and devotion, dear Mother . . .

Dear Mother, know that my eyes are again hurting a lot and they are completely red. Would you send me a green silk patch to wear over them at night by the light? And would you see if you might have some eyewater sent from the surgeon on the hill?

I wrote you a week ago for paper and parchment and slippers, all of which you should send me. I do not know if you have received my letter, as I have gotten no reply. On Wednesday people here were saying that someone had hacked off the legs of Kolb's horse in the forest.[44] These lies I well recall were all the talk here. They were exposed as they were being spread, when the horse, praise God, returned alive and well.

Please send me a daily diary for the coming new year.[45] Nothing more, except greetings to all the household and to all our good friends. God bless. 27 November, 1578.

> Y[our] L[oving] S[on]
> Friederich Behaim.

20 ❦ Mother to Friederich, undated 1578[46]

Know, dear Friederich, that your last letter has arrived. The reason I have not written or sent anything to you until now is that I have been

44. See n. 30.
45. "Ein schreibkalender."
46. Clearly a response to Friederich's letter of 27 November.

waiting for the slippers, as I wanted to send them to you with the other things. But they are still not ready, so I will have to send them later. With this letter I am sending you paper and parchment, a daily diary, and an eye patch.[47] As soon as the weather is warmer, I still want you to be properly bled. I am sending you eyewater from both the Rogganbachs and the surgeon.[48] I will write again soon.

[unsigned]

21 ❦ Mother to Friederich, 6 December 1578

Dear son Friederich. Since I last wrote, I have been too busy to write. I would like to know how your eyes are now. Has the water helped a little? If not, I want you to let Herr Heft bleed you.[49] If, after two weeks, bleeding also has not helped, then I will have some pills made and sent to you. Let me know how you are doing and keep yourself warm.

I am herewith sending you the slippers, which the shoemaker has made large [per your instruction].

No more for now. God bless. 6 December, 1578.

[unsigned]

22 ❦ Friederich to Mother, 8 December 1578

Filial love and devotion, dear Mother. I have your last letter in which you ask me to let you know if the eyewater has helped. Know that I applied the surgeon's water three times and, praise God, got quick relief, so that I am no longer in pain. Should my eyes become bad again and the water does not help, I will seek the counsel of a new surgeon who has recently moved here and advertises himself as an eye specialist. Be assured that I am keeping my bleeding date.

Herr Kolb, the carter here, died today, 8 December. If you have something you want to send me, you may give it to his servant, who will continue to cart regularly from here in Herr Kolb's place.

47. "Augendiegle."
48. The Rogganbachs are friends of the family. See Steinhausen, *Briefwechsel Balthasar Paumgartners*, 19, 199.
49. Heft is apparently the surgeon in Altdorf.

I am again in need of a roll of tapers, so please send me one. Nothing more. Greet all the household. 8 December, 1578.

> Y[our] L[oving] S[on]
> Friederich Behaim

23 ❦ Mother to Friederich, December 1578

Dear son Friederich. Your letter has arrived with the news, praise God, that your face has gotten better. But I also learn from it that Herr Kolb has died. May God grant him and us all a happy resurrection.

But you do not tell me whether you have gotten the slippers and whether they fit. If they have not yet arrived, let me know soon, so I can inquire after them. If they have arrived, you need not write me just on their account.

On 6 December they laid Herr Bergner to rest. He died at his brother's, Doctor Balm. Surely you have met him.

Know that Gabriel Muffel's widow is engaged to Christoph Kress who is living in Kötzel's house.[50]

With this letter I am sending a roll of tapers. Would you return the coop in which I sent the chickens for Herr Oertel? And also the carton in which I sent the slippers. God bless. December, 1578.

> [unsigned]

24 ❦ Friederich to Mother, 8 January 1579

Kind, dear Mother. I am herewith sending you the sack with my trousers and shirt. Will you send me the book and the satchel next time? Otherwise no news. Greet all the household. 8 January, 1578.[51]

> Y[our] L[oving] S[on]
> Friederich Behaim

---

50. The widow of Gabriel Muffel von Eschenau (d.1570), Maria Plodin, married Christoph III Kress (1541–83) on 3 February 1579. Kress was the *alter Burgermeister* and held other powerful positions.

51. With the turn of a new year the letter is misdated.

25 & Mother to Friederich, undated

Dear son Friederich. I am letting you know that I sent for the books you want and the bookbinder tells me that in one of the books, namely the small one, a page is missing, and that you should let him know where you bought it, so that he can get the page and include it in the book when he binds it.

I have received that sack and trousers, but not the old coat. If you no longer need the coat, send it to me, and I will make a New Year's gift of it to the schoolboy.[52]

Herewith I am sending you shirts, caps, and handkerchiefs. The book satchel is not yet ready. I will insist that it be finished and send it to you another time. God bless.

[unsigned]

26 & Friederich to Mother, 12 January 1579

My willing service and filial obedience, dear Mother.[53] I have received your letter with the news about the book. I bought the book at Lamprecht's, which was formerly Dieterich Gerlazen's shop. I bought both books there from Dieterich Gerlazen's workers. His widow was also there at the time. One can ask any of them about the book.

Regarding the coat, I have already given it to a poor student here.

No more for now. Greet all the household. 12 January.

Y[our] L[oving] S[on]
Friederich Behaim.

27 & Friederich to Mother, 26 January 1579

My willing service and filial obedience, dear Mother. I have received the sack with the satchel, candle snuffers, and book. I am returning both sacks with this letter. Nothing more at this time. Greet all the household

---

52. Apparently Friederich's eleven-year-old brother Georg is meant.
53. A new, more formal salutation, perhaps because Friederich has just turned fifteen (on December 29).

and all other friends. 26 January, 1579, the second day after the conversion of St. Paul, at 6:00 A.M. by the small clock.

Y[our] L[oving] S[on]

Friederich Behaim.

28 🐝 Friederich to Mother, 2 February 1579

Filial love and devotion, dear Mother . . .

Dear Mother, because it is now Candlemas[54] and the end of the quarter, I want to let you know, as you have requested, what I owe Herr Oertel for beer and laundry. A pint of beer [a day][55] is no longer enough for me, for when I am studying my mouth becomes very dry from reading, and I must moisten it with a pint of beer. So I now owe six pounds for beer and also six pounds for laundry.

I have spoken with Frau Oertel about what she would charge to do my laundry for a full year [with the proviso] that she wash everything over again if it does not come out clean. On this account, she has asked for two gulden.[56] If that pleases you, let me know.

Know also that although I have had four Zwelfer left over from the money you have sent me since I moved here,[57] I still must pay the stoker for a new year, the bath-surgeon for bleeding, and the barber for cutting my hair. So I ask if you would send me an additional one for this quarter.[58] You need not worry that a single pfennig will be badly spent.

Nothing more for now. God bless. In haste. I had no more time, and—in addition—a bad quill. 2 February.

Y[our] L[oving] S[on]

Friederich Behaim.

29 🐝 Mother to Friederich, 4 February 1579

Dear son Friederich. Your letter about money has been delivered to me. I am herewith sending you thirteen gulden: nine for Herr Oertel for

---

54. 2 February, the feast of the purification of the Virgin and presentation of Jesus in the temple.

55. "Ein seidla." See n. 11.

56. Sixteen pounds, twenty-four pfennigs.

57. Forty-eight pfennigs, or about a pound and a half.

58. An additional gulden is probably meant, a doubling of his normal spending money.

board, two for Herr Zan, and one and a half for laundry and beer. Meanwhile, pay your other expenses from the remaining half-gulden until more comes. God bless. 4 February, 1579.

Mrs. Paul Behaim.

30 🦉 Friederich to Mother, 5 February 1579

My greetings, dear Mother. I have your letter with the money and I have paid Herr Oertel and Herr Zan from it. But I cannot tell whether or not it pleases you to pay Frau Oertel the two gulden she demands to do my laundry for an entire year. Would you let me know at the earliest?

When I was still in Nuremberg, you indicated that you would send me a half-gulden at Candlemas to give the person who makes my bed. Do remember to do this.

Otherwise, nothing more, except write again at the earliest. God bless. 5 February, 1579.

Y[our] L[oving] S[on]
Friederich Behaim.

31 🦉 Mother to Friederich, undated

Friederich, I have received your letter in which you indicate what you should be doing for this or that person. I am surprised that you do not settle these matters yourself. It appears from your last letter[59] that Frau Oertel is just as happy to be paid for your laundry at the end of the year or when the [school] year is up, so forget about your laundry for now and take a half-gulden from the money I sent you [for laundry and beer] and give it to the girl [who makes your bed]. Then, give Frau Oertel only what is left over. If Frau Oertel wants it [all in advance], let me know, and I will send you more, although money is very tight with me now. No more for now.

[unsigned]

32 🦉 Friederich to Mother, 9 February 1579

Kind, dear Mother. I have received your letter. Know that I have paid Frau Oertel for the laundry she has done for me over the past quarter-

59. Apparently letter 28 is meant.

year. In the future she will do all my laundry over the entire year for two gulden. Therefore, please send me the half-gulden I still should give to the servant who makes my bed. Nothing more for now except God bless. 9 February.

> Y[our] L[oving] S[on]
> Friederich Behaim.

33 ❦ Friederich to Mother, 12 February 1579

Filial love and devotion, dear Mother. If you are well and hardy, it is a great joy for me to hear it.

Dear Mother, I last wrote you on 9 February, but I cannot know whether the letter has been delivered to you, since Frau Kolb has a new carter. I worry that he did not deliver the letter. Since you do not write or send anything, I am writing you about these same matters again. Know that I paid Frau Oertel for the laundry she has done for me over the past quarter-year. Henceforth she will do my laundry for the entire year for two gulden. So send me the half-gulden I should give the servant who makes my bed.

Write me again when you can. Nothing more. Greet all the household for me. Written in haste. I had no more time. God bless. 12 February, 1579.

> Y[our] L[oving] S[on]
> Friederich Behaim.

34 ❦ Mother to Friederich, 14 February 1579

Dear son Friederich. Both your letters have been delivered to me,[60] and I am aware that I have not yet answered the first. I had resolved to send you a gulden with the carter. Then I forgot about it. When I remembered, he was gone.

Herr Oertel and his wife were here last Thursday and they told me about what has apparently happened with the nobleman and Mühlholtzer, which you will surely know all about.[61] He no longer wants those

---

60. Letters 32 and 33.
61. The second reference is to Antonius or Johannes Mühlholtzer. The two were brothers who enrolled in 1578.

two [in the college]. But he has no complaints about you, only satisfaction. [However, we fear that] you might be misled by those two. He wanted to tell me himself about their goings-on so that we might restrain you, lest you are tempted to do such a thing. You know that we have always done well by our maids. But if something improper is going on for many days or weeks, then you might let me know so that I can protect your reputation for the sake of your good name. If you maintain your reputation, then all is well.

I hurriedly gave Frau Oertel the gulden to bring to you [when she returned to Altdorf].[62] The carter did not bring your letter [requesting it] until Friday.

Greetings from the household. God bless. 14 February, 1579.

[unsigned]

35 ❦ Friederich to Mother, 21 February 1579

My greeting, dear Mother . . .

Dear Mother, I wrote you a while back, but I am always missing the carter. Since my roommate, Paul Gaismair, who is one of the Twelve Orphans, had planned to go [to Nuremberg] today, I wanted him to give you this little letter.

Know that my face is again inflamed,[63] and my left eye is very red. If the swelling leaves my eyes, it is only to go to my ears, so that I can no longer hear. So I wanted to ask you if there were pills or something that might help.

You write in your last letter that the Chef[64] has been to see you and told you about Mühlholtzer and another, who are planning to move. It is indeed true that everywhere [in Altdorf] one can find better fare for thirty gulden then Herr Oertel presently serves for thirty-six.[65] As several here can attest, he now serves us meat and other food that one must

62. Frau Oertel was returning before the next mail.
63. "Mit der fluss hinein komen ist."
64. "Speisemeister." The term is used for the college's Oeconomus, or steward, although in the context of this letter, it is surely also being applied sarcastically to Herr Oertel.
65. An annual cost is here estimated. Frau Behaim paid flat boarding fees of between nine and ten gulden a quarter, to which were added additional charges for beer and laundry. Itemized bills are extant from Jacob Gruner, with whom Friederich later boarded. See letter 44.

often return after the first bite. I want you to recognize the kind of man he is. My preceptor, Herr Zan, has often advised me against doing the things I nonetheless do for him. That I can get a much better table for the money will be shown in God's time.

Nothing more. Greet all the household for me. 21 February, 1579.

Y[our] L[oving] S[on]
Friederich Behaim.

36 ❦ Mother to Friederich, undated[66]

Friederich. With this letter comes a bottle of rosewater. There is also more eyewater, which should be applied in the following manner. Place your forefinger on the mouth of the opened bottle, turn it over, and shake it. Then take what remains on the finger that was over the mouth of the bottle and smear it on your upper eyelid. Then, lay your finger again on the mouth of the bottle, shake it, and this time apply what remains on your finger to your lower eyelid. Try not to get any in your eye, for it does not need it. But if a little does accidentally get in your eye, it will not harm it. Do this three or four times a day.

Know that Christoph has arrived with his lord and is staying at Bitterolf's.[67] He leaves again on Wednesday.

I will have no peace until the new eyewater is delivered to you. Ela had taken the bottles and my letter and thrown them in a corner where they lay unnoticed until I happened upon them. By then, the carter had already gone. So we gave them to another messenger at the livery; [I am wondering] if he has delivered them to you.

No more for now. God bless.

[unsigned]

66. Letter 36 (Behaim Archiv no. 35) and 55 (Behaim Archiv no. 54), both undated, are incorrectly ordered in the archive. I have reversed them, as is clearly justified by their content.
67. Friederich's mother writes in her housekeeping book on 10 June 1576 that Christoph (1562–1624) was apprenticed in Regensburg to Jorg Ilsing, Vogt (warden) in Schwaben, "who wanted a youth who could inventory all kinds of things for him and serve him." "Aus Nürnberger Haushaltungs- und Rechnungsbüchern des 15. und 16. Jahrhunderts," MVGN 7 (1888): 137.

37 ❦ Friederich to Mother, 11 March 1579

Kind, dear Mother. Know that Herr Oertel and I have calculated my expenses and I still owe him sixty-four pfennigs. Would you send them to me? Know that I also talked with the person who will be my music teacher and he wants six gulden a year. So would you send me the small instrument?[68] I will practice it diligently. 11 March.

Y[our] L[oving] S[on]
Friederich Behaim.

38 ❦ Mother to Friederich, undated (before 18 April)

Dear Friederich. I have sent you two gulden with Hans.[69] You should buy wood with them and apply what is left over to your needs. Be thrifty with this money[70] because we do not have a lot.

I am sending you the trousers. Should the cost of fabric double in two weeks, it would pay to send the leather trousers here, so that we can see if they can be let out. I cannot always be buying [new trousers]. I believe you still have a pair of woolen trousers. So send them also.

I am also sending you the laundry.[71] You sent it here in a coarse cotton sack. Is that sack yours? The proper laundry sack for the shipping crate is coarse linen, not coarse cotton. [I hope] you have not lost it. There are also a dozen laces to tie up your jacket.[72]

[unsigned]

39 ❦ Friederich to Mother, 18 April 1579

My greetings, dear Mother. I have now received the money, trousers, and laundry. But I am returning these trousers because they are much too short and too tight. The stockings [that go with them] are so tight I

---

68. "Das kleiner Instrument." This could be a viol, lute, or guitar.
69. Another carter.
70. "Genau mitt umb gen."
71. Friederich is beginning to send some of his laundry home. Later his mother will do all his laundry, both for economy and to satisfy Friederich. See letters 50 and 51.
72. These are decorative ties for the waist and arms.

cannot get them on at all. And the breeches are also too tight.[73] The jacket is a complete misfit. Would you have it let out and lengthened for me? I prefer it too loose than too tight. The leather trousers I am sending to you are much too short and the seat too tight ever to be much improved.

It is [however] good that you have had leather stockings put on the new trousers. I had the woolen ones for winter and they [now] are too warm. I must [have] a fustian jacket, for I now have no such jacket at all. The ones I do have are too small for me.

Nothing more. God bless. 18 April.

Y[our] L[oving] S[on]
Friederich Behaim.

[P.S.] Last time I sent the [linen] laundry sack with the assembled laundry [that is, inside the cotton sack]. I have always had this [cotton] sack here with me.

40 ❦ Friederich to Mother, 24 April 1579

My greetings, kind, dear Mother. I am herewith sending you the [laundry] sack with the table cloth in it. I would have sent it to you sooner, but I forgot, and I have not had a lot of time. I am also sending a prayer book for Georg.[74]

Would you please send me what is needed to have my hat lined? And also let me know when brother Christoph is arriving from Augsburg so that I can plan a visit around my studies. If I do not write again within the week, would you [remember to] send the money to pay Herr Zan for the tutorial? Also the gulden which I may otherwise spend freely on my needs, for I do need it. Because I am now bathing often, my skin has become itchy. Would you also send me a mengel root with the carter [so I can treat it]?[75]

No more. Greet the household. 24 April, A.D. 1579.

Y[our] L[oving] S[on]
Friederich Behaim.

---

73. "Gesess" or "gesäsz." Connotes one's rear or the seat of one's trousers or clothing, like ballooned (knee) breeches.
74. "Die Vorschryt," that is, "Fürschrift" or "schriftliche Fürbitte." Possibly a belated Easter or confirmation gift for Friederich's twelve-year-old brother.
75. "Mengwurz." A species of sorrel.

41 🐝 Mother to Friederich, 2 May 1579

Dear son Friederich. I am letting you know that Christoph arrived yesterday, Friday, evening. So if you are free, would you make your way home tomorrow with your carter, or come with another for a small gratuity? You will travel more comfortably and assist the carter if you pack up what you are not wearing—like your buckram smock, fustian breeches, felt hat, and whatever else, your new jacket.

I am sending two gulden with the bearer of this letter. Would you give them to Herr Zan? No more. 2 May.

     Mrs. Paul Behaim.

42 🐝 Friederich to Mother, 24 May 1579

My greetings, kind, dear Mother. Know, dear Mother, that I forgot to bring a tankard back [to school][76] with me [which I need] because my pitcher is broken. So would you send it to me next time, if possible by cart?[77]

I am sending you my leather trousers.[78] Do with them what you will.

Know also that although I have often refused, I must now be in a play on Peter-Paul Day.[79] I must play the role of the queen. You need not worry about [buying new] clothes [for the play]; I only need necklaces, a wig, and a skullcap.

I know nothing more to write at this time. I cannot write a better letter because I lack quills. I also cannot devote time now to anything because I have to study so much for exams. God bless. 24 May, in the year of the Lord, 1579.

     Friederich Behaim
     F[ilius] T[uus] C[larissime][80]

76. Friederich has been home for a visit.
77. That is, by the daily carter.
78. See letter 39. Friederich had apparently neglected to send them earlier because of his skepticism that they could be repaired.
79. 28 June.
80. Friederich was preparing for his examinations in Latin and was presumably immersed in the subject.

43 ❦ Mother to Friederich, undated

Dear Friederich. I am herewith sending you your trousers. I could not get them from Martin any sooner.

I am letting you know now that I will not send you any fine necklaces. You are well aware of what has happened with finery there. So I do not intend to help you decorate the stage. No one any longer likes to have their [fine] things circulating there.

Matthias Löffelholz has died and nowhere else than at the Gibitzen palace.[81]

I will send your board money with the next cart.

> [unsigned]

44 ❦ Friederich to Mother, 10 June 1579

My friendly greetings and willing service, dear Mother. If you and all the household are well and hardy, it is a great joy for me to hear it. Know that I, too, praise God, am now in good health. Amen.

Dear Mother, enclosed is [Sebald Gruner's] bill for my board.[82] Would you send the money as soon as possible? The tailor has not yet made out his bill, [but I know] the amount is one gulden, four pounds, and six pfennigs, for mending and patching. I also owe the laundress half a gulden for washing, etc.[83]

I have no more time to write, as I must study for exams. Greetings to all the household. 10 June, 1579.

> Y[our] L[oving] S[on]
> Friederich Behaim.

81. See note 19.

82. After his letter of 11 March (letter 37) Friederich mentions the Oertels again only to announce their daughter's wedding. See letters 84, 88, and 92. He began taking his meals with Sebald Gruner during the spring term of 1579. There are two extant letters from Gruner to Frau Behaim, dated 15 June and 10 December 1579, requesting payment of quarterly bills for Friederich's board and beer. The bill of 10 December was for ten gulden, six pounds, twenty-nine pfennigs, overall somewhat less than the amount charged by the Oertels, although not the savings Friederich had projected in letter 35. But the fare may have been much improved.!

83. Friederich has a new laundress, but he has also begun to send his laundry home.

45 🐝 Friederich to Mother, undated[84]

Kind, dear Mother, I am returning the necklaces to you by way of Frau Geuder and I will send the clothes to Herr Baumgartner at the earliest.[85] I am also sending you a *groschen* I received because I have been promoted. I want you to have it made into a charm and returned to me.[86]

I have bought five books for one gulden, four pounds, twenty-four pfennigs. Would you send me this amount? The money for my music teacher has fallen due. Would you also send a quire of paper?

Nothing more. God bless. In haste. I had no more time.

> Y[our] L[oving]
> Friederich Behaim.

46 🐝 Mother to Friederich, undated[87]

Friederich. Here is the money for your books. See that they are worth it, and advance in your studies, so that you are not a student with a lot of books, but one of the learned ones.

I am also sending one and a half gulden for your music teacher and returning the charm.[88] And there is a quire of paper. Would you return the coarse cotton sack, the basket, and the box?[89] God bless.

> [unsigned]

84. Probably written late in June, just after the Peter-Paul Day play.

85. Despite her initial protest, Frau Behaim had sent Friederich necklaces and other articles for the play. The Frau Geuder here mentioned may be Friederich's future mother-in-law. Herr Baumgartner was evidently a source of costumes.

86. "Ein örlein" or *Henkel*. Friederich wants a hole drilled in the groschen so that it can be worn as a charm.

87. Presumably Frau Behaim had already received Friederich's letter of 1 July (letter 47) and wrote this soon after.

88. "Das zaigen" or *Zeichen*—that is, a token, which the drilled groschen has now apparently become.

89. Frau Behaim crossed out the words "the basket, and the box" and wrote under them, "I have crossed this out, received." The basket and box had arrived with Friederich's letter of 1 July (letter 47), just as Frau Behaim was preparing to post this letter.

47 ❦ Friederich to Mother, 1 July 1579

My friendly greetings and willing service, dear Mother . . . Dear Mother, I am herewith sending you by the carter the basket and the box.[90] I thank you for the roses, although there were too many of them. Nevertheless, I will dry them and lay them in my linen chest. I am also returning the box with the wig and skullcap. I could not get the other costumes into Herr Baumgartner's trunk. But if the carter makes a run [to Nuremberg] on Friday, I will send them to you then. But you need not worry about them; they are neatly and safely stored in my trunk. Absolutely no harm was done them during the play. Although it rained here at noon [on the day of the performance] (as it must have done there also), the play did not begin until three in the afternoon because of Herr von Birbaim's leisurely lunch.[91]

I have nothing more at this time, except to ask you to send me [the money] I requested in my last letter.[92] God bless. 1 July. In our city of Altdorf.

> Y[our] L[oving]
> Friederich Behaim.

48 ❦ Friederich to Mother, 10 July 1579

My friendly greetings and every good wish, dear Mother. If you are well and hardy, it is a great joy for me to hear it, etc.

Dear Mother, I now need shoes. Would you therefore send me a good, strong, large, wide pair, if possible with double soles. Know also that as we now have a three-week break and no classes, I am planning to travel with several others (if you are not opposed) and visit my old relative Caspar Reach at his home.[93] So I want to beg some traveling money from you. Send it to me with the carter. And would you let me know if brother Paul is coming or not, so that once he has his feet on the ground in Nuremberg he may visit me here in Altdorf, and you too.[94] Now is the most pleasant time to be here.

---

90. The containers in which the roses and other accessories for the play had been sent.
91. Von Birbaim must be either an important visitor or a school official.
92. Letter 45. Letters 46 and 47 have crossed.
93. Reach was a Lutheran pastor trained in Wittenberg who lived in the village of Ezelwant, near Nuremberg.
94. Paul was then working in Prague. See n. 40.

I know nothing else to write at this time except to [ask that you] greet all our good friends for me, especially Sebastian Imhoff.[95] God bless. 6 [   ],[96] that is, 10 July. This letter was completed between eight and nine o'clock.

Y[our] L[oving]
Friederich Behaim

[P.S.] The cotton sack is not here, but was sent to you. If the morello cherries are getting ripe, I want to pay you a visit, so that I do not miss out on them.

49 ❦ Mother to Friederich, undated

Dear son Friederich. I have received your vacation plans [and I have no objection] so long as it costs nothing. There is not much money now, so you may not, like everyone else, simply do as you please. But if Caspar has offered you lodging and invited you to be his guest, you should give him, his children, or his wife an appropriate token of appreciation.

I am herewith sending you a pair of shoes and a gulden. Make it last a long time. I have not yet seen Paul.

There are few cherries in the garden. But when we have the pleasure of picking them, we will send you all [you want]. But let's see how much [of a harvest there is].

If you will send your two pair of woolen trousers, we will see what can be done to fix them. No more.

[unsigned]

50 ❦ Friederich to Mother, 10 August 1579

Filial love and devotion, dear Mother. Know that I have paid Gruner ten gulden, five pounds, and twenty-four pfennigs for my board and everything else, the laundress a gulden, and my music teacher one and a half gulden. As you now want me to send my laundry to you, would you let me know how and when you want it sent?[97] I am herewith sending

---

95. Sebastian IV Imhoff (1536–82).
96. An uncertain Latin date.
97. Friederich had been sending some of his laundry home since leaving the Oertels, apparently in mid-March. From this time on his mother did all his laundry.

you the two sacks and a heraldry book that belongs to one of my mess-
mates, who is moving away and wants my coat of arms emblazoned in
it. So would you have it painted ever so simply in his book right away?

Would you also send me a gulden that I may spend freely as my needs
require? Although I have not yet spent the quarter-gulden you gave me,
I may not and cannot write to you every day [for money as I need it].

Nothing more except [to say that] if you have harvested something
[from the garden], please send me half of the pick, and let me know
when it is coming. 10 August.

> Y[our] L[oving] S[on]
> Friederich Behaim.

51 ❦ Mother to Friederich, undated

Friederich. I am herewith sending you the [heraldry] book. You should
know that in the future you shall not trouble me with such rubbish. You
may not engage in such trifling and folly. Otherwise, you can squander
[our] money until there is none left. It helps neither you nor him when
one spends or wastes money [in this way].[98] If you send me another such
book, I will not return it, but throw it away. Do take note of this.

As you already want more money, I would like to know what there is
that you still need to buy. You have your evening beer. You have the
laundry. You have the shoes. And you are supposed to make a gulden
stretch for all the [other] things each quarter. Certainly not every [student]
is given so much for such things.

Further, you ask whether you should send your laundry home. I told
you last time to do so, so that we save this money.[99] The more I try to
find ways to save, the more you look for something useless to spend
money on.

I am herewith sending you a half-gulden. Just do not come to me again
too soon [for money].

> [unsigned]

98. The reference is to Friederich's messmate. See letter 50.
99. Apparently in a letter that is not extant.

52 ❦ Friederich to Mother, 27 August 1579

My greetings, dear Mother . . .

Dear Mother, my preceptor has given me this book [which I am here-with sending you] for which I still owe him one gulden. However, there is an additional part to the book which I need and which he did not have at this time. So would you send this note to the bookstore, buy [the additional part], and have the book bound with it?

Dear Mother, the students who live in the college must buy their own wood in the coming winter. Since two of my roommates have a room in the city and the third is one of the twelve orphans, I alone must buy my wood for the winter, and three gulden will hardly cover the cost. So my two roommates want to take me into their room in the city at a cost of eight gulden a year, and they also buy their own firewood. I also do not want to stay in the college any longer. The servants hang around here all day and I can get nothing done. But the main reason I want to move out is that when I was last in chapel, someone stole my schilling from my locked trunk,[100] and also several books from my comrades. I do not know if the schilling will ever be returned. I reported it to the rector, but after much searching, it cannot be found.

If you approve of my moving, I must have a sofa bed. So would you either have one sent to me or send me one and a half gulden so that I can buy one? I am also in great need of paper, so would you send a quire or two? And candles, with the shipping crate?

No more. God bless. 27 August, in Altdorf.

Y[our] L[oving] S[on]
Friederich Behaim.

53 ❦ Friederich to Mother, 5 October 1579

My greetings, dear Mother . . .

Dear Mother, know that it is still the intention [of the school authorities] to require us to buy our own wood for the winter. However, I now have a roommate who must share this expense with me.[101] Since we cannot hope to have any more warm weather, and winter is already at hand, and

100. Presumably the prized groschen that had been turned into a charm.
101. Frau Behaim did not now permit Friederich to move out of the college. See let-ter 66.

a warm room is a necessity, I would like your advice on whether I should now buy two loads of wood and then have my roommate buy the next two, after these have been burned. I believe this would work out well.

There is reason to worry that wood will henceforth be very expensive here. As the peasants learn that we [students] must ourselves buy the wood for the college, they will sell it for whatever price they please. So whereas wood previously sold for around four pounds [half a gulden] at the most, one now sells oak at not a heller less than three-quarters gulden, almost six pounds. Logs and plain brush wood run five. In addition, there is [the fee for] cutting, etc. Also, I truly cannot nor wish to attend the fire. Should I make the fire first thing in the morning, I might freeze to death before the room is warm. And when I return from class for my tutorial, I will have to go back and forth to the fire, and what will remain of my studies? So we in the college have agreed among ourselves to hire some-one to tend fire for us during the winter and each of us pay him half a gulden. As you can see, a load of wood costs more than a gulden even before it is in the fireplace.

Would you let me know what you think about these plans as soon as possible? And send my laundry soon because I have no shirts to wear.

No more. God bless. 5 October, 1579.

Friederich Behaim.

54 ❦ Mother to Friederich, undated[102]

Friederich. I am herewith sending you your laundry and an old piece of fabric you had asked for and I had since forgotten about. I am also sending you a gulden for wood. You should not, however, buy wood as you have proposed, [namely] that you now buy two loads and, after they have been burned, your roommate then buy two. You cannot be so sure of the future. [Consider] what would happen if you and your roommate had a falling out, or if for some other reason he moved out of your room. Who would then buy wood for you, after your roommate had occupied the warm room? Think about this and do not enter into such an agree-ment. Rather, when you buy wood, let each pay for his half from the start. Then, if someone is [un]willing to pay his share, you will know, and you can press him to do his duty. Beyond this, do not bargain with your roommates.

102. In response to Friederich's letter of 5 October.

I cannot advise you to buy more than a single load or cord of wood at a time. For where will you store all that wood? If you and your roommate stack it on the floor, then others can take it and burn it as easily as you. So buy only one load, and put it under one of your beds. Then, you need not worry.

When you hire a stoker, hire him at one-half gulden per fireplace, regardless of how many students occupy a room. He will have no more work to do. A quarter-gulden each is enough for you and your roommate to pay.

As for your behavior, just do not venture behind any castle, regardless of what your roommate wants to do.[103] And always keep a clean shirt on your back.

Before you send laundry here to be washed, it is best to dry it out first. And we cannot always do it immediately.

No more. God bless. Amen.

[unsigned]

55 ❧ Friederich to Mother, 19 November 1579

Filial love and devotion, dear Mother . . .

Dear Mother, I am saddened to hear that the Lord God has called our dear relative and friend Jacob Schleicher from the world so suddenly.[104] May He grant him and all of us a happy resurrection.

Dear Mother, I am completely at a loss to know what to do about my eye. It is again as it was before, only worse. If I take a day or two off to rest it, when I begin to read again, as I must, for I cannot discontinue my studies, the pain starts all over again after a day. My vision has become so darkened that I worry that a blemish is developing over my eye. Personally, I would like to come home, but I must stay another week or two for exams. Although I am treating my eye as best I can, when I begin again to read and study, it hurts even more.

Know that a bookbinder has recently moved here. I have given him a book to bind which was in such a complete mess that it shamed me for

103. Prostitutes were to be found behind the castle.
104. See letter 10.

anyone to see it. Would you send me the money to pay for it, namely, forty-two pfennigs?

No more. Greetings to the household. 19 November.

> Y[our] L[oving] S[on]
> Friederich Behaim.

56 ❦ Mother to Friederich, undated[105]

Dear son Friederich. I have received your letter and I am unhappy to learn that your eyes are bad again. Would you come home as soon as possible so that we can see what can be done? I do not know what else to advise you. Nor do I know whether you can endure still another week or two of this. You must yourself take steps so that your eyes are not seriously damaged. You know what to do.

I am herewith sending you a gulden. Use it to pay for the book and to buy the other things you need. Veit will bring the instrument [home] next Sunday. My advice is that you bring the small instrument home when you come. If someone gives it to Veit, then take the other one. If Veit overlooks it, let someone else do it.[106]

I fear that you will have to take a heap of pills to get rid of the swelling.[107] But I will continue to seek advice.

> [unsigned]

57 ❦ Friederich to Mother, undated

Dear Mother. You will no doubt know that Herr Dr. Flick has often asked me sometime to write him a little Latin letter so that he may see what I am studying and how well I am doing.[108] So I could not neglect writing him a little letter, which I ask you to send on to him.[109]

---

105. Notwithstanding the misfiling by the Behaim Archiv, this is a response to Friederich's letter of 19 November, not his letter of 21 February.
106. Veit is obviously a servant. It is unclear what this second, apparently larger, instrument is.
107. "Haip pilela." *Haip* is related to *happ, hab, Haufe.*
108. Dr. Flick is Dr. jur. Bartholomaus Flick, a *Genannter* (member of the Large Council) related to the Behaims by marriage: like Frau Behaim, his wife was a Römer.
109. This was enclosed but is not extant.

Would you send me a pair of shoes as soon as you can? I have worn my present ones since St. James Day [25 July].

No more. Greet all the household for me. Amen. God bless. In Altdorf.

Y[our] L[oving] S[on]

Friederich Behaim.

58 🐝 Mother to Friederich, undated[110]

Fritz,[111] I thought I could wait no longer for the carter, so I am herewith sending you the money [for Herr Gruner] in the oaken box together with the bill indicating how much you should pay him. Return the bill to me and send me your blanket. If you have dirty laundry, send it along also in the blanket. Do not keep the box any longer than it takes to gather up your laundry.

Your jacket will not be ready before the new year because the tailor has taken ill. Meanwhile, I will send you the other one. I am sending you the trouser ties now.[112]

[unsigned]

59 🐝 Friederich to Mother, 21 December 1579

My greetings, dear Mother . . . I am herewith sending you the sack with my blanket and laundry and also the tailor's bill.[113] He wants to be paid before the holidays. Know that the money due Herr Gruner was short by more than four Zwelfer, which I have had to make up. Would you send my shoes at the earliest?

I am not very happy with the trouser ties. I wish you had mended

110. Posted on 10 December, the date of Herr Gruner's bill for Friederich's quarterly payment.

111. Only twice in the entire correspondence does Frau Behaim address Friederich this way. See letter 76.

112. These are apparently knee bands or laces.

113. The bill, for five pounds, six pfennigs, was for mending or sewing trousers (three times), coats (three times), gesess (twice), and stockings (once).

them with old taffeta and saved the new. They are entirely too short; I can hardly make a loop, much less tie them in a knot.

No more. God bless. 21 December.

Y[our] L[oving] S[on]

Friederich Behaim.

60 ❦ Mother to Friederich, undated[114]

Friederich. I am herewith sending you a gulden to present to your boarding-house keeper as a gift on New Year's Day.[115] There is also a half-gulden for the maids. If [Frau Gruner] has only one maid, change the half-gulden and give her seventy-two pfennigs. If there are two, give each a quarter-gulden[116] or simply give them the half-gulden [to share equally].

Meanwhile, I am sending you the two clean shirts. The others will follow. No more for now. Happy New Year. Would you greet the Gruners for me and wish them a happy New Year? God bless.

[unsigned]

61 ❦ Friederich to Mother, 3 January 1580

My friendly greetings and every good wish together with a happy and joyous new year . . .

Dear Mother, I have now received a shirt, then another, and thereafter two shirts. But I am puzzled why you do not send my shoes. Would you let me know about them?

When the carter, Fritz, comes again, would you pay him off, and thereafter use the carter who brings [this] letter to do our carting? Would you also buy me the book that is on the enclosed note? I urgently need it, and if I do not buy it, I cannot do much useful work here. Just ask Jacob Schleicher to buy it for me.[117] It costs one and a half gulden unbound.

114. Before New Year's Day 1580.

115. The boarding-house keeper is now Frau Gruner.

116. About sixty-three pfennigs. The discrepancy between seventy-two pfennigs and sixty-three may reflect a desire to pay no more than half a gulden, but to give one maid more than she would receive if she were assisted by another, because of the increased labor.

117. This is the son of the Schleicher mentioned in letters 10 and 55.

There is a bookbinder living here now who charges a flat fee of a half-gulden per book. After I buy this book, I will not soon need to buy any more and I can return [full-time] to my studies.

No more. Greet all the household for me and wish everyone a good new year. 3 January, 1580.

> Y[our] L[oving] S[on]
> Friederich Behaim.

[P.S.] When you can get quills for pens, send me some. I do not have a good pen and there are no quills here.

62 ❦ Mother to Friederich, undated[118]

My greetings and wish for a happy new year, dear son Friederich. I have received your letter about the shoes from the carter. As I had never given shoes a thought and had no recollection [of your previous request], I went back through your letters and, sure enough, found that you had written me for shoes.[119] I simply overlooked it. I have now visited the shoemaker, but he had no finished pair. He will have a pair ready for you by Friday and I will send them out to you later. I am also unable to send the book to you until the next shipment. But I am herewith sending a dozen quills. They are the best I can find here. God bless.

> [unsigned]

63 ❦ Friederich to Mother, 14 January 1580

My greetings, dear Mother. If you and the household are still well and hardy, it is a great joy for me to hear it. Know that I, too, am still in good health, etc. Amen.

Dear Mother, I am herewith sending the sack. I need the scouring brush for myself.[120] Perhaps you will not miss it too much.

Know that I am constantly in need of the book. So if you would give me this money I will take the book to another [to bind it].[121] It can only

118. A response to letter 61.
119. Friederich's letter of 21 December. The comment suggests that his mother carefully saves all his letters and perhaps files them methodically.
120. "Spülfleck" or "Spielfleck." This could possibly be a mending tool.
121. Because his mother had ignored his request in letter 61 for a half-gulden to bind the book in Altdorf, Friederich again raises the subject.

be bound in boards and covered with leather. That is why it costs half a gulden.

Would you also send me a roll of tapers? And if the laundry is ready and you want to send it, you can save a shipment by sending the shirts with my whites.

The only other thing I have to report is a terrifying sight that occurred here on Tuesday and was doubtlessly also seen in Nuremberg. At 1:00 P.M., three suns with well-nigh four rainbows appeared in the sky, which, although a natural occurrence, portends violent storms and riotings among the princes.[122]

Know that I have learned from the barber-surgeon who treated Gabriel Muffel that Muffel was struck with a tankard on the road to Nuremberg by a shoemaker named Hans von Schenbach, who runs a store here.[123] In addition, Muffel has syphilis. That is no surprise. A great many people here suffer from it. No one may go securely into the bath. But I always bathe in the castle so that I may be safe.[124]

God bless. 14 January.

> Y[our] L[oving] S[on]
> Friederich Behaim.

64 ❦ Mother to Friederich, undated

Friederich. I am herewith sending you the book and the shoes with Milholtzer because the devilish carter left on Tuesday as soon as he arrived, and I did not have the book and the shoes ready to give him.[125] I then arranged for Fritz to deliver them, but I could not get them to him soon enough either. So I have given them to Milholtzer to deliver without

122. A contemporary broadsheet bears a portrayal of the apparition by the artist Hans Mack. According to the accompanying commentary, it portended "violent changes in government and divisions within the church." Walter Strauss, ed., *The German Single-Leaf Woodcut, 1550–1600*, vol. 2 (New York, 1975): 656. The phenomenon, commonly known as "sun dogs," is a parhelion, a bright spot appearing on either side of the sun, often, as here, on a luminous ring or halo.

123. Gabriel Muffel von Eschenau (1546–82) is the son of the Muffel mentioned in letter 23. He died in Siena.

124. Friederich arranged to bathe privately and avoid the temptations and diseases of the public bath.

125. Milholtzer may be the Mühlholtzer mentioned in letter 34, now returning to school. This letter is a response to letter 63.

Fritz's knowledge. When you send back [the box in which they come], return the scouring brush. I have also put the paper in it and the sack in which I am sending you the book. Have the book bound and write down the cost. But read it for a while first and then have it bound as cheaply as possible. [The binding you propose] renders the book no more useful than otherwise and it also costs a lot.[126] And hereafter, stop spending money for a while. Since All Saints I have spent altogether twenty-five gulden on you. So it is time for you to cut back.

I think you will still have a white shirt to wear this Sunday. I will send two new shirts next week. Send your dirty laundry home soon to be washed. No more for now.

[unsigned]

65 ❦ Friederich to Mother, 10 March 1580

My friendly greeting and wish for every good thing for you, dear Mother . . .

Dear Mother, I am herewith sending [Gruner's] bill.[127] Although there is much beer on it, I swear to God that I have not drunk as much as I did last quarter. Would you henceforth stop sending [Gruner] money, because I do not want to deal with him [any longer]. I will take nothing from him in the next half-quarter.[128]

Would you send the money for my music teacher and, as you have done in the past, a gulden [for my free use]? When I am able, I will work diligently to repay it. I am sending you the wheat flour. Would you distribute it? If [those you give it to] will grind it finely, they will never forget it. No more for now. God bless. 10 March.

Y[our] L[oving] S[on]
Friederich Behaim.

126. Frau Behaim warns against making a book more for exhibition than for study. See her similar chiding in letter 46.
127. For the quarter from 11 December to 11 March: nine gulden, four pounds, six pfennigs for board, three gulden, nine pfennigs for 127.5 measures of beer (at a little more than a quart a measure).
128. An apparently idle threat, for Friederich sent his mother another quarterly board bill from Gruner in mid-June. See letter 77.

66 ❦ Friederich to Mother, 5 April 1580

My greeting, dear Mother . . .

Dear Mother, I am herewith sending you the laundry and the box. I thank you for the Easter cakes and pancakes. I have eaten them all.

Know that now is the time one pays for wood, namely four gulden for each room. There are only three of us in our room, but we still must pay the full amount, which comes to one gulden, two pounds, twenty-four pfennigs each. Send me this money next time because someone has already asked me for it. One must pay the same amount for the room,[129] but not until Peter Paul [28 June].

I cannot wear my trousers any longer. The more I wear them, the more ragged they become. So would you send [another pair] soon?

God bless. 5 April, [15]80.

      Y[our] L[oving] S[on]
      Friederich Behaim.

67 ❦ Friederich to Mother, 20 April 1580

My greeting and wish for all that is good for you, dear Mother. Herewith I am sending this little bill for the room rent.[130] Seldom does one pay anything for the room when one lives there in the summer, but for the winter one must pay this much. The Pfleger has asked me to give him this [payment] soon, because he must make an accounting. So would you send the money soon?

I am also sending you an old pair of trousers and a jacket. You can certainly have the trousers mended so that I can wear them when I come home. God bless. 20 April, 1580.

      Y[our] L[oving] S[on]
      Friederich Behaim.

129. Friederich has now moved into a room in the city with two of his roommates. See letters 52 and 78.

130. "Stubenzins." The bill, for five gulden, was for Friederich's room in the college over the winter quarter. It came from Balthasar Baumgartner, Pfleger in Altdorf, who became Friederich's relative in 1583, when Friederich's sister Magdalena married his son.

68 ❦ Friederich to Mother 4 May 1580

Filial love and devotion, dear Mother. I cannot marvel enough that you
do not send the trousers and the money that belongs to the Pfleger here.
I would like to know if you have received my two letters and the sack
with my old clothes, which I recently sent you.[131] Please send the money
and the trousers at the earliest. May almighty God keep you under his
protection and care. 4 May.

> Y[our] L[oving] S[on]
> Friederich Behaim.

[P.S.] The students controlled themselves well today when in the evening
two peasants fought. One waits every hour for one of them to die, and
not without reason.

69 ❦ Mother to Friederich, undated

Friederich. I am herewith sending you the trousers and the money.
Have the trousers cleaned. There is no need to alter them until the [at-
tached] stockings become torn. However, you may not mischievously
tear them, for they cost a lot. Keep them clean and they will still last you
a long time. No more for now.

> [unsigned]

70 ❦ Friederich to Mother, 22 May [1580]

Kind, dear Mother. I am sending all the laundry I was unable to send
last time, together with my old coat. You need not send any more [clean]
laundry as I do not need it now. No more. God bless. In Altdorf, 22 May.

> Y[our] L[oving] S[on]
> Friederich Behaim.

71 ❦ Friederich to Mother, 25 May [1580]

My greeting, dear Mother. I am now in need of shoes. Please send
them at the earliest. Also, it was almost Easter when anyone last did

131. The letters are those of 5 and 20 April.

anything to improve my clothing a little. My stretched-out trousers become smaller each day. When I walk or bend over, they split on every
side. If you do not let them out, I maintain they will become completely
useless. If you will allow me [to buy] the cheapest fustian breeches or
galliot without any trim, that would be good enough for me on workdays
during the summer.[132] And you could repair the other trousers so that I
might have them on holidays and spare my new ones. No more. 25 May.

Y[our] L[oving] S[on]
Friederich Behaim.

72 ❦ Mother to Friederich, undated

Friederich. I am herewith sending you five eln of fustian for breeches
and four eln for a jacket. Line the jacket sleeves with the bleached cloth
and the jacket body and skirt with the unbleached. I will send buttons
next time. Do have it made large enough, for you are now having your
greatest growth.[133]

[unsigned]

73 ❦ Friederich to Mother, 30 May 1580

My greeting, dear Mother. If you are well and hardy, I am happy to
hear it.

Know, dear Mother, that my eye will not get better. Although the
[eye]water takes the redness away, there is still pain and swelling. I have
therefore sought the advice of the [new] surgeon here in Altdorf, who is
an experienced eyedoctor. His good response is that he would very much
like to help me and that he [could] rid me of the inflammation altogether.
I wanted to inform you of this. Would you give me the money for it? I
hope that [his treatment] will reverse [the inflammation]. He knows the
true cause of what is troubling my eye.

No more, except that there is to be absolutely nothing, not even a play,

---

132. A *galliot* is a sailor's shirt or light jacket.
133. Friederich is now sixteen years old.

on Peter Paul, because it has been moved to St. James [Day], when one will then allow it.[134] God bless. 30 May.

> Y[our] L[oving] S[on]
> Friederich Behaim.

74 ❦ Mother to Friederich, undated

Friederich. I have learned from your letter that the surgeon there wants to help you, which I did not know [before]. I have instructed the carter [to tell you] that you should let him help you, if he can. I would like [first] to find out what medicine he uses. Would you let me know? And tell him that when he has an occasion to be here in the city to come and see me, and I will talk with him about [your treatment].

God bless. I did not now have time to write you [any more], as the carter was so soon off.

> [unsigned]

75 ❦ Mother to Friederich, undated

Friederich. The servants have just given me your note. Since we are just getting around to the laundry, I have been unable to send you anything.

Although you know from my previous letter[135] that you should come home if you can do so without getting behind [in your studies], I do not know what you mean when you write that you are bringing the doctor with you.[136] Are you saying that he shall be rooming and boarding with me or only that I should talk with him while he is here? Do not [commit]

134. 25 July. On this day in 1580 Altdorf officially celebrated its elevation to the status of an academy. This academic "privilege" had been bestowed on the school on 26 November 1578 by Emperor Rudolf II, empowering the school to award bachelor's and master's degrees in the arts and philosophy. Horst Claus Recktenwald, *Die Fränkische Universität Altdorf* (Nuremberg, 1966), 16–18. As part of the celebration students gave special orations, debating among other topics the usefulness of the privilege. Frederick John Stopp, *The Emblems of the Altdorf Academy: Medals and Medal Orations, 1577–1626* (London, 1974), 35–36.

135. Not letter 74 but a letter that is not extant.

136. Also a reference to a letter that is not extant.

me to providing quarters for him; I am not yet indebted to him.[137] But if I can talk with him, I will be happy to do so. So arrange for me to do this.

      [unsigned]

76 ❦ Mother to Friederich, undated

Son Fritz. The carter informs me that he has heard that you are now being treated [by the surgeon]. I do not know what it is with you that you do not let me know this in advance, as I had previously written you that I wanted first to talk with him. He gladly takes you now [as his patient] and afterwards he will think that one must pay him whatever he wants.[138] So think more about the cost. If his [fee] is not [agreed upon far] enough in advance, I can never pay it.

      [unsigned]

77 ❦ Friederich to Mother, 16 June 1580

My greeting and wish for every good thing for you, dear Mother . . .

Dear Mother, I am herewith sending you Gruner's bill. Since there is again so much beer on it that I [am alleged to] have drunk,[139] you might be thinking that all I do is drink beer and never study. Know that I have written down all the beer I have had until now. When Gruner gave me the bill a week ago, I told him then that he had charged me for more that forty measures of beer that I did not drink. He answered, to the contrary, that there was never a day when beer had not been served to me and the others. However, he did not know whether it had been

---

137. This means the letter was written before treatment began.

138. Frau Behaim had had such experiences earlier when Friederich's brother Paul was in Padua (1576–77). During time of plague, what Paul feared most apart from disease was being preyed on by the "medicis, who know well how to reach into one's pockets." He claimed to have got the services of physicians and surgeons "only by great pleading and paying double." Loose, "Deutsches Studentenleben in Padua," letters 17–18, p. 25.

139. Gruner's bill includes charges for 132 measures of beer (four and a half more than on the preceding quarter's bill) at seven pfennigs each (one pfennig a measure more than in the preceding quarter).

served at my command or not. But should he now have to forgo payment
for so much beer because he did not know [who ordered it], it would
be too great a loss for him. So he is going to inquire about a thief [who
orders beer in my name]. If I find him, he must pay dearly, and I will
find him.

As for the doctor, dear Mother, know that he has not yet begun to
treat me. For after I wrote you, the swelling soon went away. The doctor
wants to wait until it returns before he treats me.

Would you, as in the past, send me a gulden [to spend freely] and
meanwhile not let me suffer on account of the [extra] beer, which is an
injustice that has befallen me? Also, as we are now beginning to read new
books and I am entering a new class, I bought two books for a gulden
that would have cost me two, had they been new. But, as I have had no
money, I have not yet paid for them. And I must have still more [money],
for I will now settle accounts for other books I had previously gotten
from the bookbinder, who also runs the bookstore here. Altogether, the
cost comes to three gulden. If I may have this [money], I will want no
more, and it will restore my studies. I have perhaps wasted too much of
my time this half year. But I will now be a different person and henceforth
more exacting. It is only out of great need that I have bought these books.

Would you also send another quire of paper? No more except to commend you to God's care.

> Y[our] L[oving] S[on] A[lways]
> Friederich Behaim.

78 ❦ Friederich to Mother, 27 June 1580

My greeting, dear Mother. Your letter scolding me for my excessive
table[140] has been delivered along with the money. I wrote you in my last
letter that I did not in fact drink [all] this [beer]. It would be impossible
for me to do so. Rarely have I ever drunk more than two measures a day
(and I am willing to swear an oath to that). And [drinking beer] is not the
cause of the swelling in my eyes.[141] I do have some understanding of what
is causing that. But what I cannot now understand is how I should have
lost all trust and faith [with you]. I have so far conducted myself here in

---

140. "Meiner ungepürlig Reicht [Richt, Gang bei Tisch] halben." The letter is not extant.
141. On Gruner's bill of 11 June 1580 Frau Behaim, obviously impressed by the quantity
of beer consumed, has written "5 pints a day" next to the total figure for the quarter.

such a way that neither the preceptors nor my other companions have ever been spiteful or hostile toward me or lodged a complaint against me. I do remain over my books, which are my dearest possessions. But since you think I do nothing but eat and drink to excess and lead the life of a dissolute youth, when I am next home, I want you to put me to the test with others. Would you [until then] hold no evil suspicion of me whatsoever, as if I were some deceitful and cunning person! I [too] would rather save the money.

I recently wrote you about the rent, the eight gulden, which is a lot, that one must pay for a room. Since we are [only] three, each of us must pay one gulden, two pounds, twenty-seven pfennigs, and it is due on Peter Paul.[142] Would you please send this money?

Dear Mother, I wanted to point [all this] out to you, not to scold you for your letter, but only to defend myself, so that when I come home during the Reichstag, I may not be there amid anger and discord.

God bless. 27 June. If you still have a few roses left over, would you keep them for me? And would you also send me paper?

Y[our] L[oving] S[on]
Friederich Behaim.

79 ❦ Friederich to Mother, 12 July 1580

My greeting, dear Mother . . .

Dear Mother, I have long planned to come home, but on the very night [I was to do so] a blemish spread over half my eye, so I have remained here. The doctor has begun to treat me first with a pill, but not like those one gets at the apothecary. He used several of these pills to drive a great filth from me and almost as soon I found myself feeling better. He is now putting a water [in my eye], which also helps a lot. He is experienced; for twenty-nine years he was the chief military surgeon on land and sea. And he has been the pupil of Theophrastus,[143] from whom he learned most of his craft. I would choose him over all the doctors and surgeons in Nuremberg.

142. See letter 66. The eight gulden pays for both wood (four) and room (four), each divided equally among the three boys. Wood had earlier been paid for; here only the rent is falling due.
143. Theophrastus Bombastus von Hohenheim (1493–1541), Swiss alchemist and physician, known as Paracelsus.

That I have not written until now is in part because I could not do so. I have had to wait for my eyes [to mend] and have been unable to meet the carter.

Otherwise, I know nothing to write you at this time except that the school will celebrate its [academic] privilege on St. James Day.[144] If you want to see it, you may do so. There will be four successive days of activities such as can never again be seen here. Would you tell Magdalena to tell [Paul] Ketzel, if she sees him, that when he has too much money again, he should come back to Altdorf? He and some comrades were here last Sunday, and he, Paul Scheurl, and Hans Imhoff won one hundred and fifty gulden gambling.[145]

I have no more paper, so would you send me a [quire]? No more. God bless. 12 July.

      Friederich Behaim.

80 ❦ Friederich to Mother, 21 July 1580

My dear Mother and dear sister Magdalena. You will without doubt know what this little wreath signifies on 22 July and therefore also know to place it.[146] Dear Mother, if it is not repugnant to you, I plan to be here next Friday to collect the *presenz*, not for the sake of the *presenz* itself, but rather because of the fireworks, which are going to be spectacular.[147] If

144. "Die schule priviligirn." See n. 134.

145. Paul Ketzel (d. 1588) was the son of the *Stadtrichter* (city magistrate) Georg Ketzel, and the last of the Nuremberg Ketzels. His cousins Paul Scheurl von Defersdorf (1555–1618) and Hans III Imhoff (1563–1629) appear several times together in the correspondence of Friederich's sister Magdalena. *Briefwechsel Balthasar Paumgartners*, 150, 260–61, 274–75. So does Paul Ketzel. *Briefwechsel Balthasar Paumgartners*, 12, 15, 31–32, 36, 211. The Scheurls and Behaims were related to the Imhoffs by marriage. The sum Friederich mentions is enormous, even for well-to-do boys. Assuming he is not exaggerating, the three Nuremberg boys must have been gambling with Altdorf's most aristocratic youths.

146. 22 July was Mary Magdalene Day. A wreath on that day symbolized purity and forgiveness.

147. A *presenz*, or *präsenz*, was compensation for assisting at a religious service, particularly commemorative Masses. Because Altdorf was the major Protestant school in southeastern Germany, Friederich must have been using the term in reference to services commemorating the school's academic privilege. Knowing his mother's opposition to ostentatious display (see letter 43) and her suspicion of his overindulgence, Friederich

you hate the idea (almost all the students are coming here [for the cele-
bration]), would you let me know? I am just as happy not to be here;
indeed, I prefer to be there [with you]. God bless. 21 July, the day before
Mary Magdalene.

> Y[our] L[oving] S[on]
> Friederich Behaim.

81 ❦ Friederich to Mother, 22 September [1580]

My greeting and willing obedience, dear Mother. I am writing to let
you know briefly about my board, which I should have done long ago.
Gruner has calculated it up to the present, but because he was working
he could not make out a bill. However, he told me that my board had
fallen due on 11 September, in the amount of nine gulden, four pounds,
and six pfennigs. As I wrote in my last letter, there is also four measures
of wine at a cost of twenty-four pfennigs. As for my other [expenses], you
will know well what to send me. I must now pay eight pfennigs for beer,
so I just get by on two gulden.[148] Otherwise [I still need] one gulden. Do
send me this money when you can.

I, too, am disappointed that the emperor did not come.[149] (But if [Paul]
Ketzel cannot help you consume all the partridges and ducks [gathered
for the occasion], I will also do my best to see that you are free of them!)

Our school increases in importance; today, for the first time, two English counts arrived.

Would you send back some candles in this box? There is less daylight
now and the night is coming on.

---

anticipated her opposition to his remaining in Altdorf for the school's four-day celebration. Clearly the spectacle was more important to Friederich than any remuneration.
148. This increase of a pfennig in the cost of a measure of beer is the third in as many
quarters.
149. A visit by the emperor to a diet of the electoral princes in Nuremberg was planned
but ultimately canceled. The emperor's fear of rumored disease in the Nuremberg area
apparently led to the cancellation. Because the emperor had not visited the city since
1571, elaborate preparations had been made. Albrecht Kircher, *Deutsche Kaiser in Nürnberg.
Eine Studie zur Geschichte des öffentlichen Lebens der Reichsstadt Nürnberg von 1500–1612* (Nuremberg, 1955), 143–44.

God bless. 22 September, the day of [St.] Mauritius, the holy martyr.[150]
      Y[our] L[oving] S[on]
      Friederich Behaim.

82 ❦ Mother to Friederich, undated[151]

Dear son Friederich. I have received your letter and learned of your
willingness to help remove the provisions [gathered for the emperor's
visit]. The partridges have removed themselves, having died from disease,[152] while the ducks and hens have been sold. [Only] the hay and
straw are still there. Nothing is left but drink. If you still want to come
and consume that, it is up to you. It may be too harsh for your mouth.[153]
The emperor's arrival is again postponed until 16 October or 6 November.

The matter of [your] board still hangs in the balance. I wish you had
talked with Herr Gruner about a three-week delay, so long as he has
nothing against it. I am now hard pressed to pay, as you know. I will
receive some money again on All Saints. I will ask to have it two weeks
early and send it as soon as I get it. But if Gruner is against [any delay],[154]
let me know, and I will see how you [can] still pay him. Meanwhile, I am
sending a gulden for your needs and six pounds of candles.
      [unsigned]

83 ❦ Friederich to Mother, 13 October 1580

My greeting and wish for every good thing for you, dear Mother.
I am herewith sending you a letter for Paul. Would you send it on to

150. Maurus, a third-century martyr. In another hand is written at the end "In Altdorf,
Ao. 81." But Friederich was in Venice in September 1581; because Gruner was paid in
full in August for the corresponding quarter in the preceding year (1579), the board
here discussed can only be that for 11 June to 11 September of 1580, not 1581.
151. This is clearly a response to letter 81.
152. "Am schelm gesttorben."
153. Either Friederich is suffering from some mouth ailment (canker sores?) or the
wine is very strong.
154. Frau Behaim had paid Friederich's bill for the preceding quarter a full month after
it had fallen due. As a widow with children, Frau Behaim received money from appointed male trustees (actually relatives), who oversaw her late husband's estate with
her and for her.

him at the earliest? And would you also send me his letter when he writes back?

Dear Mother, know that Herr Baumgartner was here last Sunday to set up the deposition[s] by which one becomes a student.[155] I, too, must so become one. It costs money, and it is of little use to anyone. Still, the old regulation must be observed. Each student is obligated in the amount of two gulden: one for the banquet to which the students are invited, one-half for the person who "deposes," and one-half for a new inscription [into one's records]. I will let you know how it otherwise goes. I had to borrow this money from Gruner, so would you again send it to him with the other money [we owe]?

I have received the laundry, but there were no linens in it. Do you still have them there with you? Would you let me know right away? No more. God bless. 13 October, in haste.

> Y[our] L[oving] S[on]
> Friederich Behaim.

84 ❦ Friederich to Mother, undated, 1580

Dear Mother. In my last letter I said nothing about the money you customarily give me [at this time], namely the gulden for [free] spending,

---

155. At sixteen, successful students were ceremonially "acquitted" of their preparatory studies and advanced to public (professional) lectures or university study, or into a vocation. Friederich, now almost seventeen, was at this point in his studies. Before "deposition" a student was know as a *beanus*, a derogatory term for a beginner. The ceremony of acquittal marked the transition to more serious professional study or work, a laying aside of the easier, youthful regimen. It took many forms. Very often the *beanus* was outfitted with horns or donkey's ears. During the ceremony the "deposer," usually an older student (although Martin Luther played the role of deposer in Wittenberg), rubbed salt on the student (a reference to Jesus' "You are the salt of the earth") and poured wine over his head (an anointing), or simply handed these weighty symbols to him at ceremony's end. Older students hazed the *beani* throughout the deposition. Mertz, *Das Schulwesen*, 444; Oskar Dolch, *Geschichte des Deutschen Studententhums* (Leipzig, 1858), 156ff; C. Beyer. *Studentenleben im 17. Jahrhundert* (Schwerin in Mecklenburg, 1899), 29ff.

and the two for beer. Would you send this money at the earliest? In haste, [15]80.

> Y[our] L[oving] S[on]
> Friederich Behaim.

[P.S.] The Speisemeister's daughter is the bride of the city secretary here.[156]

85 🐝 Mother to Friederich, undated[157]

Friederich. I am herewith sending you Gruner's money: nine and a half gulden for board, two gulden for "becoming a student,"[158] as you write, and two gulden for beer. For the time being, pay him also from this money for the four measures of wine. And do stop eating and drinking at the other house as long as it goes on.[159]

The linens were given to the carter last time. He still has them [   ] and he says he will deliver them to you. Just ask him for them.

> [unsigned]

86 🐝 Friederich to Mother, 13 November 1580

My greeting, dear Mother . . . I am herewith sending you my laundry. I thank you for the chickens. Would you send me paper at the earliest? I am completely out.

I do not know anything else to write you at this time. So God bless. I would write more often, but I have nothing to write about. Also, I do not have much spare time for writing. 13 November, [15]80.

> Y[our] L[oving] S[on]
> Friederich Behaim.

[P.S.] If the Spitzwerk is ready, would you let me try it?

---

156. This is Herr Oertel's daughter. See letter 88.
157. A response to Friederich's letter of 13 October.
158. "Fir den sttudenden."
159. That is, as long as the depositions last: Frau Behaim is paying a gulden for banqueting.

87 ❦ Friederich to Mother, 26 December 1580

My greeting, dear Mother . . .

Dear Mother, I wanted to write you before the new year and let you know that in the past we [have given] Frau Gruner a gold gulden and the maid[s] a half-gulden [for New Year's].[160] You may do as you wish. I received the money from the carter with the last mail, namely thirteen Zwolfer.

I would have written more, had I a good quill. Would you be sure to send the letter on to Paul? No more. God bless. 26 December.

> Y[our] L[oving] S[on]
> Friederich Behaim.

88 ❦ Friederich to Mother, 18 January 1581

My greeting and wish for every good thing for you, dear Mother.

Know that I have received my laundry and the trousers. I also talked with the surgeon. He is supremely confident that he has helped me.[161] He blames it only on the air that my eyes became bad again after I had traveled for a while. He now demands four crowns [to continue treatment], with the warning that my eyes might become bad [again], for he knows that a change in the air can excite all kinds of illness. So he would still give me pills and [eye]water, and he assures me that the swelling should go away completely and never return. I have bargained long with him over what he demands for what he has done for me up to now. But he will have it all and not be denied a single pfennig. He is prepared to help me so that my eyes are never bad again, which is also what I want. I would so like to be free of bad eyes (as I am now, [at least] until I travel again) and have real peace of mind. I have remained inside studying and reading. But were there to be no [further] treatment, I would see how I might endure with God's help.

Although the money [he wants] is in itself a lot, when one compares it with other [of his cures], for which he often took again as much, it might be [considered] reasonable. He helped Clement Khun's son survive [urinary] gravel after he had lain near death three times in Jena. [Although]

---

160. Cf. letter 58.

161. He first started to treat Friederich's eye in July. See letter 76.

he treated him for only three weeks, Khun had to pay him eight gulden. My hope is that, with God's help, he shall also [continue to] help me. God bless. 18 January.

> Y[our] L[oving] S[on]
> Friederich Behaim.

[P.S.] On 13 February, Oertel's daughter will celebrate her wedding here.

89 ❦ Mother to Friederich, undated

Friederich. I am herewith sending you two gulden. Give them to the slacker and tell him to stuff himself with them in [his] bed. Doctor Flick has told me that this wandering rogue is the [same] man who had wanted to cure his sister's son of epilepsy. She gave him and his wife a half-year's board, together with his fee, and even made sure that he did not have to take his meals with his host.[162] In a word, he shits on people wherever he is;[163] he is as good at it as one can be. I will not get involved with him. We will soon make an end of it. No more for now.

> [unsigned]

90 ❦ Friederich to Mother, 30 January 1581

My sincere greeting and wish for every good thing for you, kind, dear Mother. Know that I paid the surgeon the two gulden and I let it be known to him that I would not give him any more. Although he accepted the money, he has now lodged a complaint against me with the rector, something no one has ever done during all the time I have been here, and the rector has enjoined me to pay him [the remainder of his fee]. Should that not occur, he threatens to bring charges against me before Herr Baumgartner in Nuremberg. So, dear Mother, I ask you to send the money, if it is possible. Almost everywhere here people point their fingers at me, because the surgeon has reproached me all over town. I will not forgive him for this. Because of these goings-on, as I have well experienced, I cannot give my studies proper attention.

---

162. He and his wife could take their meals in private.
163. "Der rechtten land und leitt bescheiser."

I am herewith sending you my candle crate; would you return it with candles? 30 January, 1581.

> Y[our] L[oving] S[on]
> Friederich Behaim.

91 ❦ Mother to Friederich, undated[164]

Friederich, I am herewith sending you another gulden. You may give it to [the surgeon], if you cannot hang on to it. But that butcher shall get no more. If he will not be content with it, then let him come to me or file charges against me with Herr Baumgartner. When people there point their fingers at you, [remember that] they are not pointing at a scoundrel, but at one who will not suffer another's knavery. You are being a true fieni [and behaving] like a child.[165] You should have declared to the rector that you were the one in the right and informed him that the surgeon had promised you that you would owe him nothing if your eye became bad again.

Stay away from him in the future. Why does he not take action here against Herr Kress because of his son?[166] The scoundrel knows the injustice [he has done you].

> [unsigned]

92 ❦ Friederich to Mother, 15 February 1581

My greeting and wish for every good thing for you, kind, dear Mother. I am sending you my laundry with the carter and herewith letting you know that the surgeon has again made charges against me, [this time] before a plenary session of all the professors. I answered him there as best I could. Still, nothing was settled [by our exchange]. They have now set the amount due him at five gulden and enjoined me to pay it. The reason they did not want to allow anything to be deducted [from his fee

164. After 30 January; a response to Friederich's letter of 30 January.
165. The reference is to a vanquished warrior, whom his conqueror releases under a vow of continued service ("fianze"), hence a person who is free, yet conquered and still dependent.
166. The indication is that he had also treated Herr Kress's son unsuccessfully and was not being paid for it.

of six gulden] is that he had originally demanded ten gulden from me. I did not want to write and tell you this [at the time]. But now it has been reduced by half. So I ask you, dear Mother, if it can be done, to send me still two more gulden. By this little wrong a greater wrong can be avoided, and whether it is done to me or to the surgeon can be passed over in silence.

The wedding of the Speisemeister's daughter occurred yesterday, 14 February. Should you be thinking that I spent the money I now want for the surgeon at the wedding, know that I did not so much as set foot in the inn where the wedding occurred, but only in the town hall where the dance was held. I danced maybe three rounds with the heroine.[167]

I know nothing else to write at this time except what I have said above, [namely, to ask] that you send me the money [for the surgeon], because there is now a great need for it. 15 February.

> Y[our] L[oving] S[on]
> Friederich Behaim.

93 ❦ Mother to Friederich, undated

Friederich. I have received your letter about the surgeon and carefully considered it. Only extortion satisfies him. So consider your situation and have nothing more to do with him. I am herewith sending you two gulden. Give them to him. If he does not want it, let him leave it. There is already injustice enough. No more for now.

> [unsigned]

94 ❦ Friederich to Mother, 12 May 1581

My greeting, dear Mother. Know that I have received the eyewater and, praise God, my eyes are getting better.[168] I wish you had also sent me shoes. If I have the ones here repaired, then I have none to wear [while they are in the shop]. So would you send shoes with the carter? They

---

167. That is, the bride.
168. Friederich is resorting again to self-treatment, which had proved successful.

need not be double [soled], for they are then too warm. I am herewith
sending you my laundry. No more. God bless. 12 May.

> Y[our] L[oving] S[on]
> Friederich Behaim.

95 ❦ Friederich to Mother, 5 June [1581]

Filial love and devotion, dear Mother. I am herewith sending you my
trunks with books, and, since the time [of my departure] is at hand,[169] I
wanted to indicate to you the money I have spent. First, there is the nine
and a half gulden for my board. In accordance with law and custom here,
I have paid the rector three crowns, or four and a half gulden, for the
knowledge and training I have received.[170] This money goes into the
common chest and the preceptors thereafter take it for their effort and
work. I recently traveled with forty other students to Neuenmarkt. There
I watched two noblemen celebrate stately wedding[s] and while there, I
spent a gulden loaned me by [my] host. As a fitting conclusion, I have
attended a student wedding here, which cost me [another] gulden. My
traveling back and forth has created still another small debt of a half-
gulden. As I will now be moving away, I must secure my good name by
inviting several of my comrades out, which will cost me almost a gulden.
And, dear Mother, I also need a half-gulden immediately to meet my
daily expenses. Altogether it comes to eighteen gulden.

This is a lot of money, but one cannot always be spinning silk. One
must at some time in his life live it up, although I have done so more
out of necessity. I ask you not to be annoyed with me and to send me
[the money] at the earliest. May almighty God keep you. 5 June, Altdorf.

> Y[our] L[oving] S[on]
> Friederich Behaim.

169. Friederich is leaving Altdorf and will travel to Italy by summer's end.
170. "Lehr undt disciplin."

96 ❦ Friederich to Mother, 15 September 1581

Kind and much beloved Frau Mother. I arrived safely in Venice on the tenth of this month.[171] Since I cannot bring my horse [into the city] and must pay around three gulden a week to stall and feed him,[172] I have borrowed twenty ducats from Wilhelm Imhoff, which, at six batzen, four schilling [interest], comes to around twenty-eight gulden.

The [Spanish] empress will come in two weeks. Everyone brings his horse here, but no one can sell them. On 16 September, I will be off to Padua, where I have a prearranged meeting. As for what opportunities there are, I will let you know in my next letter.[173] God bless. 15 September, [15]81.

> Y[our] L[oving] S[on]
> Friederich Behaim.

97 ❦ Friederich to Mother, 29 September 1581

Very kind and much beloved Frau Mother. In my last letter you will have learned of my arrival in Venice on 10 September and of my travel to Padua on 16 September. The lords Otten in Venice have given me a letter [of recommendation] to a man [in Padua] named Cyprian, who provides board.[174] He can speak German well, although his entire household is Italian. He has accepted me, and I shall pay him seven crowns a month for everything. There is no cheaper board. Since I cannot yet speak Italian, I must in the beginning be patient and stay with him for a while. But thereafter I can shop for myself, as is the custom here, and get by on less.

Know also that, as others advised me, I have borrowed nothing from

---

171. Friederich, en route to Padua via Venice and three months away from his eighteenth birthday, is following in the footsteps of his brother Paul, who studied law in Padua between 1575 (when he was eighteen) and 1578.
172. Within two weeks the horse was sold.
173. That is, opportunities for accommodations.
174. The lords are Friederich's contacts in the "German House," the Fondaco de' Tedeschi, where the German merchants lived and worked.

the Jews, but instead purchased a note for four crowns.[175] I should otherwise have paid the Jews forty schillings a month, which would have come to four crowns or more a year [in interest]. When the note has been repaid, I can always resell it.

It has gone badly for me with my horse. I could sell him for no more than seventeen crowns, and I had to take him to Padua to do so.

If I seem somewhat short in my accounting [of what I am spending], know that when I have put down kreuzer, six pfennigs [not four] equals one kreuzer in small change in Schwabia. When something is short, I write it all down. But because I do not yet know the correct equivalents of Italian and German coins, I always lose money [during exchanges].

Know that the empress was here between 25 and 28 September, before departing for Milan, where she will spend the winter. She was shown great honor here. Throughout their entire land, the Venetians gave her and all her servants free board.

I know nothing more to write you at this time. May God keep you under his protection and care. On the feast of St. Michael, 29 September, [15]81.

> Y[our] L[oving] S[on]
> Friederich Behaim.

98   ❦   Friederich to Mother, 29 November 1581

My greeting and wish for every good thing for you. Know, kind, dear Mother, that I am still faring well and I do not doubt that the same is true for you.

Wilhelm Kress sent me your letter on 24 November, and I have faithfully read your exhortation to Christian devotion.[176] I will act on it as far as possible. I can receive [Christian] teaching from the Italian sermon, and

175. "Ein Instrument." This is a kind of bond that provides the holder with a regular income. Friederich in effect lent four crowns to gain interest-free income without losing his original investment. His brother Paul had also avoided the interest charges of Paduan Jews by purchasing such an "Instrument" from his fellow German Jobst Tetzel for five and a half crowns, expecting to make more than his investment over several years. Loose, "Deutsches Studentenleben," 21.

176. Wilhelm Kress (1560–1640) married Friederich's sister Sabina in 1585. He is apparently sending Friederich his mail from the German House in Venice, where it first arrives in Italy.

it is useful as well for learning Italian. Together with vespers, the sermons are not too bad.[177]

I am pleased for Christoph. If it is the [same] count of Mantfort who was here in Padua and whom I met riding out of the city when I moved here, then it is an excellent, fine lord [whom Christoph now serves]. I have no doubt that he can provide him real opportunity.[178]

I know nothing more to write you at this time. Greet all the household and other good friends on my behalf. And would you send this [enclosed] letter to Paul? May almighty God keep you and us all. In haste, on St. Andrew's eve, [15]81.

> Y[our] L[oving] S[on]
> Friederich Behaim.

99 ❦ Friederich to Magdalena, 17 January 1582

My brotherly love and devotion and my wish for a happy new year and for all that is good in body and soul for you and all the household, dear sister Magdalena . . .

On 14 January, I received a letter from cousin Jacob Imhoff, to be sure, not one for the best, telling me how almighty God has called our dear Mother away, taking her to himself with the old year.[179] Although we needed her with us for our lifetime, this was best for her failing body and for the salvation of her soul and [eternal] happiness, as might happen with us all. Inasmuch as it has happened by the just judgment of God and we can do no more about it, and we have all patiently awaited it, we must now find consolation [in knowing] that we are not completely forsaken by God in heaven or by our other good friends [on earth].

Although I have nothing particular to write you, would you let me know what is going on there? Have you heard from Christoph? Is Paul still in Prague and Georg with Herr Strobel?

---

177. Friederich originally wrote: "Sampt den vespern lass ich [mir] gefallen" (I am pleased with it), but then crossed this out and wrote (less positively): "sindt mir nit zu wider," apparently to assure his Lutheran mother that he was not overly enthusiastic.

178. It is unclear who the count of Mantfort is.

179. Magdalena Paulus Behaim died on 31 December 1581. Jacob I Imhoff (1537–99) was a member of Nuremberg's privy council (alter geheimer Rat) and guardian to the Behaim children. His son, Jacob II (1572–1609), married Friederich's sister Maria in 1594.

Nothing more. May almighty God keep you and all our siblings. 17 January, 1582, in Padua.

Y[our] L[oving] B[rother]
Friederich Behaim.

100 ❦ Friederich to Sigmund Held, 4 February 1582

My greeting and wish for a happy new year and for all that is good in body and soul, esteemed, kind, dear Herr Uncle Held.[180] I have learned from Herr cousin Jacob Imhoff's letter how almighty God has taken my dear mother away to himself. He will grant her and all of us a joyful resurrection. I am dressed in simple mourning clothes because I brought no clothes whatsoever here with me. In the winter, when I could have arranged [to have clothes made], I needed only one clean suit of clothes, so I chose to have two simple articles of clothing made, the only ones since I have been in Italy.

I received thirty ducats in Venice on 19 December,[181] but I have already spent twenty-one crowns for board over the three months between 14 November and 14 February, five crowns, four pounds for the other things, and three crowns when I was in Venice [on the nineteenth], as I had to stay over there because a storm prevented my sailing. The rest of the money had to be spent on wood, shoes, and laundry. So on 2 February, in Venice, I had to take forty crowns from Herr Wilhelm Imhoff, as I needed twenty for two plain articles of clothing and a jacket.

Although I must confess that my life here is expensive, I do arrange all my affairs in the most exacting way possible. I am prepared this month to leave my German patron,[182] and, since I now understand Italian rather well, to find an Italian patron, rent a room, and care for myself. Then I may do my own shopping and take my meals in the most economical way. I will perhaps have to pay two crowns a month for a room and a cook. To be sure, I could do better in Germany with fifty gulden than I can do here with a hundred crowns. What one buys for pfennigs in Germany, one must buy with schillings here. An [Italian] schilling is ap-

180. See n. 28.
181. A Venetian ducat was worth about 1.4 gulden (see letter 96); an Italian crown, 1.5 gulden.
182. See letter 94.

proximately two and one-half pfennigs and one-sixth the size, which will not be unknown to you, kind, dear Herr Uncle.

I know nothing more to write at this time. May God keep you in his gracious protection and care. 4 February, [15]82, in Padua.

> Y[our] L[oving] Nephew,
> Friederich Behaim.

❦ EPILOGUE

In the years immediately following this last letter, Friederich was twice referred to in the letters of his brother-in-law Balthasar Baumgartner, Jr. Balthasar reports a visit with Friederich in Padua in October 1582, and he later announces Friederich's arrival in Frankfurt for the fall fair in September 1583.[183] By the latter date Friederich was out of Italy. His sister Magdalena describes him as "der Pfleger" in November 1591,[184] indicating that at least by that date he was well established in his post of town manager in Gräfenberg and Hiltpoltstein.

Unlike his brothers Paul and Christoph, Friederich never became a major political figure in Nuremberg. He retained his post in Gräfenberg and Hiltpoltstein to the end of his life. In 1588 he married into a powerful patrician family in Nuremberg when Ursula Geuder became his wife. Between 1589 and 1607 they had ten children, four sons and six daughters, all but two of whom survived their father, something against the odds on sixteenth century actuarial charts. Magdalena mentions Friederich and his children frequently and warmly throughout the 1590s, as she comments on their visits to Nuremberg. Friederich made a special effort to comfort Magdalena after she lost her only child in 1592.[185] He arranged for her to spend time with his own children, particularly his daughter Magdalena, born in 1593 and named after her. From Magdalena's description of her brother, the character of Friederich's youth—steady, earnest, and caring—remained also that of the man.

183. *Briefwechsel Balthasar Paumgartners*, 5, 37.
184. *Briefwechsel Balthasar Paumgartners*, 127.
185. Ozment, *Magdalena and Balthasar*, 106–08.

Stephan Carl Behaim

❦ ❦ ❦ ❦ ❦ ❦ ❦ ❦ ❦ ❦ ❦ ❦ ❦ ❦ ❦ ❦ ❦ ❦

Although Michael Behaim may be said to have been obsessed with success and Friederich an all too trusting soul, by every contemporary measure both were well adjusted youths who realized their goals in life. Such cannot be said of Stephan Carl. Early in his life his family and his teachers observed behavior they considered pathological, and he succeeded at nothing he undertook.

Before the summer of 1628 there are only a few fleeting glimpses of Stephan Carl. In 1622, at the age of nine, he was in a fine public school to which burgher youth were sent in Hersbruck, about twenty miles north of Nuremberg.[1] Already he was misbehaving and his academic progress was unsure. In 1624 he was summoned home by his half-brother and chief guardian, Lucas Friederich, who was twenty-five years his senior. According to Hersbruck's rector, Joachim Bonus, who seemed happy to have Stephan Carl gone, he was withdrawn from Hersbruck "out of concern to keep him in [his present] class, but to commend him to another preceptor."[2] Over the next four years he completed his elementary education and preparatory Latin studies in Nuremberg and neighboring Altdorf.[3]

In August 1628, on the eve of his sixteenth birthday, Stephan

---

1. Letter of Joachim Bonus to Lucas Friederich, 22 May 1622.
2. Letters of Joachim Bonus to Lucas Friederich, 15 and 26 January 1624. Lucas Friederich was the eldest of Paul II Behaim's children by his first wife, Ursula Sitzinger (d. 1591). Stephan Carl was the eldest of his children by Maria Magdalena Baier (d. 1641), who became his third wife in 1611.
3. He appears on the Altdorf matriculation lists for 1625 (June 29). Elias von Steinmeyer, *Die Matrikel des Universität Altdorf*, vol. 1 (Würzburg, 1912), no. 6144.

LUCAS FRIDERICUS BEHAIM . REIP.NORIBERGENSIS SEPTEM,
VIR, EIUSDEMQUE ECCLESIAR. ET SCHOLARUM CURATOR PRIMARIUS.
. NATUS XVII.IULII A: MDLXXXVII.DENATUS XXVIII.IUNII A: MDCXLVIII .

An Etching of Lucas Friederich Behaim,
by Michael Herr and Waldtreich

Gaze upon these features full of aged gravity:
   Thus did Behaim carry his eyes, forehead, and mouth.
How irksome it is that no artist's hand
   Can carve his heroic high virtue in brass!
If there is anything I know about him, it is this:
   He was an Aristides* to the fatherland of his city,
A dependable donor to the needy, and a prudent and pious man,
   Whose virtues and high Scholarch's coat of arms† befit a journey to Jerusalem.

*An Athenian renowned for his integrity.

†Lucas Friederich was superintendent of Nuremberg's schools. In the background is his coat
of arms.

Reprinted by permission of the Germanisches National Museum.

Carl began formal study in the Altdorf Academy. Between August and October he wrote four Latin letters and a most unusual birthday poem for his brother Lucas Friederich, concocted ineptly from Latin phrase books.[4] Already a transparent manipulator, he addressed his fearsome big brother as his "honey" and eulogized him as "the generous, noble, native bud" of Nuremberg.[5] There is nonetheless a certain innocence and understatement in these early letters that are not seen again—perhaps because they were written in a language Stephan Carl never mastered and he was therefore restricted in his cunning.

Stephan Carl's academic career ended once and for all with the spring term of 1629, when his tutor and his brother, a graduate of the academy, conjointly decided not to promote him after his first year of academy study. By his own later admission, he was the first Behaim so to fail. Although he begged and schemed for another chance at a university education, one was never granted.

There was also serious moral failing on Stephan Carl's part in the months between October 1628 and spring 1629. According to a letter from his mother he drank heavily and had been disciplined for stealing.[6] But his life truly began to unravel when his prying mother happened on a poorly disguised attempt to sell a schoolbook in Nuremberg for ready cash. This discovery led to others (he had also been selling his clothes and borrowing money without authorization to support his habits), and it made his mother forever suspicious of his basic honesty. Regaining the respect of his unforgiving mother became a lifelong obsession for Stephan Carl, at least rhetorically. According to the report of his preceptor in Altdorf, Magister Matthias Tydaeus, an older, married man nearing retirement, Stephan Carl's realization of his academic failure occasioned new depths of boozing, insolence, and womanizing.

---

4. See appendix 2.

5. See appendix 2.

6. Among the "excesses" of Stephan Carl catalogued between December 1628 and July 1629 in Lucas Friederich's notebooks, were the following: spending the Christmas holidays with tambourine players and consuming forty kreuzer of drink; squandering a thaler given to him to repair shoes with the help of Sebastian Löffelholz, who had begun studies at the academy in the same year as Stephan Carl (1628); making repeated flights with cronies to Grünsberg purely to carouse; purchasing a sword without authorization; throwing a party in his room while his preceptor was absent and during which thirty-two quarts of beer were consumed; and taking part in a drunken brawl at an inn in Nuremberg. Ernstberger, *Abenteurer*, 20.

Throughout his life Stephan Carl was his own best advocate and his only one. After the summer of 1629 his mother and his brother looked on him as a master of bravado and sophistry and never again believed him. But his romanticism and deceit also concealed a lonely and desperate youth. Like Michael he was haunted by the specter of seemingly endless dependency, yet unlike Michael he set his own snail's pace into adulthood. So fearful was he of his powerful brother's reaction to his lack of achievement and misbehavior that he pleaded and conspired to withhold from him all bad and even seemingly disappointing news for as long as possible. He was terrified of having his misdeeds exposed publicly and of being humiliated before his peers and teachers at the teachers' banquet that took place at the end of each year in Altdorf. He clung naively to his old preceptor Tydaeus, convinced that he was a faithful ally, while at the same time he demonized Tydaeus' wife for informing his mother of his behavior. Stephan Carl clearly sensed what the adults around him knew well: second chances were few and came hard for a youth such as he.

1 ❦ Stephan Carl to Lucas Friederich, 2 August 1628

Hail and be well.

If you are in good health and all is well, good!

Most noble Brother, I felt obliged to write and tell you that we arrived here [in Altdorf] safely and in good health. I would at the same time like to take the opportunity to inform you of books that I need. They are indicated on the enclosed note. At any rate my uncle often bade me, whenever I needed books, to write to him and send a list.[7]

Once again, I ask that you kindly forgive my perhaps straying pen. You may be sure that I shall write a better letter next year.

One more thing. I like Altdorf far more than Hersbruck and Nuremberg. Here I can make better progress with my education. I have arranged my time for both learning and play.

Be well. Written in Altdorf, very hastily, in my study,[8] 2 August, 1628.

> Your loving brother,
> Stephan Carl Behaim

2 ❦ Stephan Carl to Lucas Friederich, 22 August 1628

My fraternal greetings and readiness to serve you in whatever way I can.

Most noble, generous, prudent, and much-beloved Brother, excuse this temerity of mine (if temerity it is), which does not blush to interrupt you at a time when you are engaged in important civic business.[9] I expect my books to arrive tomorrow. I am well aware that you have gone to a lot of trouble to get them for me, setting aside your own more serious

7. The reference is to Conrad Baier, Stephan Carl's maternal uncle. That such book lists are being sent to Lucas Friederich attests to his role as the chief of Stephan Carl's four guardians.

8. "E Musaeo meo," literally, "Museum."

9. Lucas Friederich was one of the seven senior members of Nuremberg's privy council (*geheimer Rat*) and in this position he undertook a variety of diplomatic missions for the city.

business. For this and innumerable other fraternal favors I am most grateful.

I now ask you to have a talk with my most-beloved mother about sending me some money. You know well, my brother, that a student without money is a soldier without arms. Often I find myself having to ask for and spend money I never dreamed of spending. To ensure that the money you send me is not squandered or wasted (which I know concerns you), it occurred to me (although I do not mean to impose on you or Mother) that you might entrust two or three gulden to my host and preceptor, Herr Magister Tydaeus.[10] Then, when an urgent need arises, he will give me what is right and just.

Be well, most-beloved Brother. Greet my kindest and sweetest mother for me. From my study, 22 August, in the year of the Virgin birth[11] of Christ.

> Y[our] M[ost] D[ear] and Most Loving B[rother],
> Stephan Carl Behaim

3 ♛ Stephan Carl to Lucas Friederich, 13 October 1628

Greetings. I rejoice that you have returned home from your very difficult journey, a sojourn made dangerous by the depraved soldiers [along the way], in whom, as [Lucan] says, "there is no trust in or respect for God."[12] You know, best of brothers, that after God and my dearest mother, you have always been my refuge. So now, when I need books, I ask you to persuade Mother to buy Quintus Curtius [Rufus's] *History of Alexander the Great* and the *Helvetian Discourses, Latin-German*. Because they are evidently small books (I think), I can practice the Roman language with them to great profit, which I should add I am gaining command of at a good rate. I await the packet of books at your earliest convenience. Be well and happy.

Hastily from my little study, 13 October, in the year of the Virginbirth, 1628.

> Stephan Carl Behaim

10. It is unclear whether Tydaeus was the head of the *hospitium* in which Stephan Carl lodged, or whether Tydaeus' private home is here meant. In either event, Tydaeus was both a host and a preceptor during Stephan Carl's stay in Altdorf.
11. Or "Incarnation."
12. Lucan, *Bellum civile*, 10.407. The reference is to deserted and marauding soldiers fighting for various sides during the Thirty Years War.

4 ❦ Stephan Carl to Lucas Friederich, 17 October 1628

Fraternal love, greetings, and respect.

As babbling infants are at one time cheerfully listened to by their parents, who even take pleasure in their errors, so, kindest Brother, I am thoroughly convinced that my infancy [in Latin letters] will not be unpleasant to you. According to Pliny [the Elder], Book 7, chapter 40,[13] it was a Thracian custom to mark lucky days [on the calendar] with a white stone and unlucky ones with a black stone. The custom passed down to the Cretans, according to Horace, Ode 36, Book 1, "lest the lovely day lack the Cretan mark," as if to say, "a white mark indicates this to be a truly happy and lucky day." Indeed, why should I not now address you with the words of the Satirist,

"Mark this day, Brother, with a better stone. A white one you use to mark the gliding years. Pour out the unmixed wine, Brother, etc."?[14]

For I find your name (Lucas) on the calendar for the 18th day of October, in other words, today.[15] An old and noble custom endures among friends, who on their birth, or name, days, wish one another all good fortune and every good thing, and accordingly bestow gifts for good luck. But since, like Peter in Acts 3, "gold and silver have I none," I am sending Brother this [enclosed] paper gift.[16] And so that I may continue, as it were, under the cheerful countenance of Brother's respect and fraternal goodwill, I humbly ask that you consider not [the quality of] the verse my poor talent has written against the will of Apollo,[17] but rather the spirit of the one who offers it to you, and that you continue to show me your fraternal favor.

Farewell, flourish long and in safety to the increase of the State and the honor of a noble family. Written on the day before Lucas [October 17] in the Christian year, 1628.

> Your most respectful brother,
> Stephan Carl Behaim

13. *Natural History*, 7.40.41.
14. Persius, *Satiricon*, 2.1–3 (Stephan Carl has made some changes).
15. Stephan Carl writes in the epistolary present, as of the seventeenth, but in the expectation that the reader will see his words on the eighteenth. On contemporary calendars 18 October marked the celebration of St. Luke.
16. "Carthaceum." See appendix 2.
17. The god of verse.

5　🐿　Mother to Stephan Carl [March 1629][18]

Good evening. You have asked to know my thoughts about you. You can easily imagine what I am thinking. That God may have mercy; my hope is that God will be merciful to my own. I lie awake many a night because I cannot conclude otherwise than that your letters, with their citations of God's Word, are pure hypocrisy, used only to hide your shame. If your behavior were really a painful and serious matter to you, you would not be so bold and arrogant [as to say] that you have eaten with the children at the cat's table,[19] or that when the others have been sad, you have been completely happy and joyous. Neither sin nor shame gives you any pause. You have told me that the water fountain is now your greatest joy,[20] also when you hear it said in church, "give," which is as it should be for a true Christian. However, you [in fact] much prefer [to take] a little money [for yourself]. By such thoughts you are steering a course of shame and vice, which leads in the end to the gallows and hellfire. May God in his grace save you from such a fate. God will not be joked with. He has also said that one should not plunder, and he will not let you steal. If there were any honor in you, you would be thinking what I have often told you, namely, that if you see [another's] silver and gold lying at your feet, you shall take and use none of it. But my admonitions have so far had little effect on you. May God have mercy.

Because I have learned that, God willing, you will receive the Holy Sacrament on Good Friday,[21] I will again pray for you and your soul's salvation, which so far has been of very little concern to you. Humble yourself before God from the depths of your heart. Acknowledge and confess to him your great and weighty sin in true penance and suffering, and with a broken and battered heart, seek his forgiveness for the sake of the merit of Jesus Christ. Henceforth, lead a good life with the help and assistance of God the Holy Spirit, whom you must humbly call upon daily, in every hour, if you want to overcome your sin and lead a Christian

18. Five months have now passed, during which Stephan Carl's misbehavior at home and at school has alienated his family from him. There were several letters on this subject from his mother, of which only this one survives. I follow Ernstberger in dating it in 1629 rather than 1630. Ernstberger, *Abenteurer*, 16–17.
19. A small table for children. Being sent there to eat was also a punishment for unruly children. By such an image Stephan Carl trivializes the seriousness of his behavior.
20. Rather than the beer tap at the inn.
21. This would seem to date the letter in March, before Easter.

and godly life. Then, the angels, whom you have so long saddened by your many sins, may rejoice over you as over a penitent sinner. To this end may God the Father, Son, and Holy Ghost, the Holy Trinity, give you good fortune, blessing, and salvation. Amen. 1630.

Be devout, pray diligently, and from the heart.

[unsigned][22]

6 ❦ Stephan Carl to Mother, 13 May 1629

Filial love and devotion, dear Mother. I received the four thaler with your letter,[23] which I have read with such dismay that I hardly know where I am, much less how I should answer you. You write of your worry and concern. How many thousand times have I worried about this! Should I cause you heartache, I must repent it forever.

I see from your letter that you are distressed because you have read my letter to Georg Becken asking him to sell a book for me. From this you have not unreasonably become concerned that I may be involved in some wrongful doing. I tell you now that the book is not mine. It belongs to a poor student here who, apparently because of his poverty, had no money to pay the carter [to take him to Nuremberg]. So he asked me to sell the book for him when I next traveled to Nuremberg. Since he has in all other respects been a good friend to me, I had reason to do him this favor. So I ask you sincerely to strike the worry that has so seized you from your heart and not ascribe to me the mischief of selling my good and useful books. And for God's sake, strike also from your heart whatever thoughts have caused you to place so little trust in me. With God's help, you will know honor and joy, not shame and heartache, in me. I pray to God for this from my heart. Amen, Amen, Amen.

I do not say that I am completely without sin, and may dear God protect me from stubborn impenitence. But it is my sincere, filial, and fervent request that Mother will now put aside all worry and care over

22. Probably a draft, although it has the neatness of a final letter. It is possible that Stephan Carl's mother had ceased signing her name to his mail, as still another expression of her disapproval of his behavior.

23. This letter is not extant, but its contents are made clear by Stephan Carl.

this matter.[24] For it is absolutely useless. I also want to ask that she not tell Brother about this. I know him well, and he will only believe that the book is mine. If she has already told him, would she now, for sure, for sure, write me exactly what he said? And also tell him what I have here written about the book and write me his response to that also. Because this book is causing so much trouble, would you return it to me now or with the next mail?

Herewith, in great sadness, I commend you to God.

In great, great haste, 13 May, at night, between 6:00 and 7:00, 1629.

Your obedient son always,

Stephan Carl Behaim

P.S. If my health is dear to you and you sympathize with my sadness, would you, when this messenger returns to me in a few hours, for sure, for sure, send with him your answer and let me know what you think? And also tell me Brother's reaction when you told him (I will not let myself hope that you have not told him). I ask you most urgently to answer me for sure, for sure.

7 ❦ Stephan Carl to Mother, 18 May 1629

My friendly greeting and offer of every good, much-beloved Mother.

Your letter of 15 May has arrived, and I see well enough from it that you continue to believe that this book is mine. Still it is assuredly not otherwise than I have said. The book belongs to a poor student here, as I recently wrote you. I know for sure that you have never in your life seen it [among my books]. So in this case you could be quite wrong. The very person who should have sold the book in the first place is here with me now. And I never said that the book was mine, but that it belonged to another student.

You also write that you have not yet told Brother. On 13 May I had a dream that you had told him. And someone here also told me that Brother knew, although this person often does not tell the truth. But I will now discount my dream and simply hope that you will not give gossips a chance to proclaim me a bad person. For then my life would

24. Stephan Carl almost always uses the third person when addressing his brother and mother. He also addresses them invariably as "Frau Mother" and "Herr Brother." I have rendered both simply as Mother and Brother and put Stephan Carl's references in the second person when clarity requires.

fall completely apart. Therefore, I ask you very sincerely and earnestly to help me in this matter. Should Brother and his boys[25] know about this, they would only imagine it to be true. And, once begun, if the matter is pursued, it might reach all the way here, to my great disgrace. So I hope you will do me this favor. I will very soon make my innocence clear to you in a letter. But if in the meanwhile you have told Brother, do write and let me know.

I have no time to write any more, although my need is such that I should write two pages, which I shall do at the earliest possible time. Meanwhile, would you or Maria Ela[26] answer me by Wednesday for sure, and tell me how long cousin Lucas Pfintzing will still be in Henfenfelt? And would you also send my silk coat to me on Saturday? I will return it to you later, unblemished.

Herewith I commend all of you to God's fatherly care and protection and wish you continuing good health and prosperity. 18 May, 1629.

> Your obedient son always,
> Stephan Carl Behaim

[P.S.] You may expect laundry.

8 🦌 Stephan Carl to Mother, 25 May 1629

Willing obedience, filial love, and due devotion, much beloved Mother. Your letter has safely arrived and I am very unhappy to learn from it that despite my letter, you still refuse to believe me when I say that this book is not mine. However (as I have all along written) it is not otherwise. You earnestly desire that I confess to you. But I cannot obey you in this without committing a sin against another commandment, for how can I say in truth that the book is mine, when it is not? You desire proof that the book is not mine, which (although I have very little time for this) I now present briefly to you.

This book was [to be] sold to get money. Now, what does one do with, or for what does one need money? To buy food, to buy clothes, to pay debts, to gamble, and the like. Now, what need have I to turn good books into money? I have had food and drink enough, although it would not

25. "Seines Jungenk." Lucas Friederich had thirteen- and eight-year-old sons, and four-teen- and six-year-old daughters. It is possible that Stephan Carl refers here to "Lehr-jünge," apprentices, attached to Lucas Friederich.
26. "Maria Ela" was Stephan Carl's twelve-year-old sister Maria Helena.

be wrong of me, now and then, to buy one small white bun to eat in the morning in place of my broth. But I need not sell a book to do that, since I cannot complain any too harshly that you send me no money. For although it is little enough that you do send, I can certainly buy what I need with it. So much for food as justification of your uncertain suspicion.

I also have no need of money to pay debts, for, praise God, I owe no one a single heller. And, as you, who also value money, must agree, never in my life have I had any desire to gamble, nor do I now. (May God continue to suppress it in me!) Nor do I have any need to go drinking in inns. For what one gets in an inn, one can as easily get at home, inasmuch as the woman lets us have whatever we want so long as she is paid,[27] and she writes down the extras. So, praise God, I also have no need to frequent inns.

Now we come to the worst and main point of your letter: pride. You so strongly imagine that I am prideful. So long as there is time, I will now tell you what a devilish vice pride is and express my hope that it also does not befall you. You will be able to detect my atonement well enough from my words and forgive me on the matter of this book.

Now, what comes from God is good, but what does not come from Him is evil. Pride comes from the Devil, for God bitterly opposes this vice, and He soundly punishes every prideful person. The Devil is an enemy of all virtue and honor. After he forgot his place [among the angels], he wanted to be above the son of God. So God, by the most just of judgments, cast him and his companions out of heaven and into hell. Not only did the Devil lead our first parents astray, so that they, too, wanted to be like God, but he still goes about today, like a roaring lion, leaving no one untempted. By such temptation, he poisons people's hearts with the contagion [of pride] so that they are threatened with total corruption.

I have often thought very diligently about this and pondered whether I have the stuff to conquer pride. But almighty God commands humility from us on almost every page of Holy Scripture and He sternly warns that there is nothing in us He opposes more than pride. These are some sayings that are not unknown to you (I pass over others): "God resists the prideful, but he gives his grace to the humble"; "he who raises himself up will be put down, and he who lowers himself will be raised up." Such teaching [of Scripture] is so bright and clear that it should reasonably warn everyone about pride.

27. The woman is his boarding-house keeper, Frau Tydaeus.

How hostile God is to pride is easily deduced. He can tolerate it neither in heaven nor on earth. Why else has the Devil been cast out of heaven and into hell than because he began to be prideful and to hate his companions? Why have our first parents been thrown out of Paradise? Because of their pride and desire to be like God. Pharaoh, who was truly prideful, declared war on almighty God. Then, to his great loss, he discovered that what is said is true: "the vengeance of God runs down the proud." The earth swallowed Korah, Dathan, Abiram, and the rabble who followed them alive, when they wantonly revolted against Moses and the princes of Israel.[28]

I could bring forth many more such examples of this vice, but my paper, and particularly my time, are now running out. Especially [to be mentioned are] the fruits of pride, such as its ability to render creatures faithless, estrange them from their Creator, and bring God's wrath down upon their necks. No evil is borne less easily than the wrath of God. It is terrifying to fall into the hands of God. It is unbearable to lose the grace of the Highest. Who, then, would not curse pride as the very gates of hell or tremble before it as a poison deadly to both body and soul?

From these words you, not I, may now conclude whether or not I am guilty. But would you for sure, for sure let me know [which you think it is]?

Unfortunately, there is no question in my mind that once you tell Brother, the story will be told in many places, and people will look on me with greater suspicion and no longer say that I am innocent. And I do not doubt that should Brother Lucas Friederich learn about the incident, he will command Herr Löffelholz to look into it when he comes here in a week for the teachers' banquet.[29] When that happens, I would not want to be toasted [at the banquet]. For it could very well happen that before the doctors and professors make their toasts, Herr Löffelholz will have told them in his cups about the incident to humiliate me. Barring this, Herr Löffelholz could still reveal the incident because of his son, and I will then be the object of great hatred and suspected of leading [his son] astray.[30] But Herr M. Tydaeus can vouch for me, should people believe Herr Löffelholz.

28. Numbers 16.
29. "Doctermal."
30. Young Sebastian had been Stephan Carl's accomplice in various misbehavior, and Stephan Carl believed himself to be held entirely responsible by his father. Stephan Carl also resented that young Löffelholz was promoted while he was held back. See letter 11.

I leave it to you now to decide what you may or may not say [to Brother]. You have my reasons. I would much prefer that you remain quiet about it until I can come home. By then, the matter should be nicely resolved and my innocence revealed. For I will bring the student home to you so that you can question him directly. He has told the same story to [Herr Tydaeus], namely, that the book was his. He has also asked that I return the book to him. Therefore, could you send it to me on Saturday in my small trunk, together with my beautiful coat and hat? I will safely deliver the book to him. Also, buy me two eln of gold-colored ribbon for a [new] hatband. Mine is now completely worn through.

I have nothing more. You will be doing laundry this week. Would you ask Aunt Lucas[31] to ready my collars and short cape and send them out, as I have no collars? Also ask her to make two knee bands for me out of my gold-colored waist band and send them along. And would you make me a white summer jacket as soon as possible? I am also again in need of a sealing wax. And answer me for sure, for sure.

May almighty God keep you in continuing health, well-being, and good fortune. Written in great haste on 21 May, 1629.

Your obedient son,
Stephan Carl Behaim

[P.S.] Be sure to send all these things in the small trunk. I will return it to you in good condition. I especially need a collar.

9 ❦ Stephan Carl to Mother, May 1629

My friendly greeting and wish for your temporal and eternal well-being, dear Mother. When you and all the family are well, I truly rejoice to hear it. I am also well.

I cannot [tell] what, when, or whether you have told Brother. Just write me [what he knows], so that I may know how to approach him. I must, God willing, write to him on Tuesday. If he already knows, I will say nothing about my great wrong,[32] and thus [avoid] having written in vain. So could you inform me where the matter stands? Meanwhile, as I re-

---

31. The wife of Stephan Carl's brother Lucas Friederich.
32. "Meinen grossen schaden." Probably a double meaning: Stephan Carl admits to the "wrong" of assisting another to sell his books. Beyond this wrong, however, he believes the matter has unfairly wronged him, or so he argues. As becomes clear, he has lied altogether about the book.

cently wrote, I still plan to come to Nuremberg and there fully explain the matter to you, as I cannot do so from Altdorf. Then, you can tell me if I am not in the right.

Would you let me know [immediately] if cousin Weiss [is well] and will take part in the teachers' banquet?[33]

Be sure to send candles, the book, sealing wax, and handkerchiefs in the small trunk. Also a collar and small cape, for I have [none of] these. Then, I can send my laundry back to you in the trunk. I would also be pleased if you sent my jacket.

I commend you all to almighty God. Written in haste, in the month of May, 1629.

> Your obedient son always,
> Stephan Carl Behaim

10 🝖 Stephan Carl to Lucas Friederich, 6 June 1629

Greetings from Christ, the Author of true salvation.

Most beloved Brother, at last I understand what the poet Ovid meant when he sang out in Book 3 of the Ars:[34] "Then does a strong horse run well, when, the gate having opened, he passes those he had previously followed." Doubtless he meant that emulation spurs one on to the most difficult and arduous striving. But I would understand such emulation in a positive sense as the striving of those who believe themselves worthy of the good things they presently lack, as Aristotle says in Book II [of the Nichomachean Ethics]. If it is the unanimous judgment of wise men that youth should learn, foster, and exalt virtue, then it can come as no surprise to you that this is also the final goal of my studies, after which I now strive with all my might.

Dearest Brother, how do you think it makes me feel when I see so many (who are barely fifteen years old and with whom I do not at all refuse to do literary combat) attending public lectures each day?[35] Obviously, there is great shame burning deep within my heart. But I believe that I have now come to port with God's help. And I take comfort from

---

33. Hans Heinrich Weiss, one of Stephan Carl's guardians.
34. *Ars Amatoriae*, lines 595–96.
35. Stephan Carl refers here to students younger than he who have mastered their subjects and are now attending public lectures (that is, courses at university level). He believes himself to be as fully capable as they, although he has not been so promoted.

the lovely hope that I too shall, for sure, be promoted out of the class of Tydaeus, my most loyal preceptor, and into the public lectures. Only one thing prevents this from happening: Brother's consent. With due respect, I wish, yes, I must, again with this letter ask you for that consent.

Be well and completely happy. My warmest and kindest greetings to your very dear wife and [children].[36] Written rapidly in my little study. 6 June, 1629, in the year of the Dionysian Epoch.

> Your most obedient brother,
> Stephan Carl Behaim

11 ❧ Stephan Carl to Lucas Friederich, 11 June 1629

May almighty God grant you temporal and eternal well-being, much beloved Brother.

Had Brother answered my last letter, it would have given me very great pleasure. But since his travels have prevented this, I ask him now very sincerely to answer me today by the messenger who brings this letter, if his business allows it, for a great deal is at stake for me. My much-beloved preceptor, M. Jacobus Tydaeus, had to discuss my promotion with Herr Magnifico last Wednesday. However, he was unable at the time to report anything to him about my personal circumstances because Brother had not yet answered my letter. So I ask Brother very sincerely to answer that letter now. Tomorrow, God willing, Herr Tydaeus will meet again with Herr Magnifico and if possible [persuade him] not to write a rejection notice. There are many reasons [I should be promoted], which time does not now allow me to relate to Brother. But one is the fact that Sebastian Löffelholz, who enrolled at the same time as I, has taken the same courses as I, and is the same age as I, will be promoted.[37]

I herewith commend Brother, his much-beloved wife, and their dear children to God's care. Written in great haste. 11 June, 1629.

> Your obedient brother always,
> Stephan Carl Behaim

[P.S.] Should Brother be of the opinion that I am still unfit [for promotion],

---

36. He writes "libros" (books) instead of "liberos" (children).

37. Here Lucas Friederich has written in the margin of Stephan Carl's letter, "but not so dumb an ass" (doch kein so grober Esel). "Esel" was commonly applied to students who were between gymnasium and university study.

Letter from Stephan Carl to Lucas Friederich, 11 June 1629 (letter 11)

I would ask that he defer such judgment to my professors, who know best my achievements.

12 ❦ M. Jacobus Tydaeus to Lucas Friederich, 22 June 1629

My faithful service always, esteemed, honorable, very wise, and gracious Sir.

I was pleased to see from your letter that [you agree that] Stephan Carl's promotion should be held up at this time, not only because he cannot yet write grammatically—and God knows how soon he will be able to do so, given his fickle mind—but also because I think he might be helped more by leaving the class. Although he will promise to be more diligent, one can only have great concern about him so long as he is unable to control himself or break his perverse pattern of behavior. Perhaps by the time I retire he will have gotten his predilection for the fast life under control and risen completely above himself.

There is all the more reason to be worried about him at this time. Whether it is out of depression or humiliation because you have deceived his hope [of promotion], he has now begun to do things he has not done before. On the 18th of this month, when my wife refused to give him and young Pömer, his bosom buddy, more beer, he scorned her with insults and raucous laughter.[38] Then, on the 20th he spent the entire night at [the inn] Die Krone and was seen the following day cavorting at home with several unsavory young women, as you, esteemed Sir, will learn.

I can do nothing more than sincerely warn him against such behavior and point out the harm it will bring him in the future. But if no punishment or warning is to be of any help, then I must leave the matter to God, into whose gracious care and protection I herewith commend your grace and his family. 22 June, 1629.

> Your grace's servant,
> M. Jacobus Tydaeus

---

38. Georg Wilhelm Pömer (1611–39) was the son of Georg Abraham Pömer, a powerful official in Nuremberg (*Kriegsherr* and *alter Bürgermeister* in 1622, *Septemvir* in 1630) and one of Stephan Carl's guardians.

13 ❦ Stephan Carl to Mother, 23 June 1629

Grace, mercy, peace, and comfort to you and also every temporal and eternal good in body and in soul from God our Father and from the Lord Jesus Christ, our Savior, much-beloved Mother.

Had Mother written, it would have gladdened me, but since she does not write, I can easily conclude (as I have also come to understand) that I have been grossly slandered to her. If one looks at a few calendars, one will see that it is written for this week: "The Devil will rage and be set loose."[39] There is also a common saying that when the Devil does not go in person, he sends an old woman in his place.[40] The Devil has always been a liar and he tells nothing but lies, and one [of his own] has now told considerable lies about me solely to ingratiate herself [with you]. The same person who says the kindest words to my face, says the most evil ones behind my back. I want to ask Mother sincerely and as a son to write to me today by the messenger who brings this letter and briefly name this person and the matter she has lied about, and I will valiantly reply again [in my defense].

Would you, God willing, send me my good black side-coat and my gold silk knee-bands on Saturday for sure, for sure, for sure? Also, fix up my gold jacket so that the new taffeta on the sleeves juts forward. And let's risk sending my white jacket. And for sure send hand-towels, two goblets, a decorative bed-cover, handkerchiefs, and a pewter tankard— all these things for sure, for sure, for sure. And answer my letter today for sure.

May God give you temporal and eternal well-being.

Your obedient son always,
Stephan Carl Behaim

14 ❦ Georg Wilhelm Pömer to Stephan Carl, 6 July 1629

Greetings. Dear cousin Stephan Carl. I have received both your letters and see from them that you are fully aware of the outrageous lies your

39. Calendars commonly bore biblical citations for each week of the year.
40. He means Frau Tydaeus, who reported his misbehavior both to her husband and to Stephan Carl's mother. See letter 18.

accursed boarding-house keeper has told about me. Unfortunately, her slanders have reached so many people here that not only are my own parents angry with me, but your dear mother, brother, and guardians as well. They believe her every word and cannot see how shamelessly this faithless beast deceives them. (She is surely inspired by the Devil; [as they say,] "she is without doubt in the number of the witches.") Because of her, there is suffering everywhere. That I, I say I, should ever have led you astray is so false a statement that it annoys me even to write it. You know much better. Listen to your conscience and it will tell you how faithful I have always been in both word and deed. Nonetheless, your mother, brother, and uncle Baier are now convinced that I am the one who led you astray, grossly insulting them as well in the process.[41] O God in heaven! Is it really possible that one such horrible woman can in a few hours rob me of my dearest and best friend? If only it did not put the soul as well as the body at risk, how gladly would I practice what the poet [Juvenal] writes: "Vengeance is more pleasing than life itself."[42] At least the world would lose little with [the death of] this accursed encumbrance, and the sun is then spared the displeasure of shining on such an abominable creature. But when I think about the future, I cannot let anger rule me. For wrath belongs to God; He will requite. "So I cry out [to the Lord]," and there I find my consolation.

As for your part, I know that your boarding-house keeper has also told many lies about you. But, as you yourself acknowledge, you are not totally guiltless. She would have assailed your failings with lies and slanders in any event. But, "ignoring the urgings of true friends," you have also truly blundered yourself. Since you have brought so much of this on yourself, my advice, as your good friend, is that you simply confess and tell the truth. It will turn out best for you that way. If you are guilty of taking money, whether a little or a lot, I advise you, as your true friend, to own up to it and confess it before God and man. You will not regret having done so, for the truth always sees one through.

In return for my loyal advice, would you also put in a good word for me, when there is an opportunity? Then the well-entrenched bad opinion created about me may be rooted out of suspicious minds.

---

41. Pömer was a year older than Stephan Carl and had been a student in Altdorf much longer, having matriculated in 1622. He certainly knew the ropes.
42. Satires, 13.180.

I have gone on too long. Goodby. More next time. 6 June, 1629.
        Your obedient friend, not your tempter,
        Georg Wilhelm Pömer
[P.S.] Let Uncle Baier read this letter, if you will; it can do no harm.[43]

15 ❦ Georg Wilhelm Pömer to Stephan Carl, 8 July 1629

Greetings and most willing service, dear cousin Stephan Carl. I happily learn from your letter of 7 [July] that, with God helping, you are willing to go to the table of the Lord next Sunday. From a heart that has always been true and good to you, I wish you all the strength you will need for true penance. I ask you to contemplate carefully the words of the fifth petition [of the Lord's Prayer] ("As we forgive our debtors"), and to forgive your hostess. She has poisoned things that are true and she has made [failings] not so terrible in themselves out to be much worse than they are. Still, if you want God to forgive you, you must forgive her, even though it is a bitter pill. But enough of this.

On Saturday, the bladesmith will come and talk with you about the sword.[44] He is considerably confused, so put him at ease.

You write that it is very difficult for you to be confined to your quarters. Should I offer you advice, [it would be to] write a letter, in Latin, to your brother. Do it as well as you can. I believe you still have the books you need there to do it.[45] Confess the wrong you have done and acknowledge your guilt. Then, perhaps, your brother will be moved to consider the punishment you have endured up to now to be sufficient.

Recently, on Tuesday last, I wrote my mother that I wanted to lodge a formal protest with the rector against Herr Tydaeus's wife, if my father will permit it. I have not yet received a decision. Should you hear anything about it, write to me. I would especially like to know if your dear mother still suspects that I was the one who led you astray. If so, I know well

43. Georg's mother was Helena Baier, daughter of Stephan Baier.
44. Stephan Carl is contemplating buying a sword. See letter 17.
45. The reference is to Latin phrase and style books from which letters were concocted. Stephan Carl's Latin was not such that he could write an eloquent letter of his own. See letter 25.

what I will do, should the matter become extreme.⁴⁶ The shame of lies, the shame of slander and injustice! May the Lord keep me from exploding with anger when I think about it! God willing, the truth will prevail over lies. "Truth triumphs and is not oppressed." Distrustful minds are basing their suspicion on a false and groundless presupposition, namely, that Herr Tydaeus' wife has told the truth. So long as this false premise holds, my self-defense will accomplish little. But when those with greater understanding carefully weigh the matter,⁴⁷ they will surely give no credence to this presupposition, but rather reason: "In law, one is presumed good, until the contrary is proven."⁴⁸ She has made allegations, but nothing has been proven. Still, it seldom happens [that the truth prevails on its own]. Hence, if [my parents] permit me, I will strongly urge [the righting of] my injustice, and not without support [from others].

> Y[our] T[rue] F[riend],
> J. W. P.

16 ❦ Stephan Carl to his Guardians and Lucas Friederich, 9 July 1629⁴⁹

Greetings from the Source and Author of salvation!

Most beloved Guardians/Brother, if ever anyone was punished for his folly and misbehavior, truly it is I. May it now suffice, dearest Guardians/ Brother, that I have missed Altdorf's Peter-Paul festival. May it suffice that I have had a foretaste of prisonlike squalor. May it suffice that I have been confined to my room like a snail in its shell for so many days (which have seemed rather like years) and denied the common air.⁵⁰ The first punishment was great, the next greater still, [the last] the greatest.

I admit that I have sinned, but I say also that my sins have been so exaggerated by lies and malice that they appear greater than they in fact are. The devilish tongue of my female accuser has alleged many things

---

46. In addition to lodging a protest against Frau Tydaeus with the Rector, Georg Wilhelm may have contemplated going directly to Stephan Carl's mother. He clearly did not intend to act out his fantasy and murder Frau Tydaeus.

47. That is, the Rector and other authorities.

48. Georg Wilhelm pursued a degree in law.

49. This is the letter in Latin that Georg Wilhelm advised Stephan Carl to send to his brother. Stephan Carl addresses it to all four of his guardians.

50. Stephan Carl means freedom to come and go at will.

of me which I have in fact not done, can truly deny doing, and condemn and hate. That foul, heedless beast,[51] who is herself more false than her own lies, has freely published not a few lies about me and others. This is a woman who ought to be poisoned. Everyone here hates her as much for her own infamous behavior as for her lies about me. But, alas, her lies have a greater power to persuade than the truth itself.

I do not deny that I frequented inns, and I frankly admit that I sinned in doing so. But overlook this one fault, most gentle Guardians/Brother. Forgive, I beg, the failings of my youth. Pardon the age, for I am still young and ignorant of the world. As you have by right been angry with me in my sin, it is only fair that you now forgive me in my penance. I am a human being, and nothing that is human is alien from me.[52] But the wrong I have done I will never do again. It will henceforth be as the German proverb says: "Nevermore to do is the best penance."

Finally, most noble Guardians/Brother, if a brother's prayer means anything to you, allow yourselves to be moved [by my plea] and restore to me my former liberty. Be well, once again, most kind and faithful guardians.

Nuremberg, 9 July, in the year of the Dionysian Epoch, from your brother in fraternal affection, 1629.

Stephan Carl Behaim

17 ❧ Stephan Carl to Mother, 18 July 1629

Sincere greetings, filial love, and due devotion, much-beloved Mother. When you and all the family are in good health, it is joyous news to me. I am, praise God, still strong and well. May the Divine Majesty long continue to keep us all well.

Much-beloved Mother, I must tell you that there is a student here who has a lot of swords and wants to sell one. He needs the money for [debts incurred at] the holy feast of Peter-Paul. He is selling it so cheaply that even if one wore it every day for a long time, one still could resell it for more than he is asking, which is five gulden. I have not seen a better sword. So I took it straightaway to a bladesmith and asked him whether he thought I should buy it. He said that I should, regardless of the cost.

51. Again Frau Tydaeus is meant.
52. A paraphrase of Seneca, *Epistulae Merules*, 95.53, quoting Terence, *Heutontimoroumenos*, 77.

Since it is to serve me for a lifetime, I asked the bladesmith what he thought such a sword should cost. He said at least six gulden. He plans to buy it himself, if I do not. The sturdy iron hilt alone is worth almost three gulden and the blade at least that much again. He has honestly advised me to buy it. Since I must have a sword, I wanted first to ask Mother to buy it for me. Brother has sent me a sword, but it is a child's sword, not a student's, and I am often made fun of because of it. It is like Fritz's.[53]

Since this sword can be gotten so cheaply, and a bladesmith has advised me to buy it, I ask you sincerely and as a son to buy it for me. Just consider that in Nuremberg I shall have to pay three or [at least] two-and-a-half gulden for a sword hilt alone, which cannot compare in the slightest degree to this one either in strength or in parrying. I will make every effort to balance the time spent fencing with time spent studying (which is otherwise all I do now). I would, however, not like for Brother to know that his sword was not good enough for me.

Another reason why you must buy me a sword is that I am leaving today or tomorrow, and I will have to pay eight gulden for one [elsewhere]. I do not want to leave it here while I am away, unless you insist that I do so out of concern that I may damage it. So I will bring it home with me over the dog-days[54] and leave it with you [in Nuremberg], to be picked up when I need it.

You must at some time buy me a sword, and they are not cheap. They are in fact becoming more expensive, and the longer the war lasts, the higher prices will climb. So I ask you once more, in total submission to your will, not to deny me this and to send five gulden. Should the sword prove not to be worth the price, I will bring you the six gulden [the bladesmith is willing to pay for it].

After you have read this letter, do not say a word to anyone about it. Tear it up as soon as you have read it, so that Brother does not find out about any of this.

We had our exams this week (praise God), and several have been promoted who did not argue as well as I. But I know well the reason I am remaining behind. As always, we owe the rector three batzen for the exams, which you should feel free to send me. Also, I need six kreuzer to contribute for the poor people at table. For everything, I need five gulden, eighteen kreuzer altogether.

53. Not a sibling; perhaps a younger cousin.
54. The summer break.

The man asks me often about the book; he would still like to have it returned.

I commend you all to God's fatherly care and protection and wish you continuing health and prosperity. 18 July, in the year of Christ, 1629.

Your obedient son always,

Stephan Carl Behaim

[P.S.] I would like again to see on your letters [the words] "My Dear Son," and also to have the first letters in the salutation capitalized.[55]

18 ❦ Stephan Carl to Jacobus Tydaeus, 18 July 1629

If you are in good health and all things are going well for you, I am pleased.

Most generous and distinguished Herr Teacher Jacobus Tydaeus, preceptor forever worthy of honor. I have learned that the last letters I wrote my dear mother have been shown to you.[56] In [these letters] I informed her that she should not believe everything reported to her by various persons, for Herr Teacher knows how people tend to exaggerate. I have also learned that you are particularly displeased by the first paragraph [of my 23 June letter]. You imagine that since your dear wife was here [in Nuremberg visiting my mother at the time] that I wrote these words against her honor. I ask and strongly insist that you not accuse me on the basis of this [one] page. And I declare to you now that I did not know that your wife was here with my mother when I wrote the letter, nor, I can say confidently, did I realize who she was at the time.[57] So I deny that I wrote these words against the honor of your wife.

There is no doubt that your wife has acted with a benevolent heart. But I really think that I have never had [such] ill-will toward her that she should have cause to set forth all my vices, or even the least of them [to my mother]. Many vices and misdeeds have been falsely ascribed to me, and I now declare that I have never done any of them.

55. Stephan Carl seems to mean the first letters of his name in the salutation or address. His mother has dropped "To my dear son" from the address and apparently written his name in lowercase letters to reflect his diminution in her eyes.
56. See letter 13 (23 June 1629). Tydaeus evidently knew also of Stephan Carl's letter of 9 July to his guardians. There may well have been others no longer extant and equally slanderous of his wife.
57. When pinned down Stephan Carl resorts to obfuscation.

But since I have recently failed to do my duty toward you as a student, and in this I have sinned against you, my esteemed preceptor, I truly have reason to be contrite. So on Sunday, God willing, I shall go to the Lord's Table and receive forgiveness for all my sins. For this reason, I want to ask Herr Teacher and his wife again to forgive me for all I have done against them. I promise, so help me God, never again to succumb to such great moral failing, and I pledge henceforth to do my duty as a good student.

May good fortune be yours. Nuremberg, 18 July, 1629.

Stephan Carl Behaim

Stephan Carl's failings in Altdorf left his guardians disillusioned and cynical about him. In autumn 1629 they began to cast about for a new career for him. As they saw it, his most immediate need was for a stern but fatherly master. In the long run they hoped he would find a position that would allow him to support himself.

Lucas Friederich turned first to an old friend in Altenburg, Saxony. This was Rudolph von Bünau, who had earlier indicated a willingness to assist with Stephan Carl. Von Bünau was the warden (hofmeister) in Altenburg and a counsel at the court of Duke Johann Philipp of Saxony-Altenburg. In 1611 he and Lucas Friederich had attempted unsuccessfully to travel together through the Holy Land. Unfortunately, von Bünau was then overwhelmed by large numbers of troops quartering in Altenburg. He did not reply to Lucas Friederich's inquiry until late January 1630,[58] and then only to say that the slot he had in mind for Stephan Carl was occupied by another youth. It was almost Easter before Stephan Carl could be properly accommodated in Altenburg.

Meanwhile, Stephan Carl had found temporary service as a courier and aide to another of his brother's friends, the Saxon electoral counsel in Dresden, Johann von Blansdorf.[59] Stephan Carl's letters describe a mission undertaken for him to the princely court in Regensburg in late 1629 or early 1630, a failed attempt to gain the release of an imprisoned lieutenant.[60] On that occasion Stephan Carl bore with him a letter on his own behalf from Lucas Friederich and was apparently seeking there as well more permanent employment for himself.

Dresden remained Stephan Carl's home until mid-March 1630,[61] when von Bünau was at last able to accommodate him at the ducal court in Altenburg. Two weeks before the move, Lucas Friederich had written on behalf of the guardians to still another powerful contact in Dresden, Johann Christoph Oelhafen, "consul to the Holy Roman Empire, the Saxon princes, and the city of Nu-

---

58. Rudolph von Bünau to Lucas Friederich, 29 January 1630, replying to Lucas Friederich's letter of 16 November 1629.
59. Lucas Friederich to Rudolph von Bünau, 11 February 1630.
60. Undated fragment (two pages), 1629.
61. Johann von Blansdorf to Lucas Friederich, 4 March 1630.

remberg." The letter frankly chronicled Stephan Carl's sad decline and assessed his present requirements. Even though circumstances made it tempting and perhaps justifiable, Stephan Carl's guardians were not yet prepared to give up entirely on their wayward ward.

For Stephan Carl the move to Dresden was the real adventure he had wanted. He got a taste of royal living while in the company of von Blansdorf, with whom he had traveled to Dresden. But he soon found himself on trial as he had never been before. A letter of censure and exhortation from his brother greeted him on his arrival in Dresden, together with a copy of the family genealogy, evidently sent to remind him of what he still had to live up to.

A youth in Stephan Carl's position could not readily exhibit aggression toward the authorities in his life. Sarcasm, however, was a weapon that could safely be employed. Stephan Carl also mastered another favorite defense, which was more of a two-edged sword: pretending conversion and abject obedience.

19 ❧ Lucas Friederich to Rudolph von Bünau, 16 November 1629[62]

My ready service to the best of my ability always, high, honorable, steadfast, very gracious Sir, and dear friend.

I will not doubt that my lord remembers well and with favor my report and request to him a short time ago on behalf of my still minor brother Stephan Carl Behaim, and also his generous offer then [of assistance].[63] According to the trustworthy remonstrance of his preceptor, my brother has very little inclination to continue his studies at this time. He thinks only of serving a master and traveling. When this is taken together with his [poor] ability, he cannot under present circumstances properly be sent either to another school or off on his own. What he now needs is the direction and assistance of an eminent master. Considering, then, my brother's present disposition, I ask most humbly in the name of my dear

62. This and many other letters by Lucas Friederich and Stephan Carl's guardians survive only in draft. A letter was composed, the draft neatly copied and mailed, and the draft kept as a record. The letter is therefore unsigned.
63. This may well have been an oral exchange some weeks earlier. No earlier correspondence on the subject is extant.

mother and coguardians that my gracious lord and dear friend honor my beloved father, who now rests in God, and graciously accept my brother into his distinguished service. To the extent that he finds my brother qualified by his abilities, I also ask that he will at his discretion recommend him for high favors.

For this great kindness, God, who rewards all good deeds, will surely not let my lord and his most dear family go unrewarded. The unceasing and impassioned prayer of our beloved and worried mother will see to that. I and my family will always remember this good deed, and we will be eager to acknowledge it by serving my lord and his family under the direst of circumstances. As I do not doubt my lord's gracious compliance, I also leave the timing of [Stephan Carl's] reception [in Altenburg] entirely to favorable circumstance there. I am willing and happy to entrust the matter completely to my lord's gracious pledge.

Regarding Stephan Carl's person, recently, at the end of September, he turned seventeen. He has progressed so far with his studies that he now writes a letter both with and without error. In terms of his physical constitution, his eating and drinking, and, above all, his fidelity and honesty (for which I am and will remain responsible), certainly no defect will be apparent. But without the necessary discipline, the smallest [fault] will be allowed to surface.

In humble trust and on behalf of the aforementioned [mother and guardians of Stephan Carl], I ask my dear friend to remember his recent offer. Humbly awaiting his desired and important answer when the opportunity permits, I commend us all most trustingly to the sure protection of God. Nuremberg, 16 November, 1629.

[unsigned]

20 🐦 Stephan Carl's Guardians to Johann Christoph Oelhafen, 2 March 1630

Our most willing service to the best of our ability, noble, honorable, very learned, very gracious, and highly esteemed Herr brother-in-law.[64]

We are not unaware that our brother-in-law is at this time engaged in very important and difficult military maneuvers in [Dresden] and that we should for this reason all the more spare him additional, vexing requests.

64. It is unclear with which of the guardians Oelhafen was related by marriage. Stephan Carl refers to him as his cousin in letter 22.

But the most pressing need sadly forces us to turn to him for assistance with our rude and prodigal cousin and foster son, Stephan Carl Behaim. Before his departure from [Nuremberg], he sold some of his books and clothes without our knowledge to pay off debts he had run up in Altdorf by his immoderate eating and drinking. And not only in Altdorf. He also left behind at the White Lion Inn here a bill for twenty-six gulden for beer and food, which, according to witnesses, he and his rowdy companions ran through and squandered in just a few days during the past Christmas holidays.[65]

We do not know whether to be more angered or surprised at the magnitude of this completely irresponsible nightly extravagance! Actually, we have all the less reason to be surprised, because it has been painfully known to us that this hopeless scamp was from an early age inclined to steal sweets, and he has since progressively succumbed to inns and pubs. Because he was not allowed money for such indulgence, he became accustomed to stealing. This was met with stern punishment and as far as possible contained. However, when he went to Altdorf, his old habits went with him, and, as described, he frequented inns and other dark corners, gambled, caroused, and raised hell. The money we entrusted him for legitimate expenses he maliciously spent on other things. By the end of his stay in Altdorf, he had demonstrated (in a word) that we could expect to hear little good about him and hope for little good to come from him.

We have better reason to be angry with this spoiled child, when we recall how many times we candidly, even emphatically, called his attention to the meager resources of his devout and honest mother, who all this time has had to eke out the most exacting and troubled existence with her young daughters.[66] We pointed out to him as forcefully and diligently as we could the great need for frugality and restraint on his part. But the more we apprised him of his small resources, the more prodigal he became. We now worry that he is so debauched that he not only cannot overcome it, but that he will continue to use every means and opportunity to indulge his bad habits. Given this state of affairs, what

65. The bill, dated 17 February 1630, covers expenditures between 29 December 1629 and 11 February 1630. Eighteen gulden were spent between 16 and 30 December, the rest between 2 January and 11 February.
66. Stephan Carl's mother had two minor daughters: Maria Helena, thirteen, and Barbara, ten.

can be done with him? Should respected and important people be burdened with him at all? Indeed, is he less a burden than a danger to them?

But if we do not now invest much in his unfit person, which we could easily let happen, what will become of him in the future? So we still have to think carefully about this maturing youth of ours, especially I, the Behaim.[67] We must resolve not to let the spoiled scamp he now is prejudice us against what he still might become. Nor should we allow him, whom we would otherwise have consoled during the dangerous and uncertain times [of youth], to become cut off from ourselves and from you.

We have no doubt that he will plead innocent to such reproach and most dramatically shed tears and promise better things. May we be forgiven for saying it, but he has so often misled and deceived us by his lying words and his crocodile tears that not only can we never again believe him, but we can no more give our brother-in-law sufficient reasons to believe him than we could other honorable people before him.

Hence, it is our collective and dutiful request that our brother-in-law extend to us a helping hand at this very difficult time, so that respected and important people do not fail again with this rude and spoiled child. May he be placed with a lord who corrects him with hunger and blows, so that he may come to forget his gluttony and sloth, and have all the less reason to turn to us and his family [for assistance]. If, in the meantime, he has already been recommended to Herr von Bünau or to another prominent person there and is now living with them, we most earnestly ask our brother-in-law not to forget the vices he has committed against past lords and to deliver the proper and necessary warnings promptly to those who now have him in their care. For doing what you can to help this fore-ill-mentioned scamp and thereby console his devout and troubled mother, we all hold you in special favor. We shall remember it and be ready to repay you diligently at every opportunity. May God be with us all. 2 [March 1630]. Devoted always to the service of our very gracious brother-in-law,

> Georg Abraham Pömer
> Lucas Friederich Behaim
> Conrad Baier
> Hans Heinrich Weiss

---

67. Lucas Friederich is writing the letter on behalf of the guardians.

21 🐚 Stephan Carl to Lucas Friederich, 4 March 1630

My sincere greeting and wish that almighty God bless you now and in eternity, much-beloved Brother . . .

Your welcome letter of 16 February has been delivered along with the family genealogy.[68] From them both, I can readily recognize your brotherly devotion to me. Because of Brother's many good deeds [on my behalf] I may, by the highest law, consider him a father.[69] And I cannot into eternity extol, honor, and praise Brother enough for all that he has done for me over so many years. Why, then, should I not, in return, heed his faithful admonitions, which help me overcome my bad life and make it good again, and draw me back all the sooner into my family? I promise again to restrain myself at all times, so that not the slightest complaint shall be heard about me.

Brother will doubtlessly have learned from my much-beloved and highly esteemed mother about my good situation here. I could not be better treated by Herr von Blansdorf. He treats me as a father treats his dearest child, indeed, better. For this I owe Brother not the smallest thanks, because it is for Brother's sake that I am being so carefully treated and watched over. Herr von Blansdorf has not a little affection for Brother. He mentions him with all due respect and remembers his health at almost every meal.

I also want to report that I will be going to Altenburg with Herr von Bünau in a week. I would like to have reported this sooner, but I had first to discuss it with the other [master] (to whom I went faithfully almost daily to offer my services, but never did see him).[70] So I was unable to inform Brother about this any sooner, as I would very much have preferred.

I ask Brother most sincerely if he might feel free the next time he has reason to write to Herr von Bünau to ask him to advance me money when I need it. There is always some need, and one can neither see nor learn anything without spending money. Brother may trust me not to spend a heller on anything that is not worth it or which does not teach

---

68. Not extant, but obviously a letter of censure and exhortation.

69. The reference is to God's law.

70. This is another master whom Stephan Carl was seeking with von Blansdorf's assistance to serve, while awaiting a firm decision from von Bünau. There must have been some tentative commitment that Stephan Carl could not break without prior consultation.

me something I need to know. May I also ask Brother to answer this letter without delay, if it is possible, and to tell me what he thinks I should know in advance about Altenburg?

I commend you all to the care of the Highest and wish you continuing health. And I ask Brother most sincerely to greet his much-beloved wife and all his dear children on my behalf. From Dresden, 4 March, 1630.

H[is] F[riendly] B[rother] A[lways],
Stephan Carl Behaim

22 🐝 Stephan Carl to his Guardians, 9 March 1630

Esteemed, wise, kind, and very learned guardians and kin. I can imagine the unhappiness that you must have in your hearts at this time. I know the great trust you have always placed in me. Your one thought has always been that I might some day follow in the footsteps of my late father. Unfortunately, my behavior in this my seventeenth year has forced you to experience much heartache and little joy. This I gather from your recent letter to Herr Dr. Oelhafen.[71] I do not know what to write to you. I feel unworthy to have a letter of mine read by you. But the almighty and merciful God says in Luke 16, "Deprecate," ask for pardon and forgiveness. And the noble and very learned Herr Johann Christoph Oelhafen, my great patron, has also commanded me to write to you. So I must obediently send you this letter.

I therefore acknowledge that I have done much that is very bad and wrong. I have not in the least heeded the honest warnings of my much-beloved mother and my highly respected guardians and cousins. I have unfortunately chosen to do the very opposite of what they have urged. And I have deeply troubled and saddened them. All of which now causes me great heartache. Truly I can say with the lost son, "Father, I have sinned against heaven and before you."[72] I am no longer worthy to be counted among the Behaims. But were I now to promise better things, one would not believe me until I had proven myself in ipso facto, by the deed itself. But so that you may know my resolve to better my life and to be more worthy, I will share my thoughts with you.

First, it is certain that I must stop behaving as I do, and if not in my

71. Letter 20.
72. Luke 15:18–19.

youth, then when I am grown. But should one try to stop bad habits when he is grown, woe to him.

2. What do I gain from such behavior? I lose the favor and trust of my best friends. I cannot get on with my life. I am an object of shame and ridicule to everyone. And in the end I must starve to death.

3. I will be the only Behaim to have failed. I now have not the slightest expectation of graduating.

4. Should God help me return home again, with what honor would I come, and what could I offer my family?

5. What kind of heartache would I bring my respected family were I to travel abroad?

6. And what punishment from God would I have to receive for it?

These are the truly painful thoughts I now have because so far I have not bettered my life. But understanding comes only with years. What has happened will never happen again, not into eternity. I have also made this promise, which is not a small one, to my noble and very learned Herr cousin Dr. Oelhafen. Up to now I have caused people heartache; henceforth, I will make hearts joyful! To this end, may God graciously send me his Holy Spirit.

Meanwhile, I ask you in complete obedience to continue to send me the money I require for my needs and always to do so as soon as possible. You may trust me to spend it most scrupulously.

Meanwhile I commend you all to the care of the Highest and to continuing health. From Dresden, in great haste, 9 March, 1630.

> Your cousin and brother,
> Stephan Carl Behaim

Stephan Carl accepted his year in Altenburg as a deserved punishment. There he claims to have known only isolation and idleness, having been reduced to waiting on tables for Herr von Bünau. "What do I do [at the court in Altenburg]?" he asks in summer 1630 in a letter to his cousin Johann Heinrich Weiss, whose support he seeks in his effort to return to the university. "What do I hear with my ears? What do I observe with my eyes? What do my feet undertake? I can embrace and express it all in one word with five letters: NIHIL."[73] To his friends in Altdorf he feigns happiness, but the opposite is all too clear. He begs a full quire of news from Altdorf and Nuremberg and is obsessed with what people there now think of him. When he happens on his kindly but hawk-eyed former master von Blansdorf in Leipzig, he cannot contain his joy over this chance meeting with a man he believes to be "still very fond" of him.

Having lost credibility with virtually all the authorities in his life, Stephan Carl found himself in the direst of situations for an early modern youth. He would not have denied that it was one largely of his own making. Apart from a certain charm and cleverness, he had little to recommend him. But even though his brother now thought him a "dumb ass," his guardians continued to care about his future. They arranged for him to get money and other assistance when he needed it from middlemen, like the merchant Georg Ayermann of Leipzig and the royal steward Valentin Sternenbecker of Altenburg. They hoped that his association with eminent lords and masters who had wide experience and contacts throughout the world of German politics might both inspire him and launch him into a new career.

But Stephan Carl was not a youth on whom to lay plans. He resisted growing up. He longed to leave the world of court politics, to travel, and to attend the university again. He lobbied in turn to be sent to Angers, Tours, Jena, Tübingen, and Wittenberg. Confronted by fresh evidence of his continuing prodigality, his guardians firmly resisted his pleas; in their minds, neither his need nor his ability justified travel to France or study at a university. But Rudolph von Bünau's sudden financial crisis and forced resignation from the court in Altenburg did move his guardians to agree that

---

73. Stephan Carl to Johann Heinrich Weiss, summer 1630 (received 2 August).

Altenburg held no future for their ward. He would be released from his "prison" in Altenburg.

Stephan Carl's joy at the prospect was real but short-lived, for his guardians had in mind another career not of his own choosing. Instead of travel abroad and university study he was to train for a clerkship at the imperial court in Speyer. The atonement begun in Altenburg was now to continue in Speyer.

Stephan Carl again threw tantrums and begged. To the shock and amusement of his guardians, he clashed with them openly for the first time. He capitulated in the end, of course, at least on this particular point. As he prepared to leave Altenburg he was no longer demanding to go to a university, but pleading abjectly to be allowed at least to plan his own itinerary to Speyer, and if possible to have a private room in the home of his new master there.

23 ❧ Stephan Carl to Master Christoph Seutzio, 14 March 1630

Greetings, "most beloved lord and truest poet."[74] I have now sent you three letters without a reply. So I herewith report further to you that I left the beautiful city of Dresden on 10 March with Herr von Bünau and I arrived here in Altenburg on 12 March. The situation here is very different than you had teasingly predicted. I am not addressed as a child by Herr von Bünau, but shown respect.[75] I do nothing except wait on him at meals for half an hour and serve when he has guests in the manor. We do not eat with the servants, but at our own table. Nor am I alone here. There are two others from the nobility, who are younger than I. After

---

74. "Poe. mere." Who is this "Jungling Seutzio"? He is not mentioned again and there are no other surviving letters from him or to him. There is a Christoph Seuter (or Seuterus) from Augsburg, who came to Altdorf in 1628, the same year as Stephan Carl (Steinmeyer, II, p. 539). But Stephan Carl addresses the letter to his "dear cousin," who is a Nuremberger. Christoph Wilhelm Scheurl (1608–89), who enrolled in Altdorf in 1624, seems a plausible candidate. But inasmuch as Georg Wilhelm Pömer was Stephan Carl's professed "best friend" as well as his cousin, the letter was most likely sent to him under a pseudonym well known among the students in the college. Georg Wilhelm also had a servant named Hieronymus: as the most expert Latinist among Stephan Carl's friends, he would also seem to merit the greeting "truest poet."
75. "Nicht gedutzet, sondern geertzet."

my lord is served the second course, we leave and go to our table. We then eat what is sent over from his table, and more. There are always five courses, not counting what comes over from the lord's table. In addition to our five courses, we have two tankards of beer with each [main] meal and one early, when we wake up, again at midday, and still again at night after dinner. But it is not so perfect for me here as it was in Dresden. I cannot praise the splendor of Dresden too much. Instead of beer, I drank wine, and more than I wanted, and I sat at the master's table. But I will write no more about it. You will have gotten my meaning from my letters. It really is true that I am having a good and glorious time here.

When you are in Nuremberg, or while you are still in Altdorf, wherever it may be, and you hear someone reproach me, always speak the best about me and praise me to them, whether it is true or not. Then they will think it must be so. For if you are not seen to be on my side, they will write still more dreadful letters to me and say that even my best friend is against me.

By now you will have received my last two letters and done all that I have asked. And if you have done your duty well, I expect and wish to receive many letters from my good friends in Altdorf with the next mail, especially from Monsieur Leidenambt.[76] Since I have written you three letters, I expect a letter three pages long in return. Just answer each of my letters fully, item by item, word for word. Otherwise, I cannot count you as my friend. Have your Hieronymus also write to me. If only we could just once get together, what fun we would have! I ask you to let it be known in Nuremberg, by Easter Day, if possible, when you will leave [Altdorf]. Do come this way, if you wish; we will get together sooner here than in Altdorf. If you go to Jena, I can be there in a day.

What is my current reputation in Altdorf? How are old Tydaeus and his flame doing?[77] Has my bursar's bill been received by my H[err] B[rother]? In sum, write me all that I wanted to know in my first letter.

I do want to write you something [new], only you do not believe me. Answer me in Latin, and tell me if there is now any good news in Nuremberg. Only write fully. Your letters are as dear to me as thalers. When I recently read one that you had written to me in Nuremberg, it made

76. Unclear who is meant. There is no one on the matriculation lists by this name; it may be a pseudonym for a friend or a term of opprobrium applied to someone who exercised authority over the boys' life in Altdorf.

77. Apparently his wife is meant, although Stephan Carl may be asking about Tydaeus's survival of a fever.

me happy and I laughed on your account. Would to God that we could meet soon in India! How happy we would be there as His little fraternity.[78] The love I have for you is great. Always think the best of me. Perhaps we will be together soon. God may work a miracle.

My master's wife is intensely beautiful and she is friendly to me. Once, while traveling, we ditched into a great mire. I and another of my lord's [servants daily] travel back and forth from the barn in his coach of six horses with the chamberlain.

As you can see, I write you absolutely everything I know! I hope you will answer me and send me some news, so that I may be at ease. Such a letter should fill a full quire of paper. Write an enormous letter, and send many more with it.

I will write to you again from the Leipzig fair. We are traveling there first before going on to Vienna and then back to Altenburg. Your letters cannot miss me. Just send a lot of them.

A mile from here, in Treben, my master has a village with a beautiful castle. We go there when the weather is beautiful.

My wish is that I receive one letter from you soon; I so long for it.

The approach to Altenburg is now most stately. The dukes of Altenburg are constantly going back and forth to the elector's castle. All the while the elector is away he maintains the castle at his own expense. (Just write to me many happy things, so that I have something to laugh about.) [At the castle] there are always three hundred Altenburg horses which the three brothers maintain in a nearby enclosure,[79] and there are twenty-six servants who are fed at the elector's expense, and each has enough to eat. And we always have enough wine.

Write me what people now say about me in Nuremberg and Altdorf, and always say the best to them about me. Send me some *verba formalia* so that I may have a laugh.[80] Internally and externally Dresden is more beautiful than Altenburg.

---

78. "Wie wir dis sein porslein sein." Perhaps Stephan Carl has been reading about missionaries to India. He probably means no more than his own personal circle of friends (in the sense that "tres faciunt collegium": three like-minded and admiring students make a fraternity, a community unto themselves). Private and informal "Gesellschaften" existed in seventeenth-century universities. They had comical names and lasted only as long as the boys who created them remained enrolled. C. Beyer, *Studentleben im 17. Jahrhundert* (Schwerin in Mecklenburg, 1899), 93.

79. Apparently a local family tended the horses.

80. The reference is to tedious Latin exercises, perhaps conjugated verbs, about which the boys joked and which "Seutzio" was evidently adept at mocking.

God bless. Greet all known good friends, particularly all those in the castle, and also Diether, who still owes me a letter. Does the *Pfleger* know about my excess?[81] What does he say about it? Altenburg, 14 March, 1630.

Your loving friend always,

Stephan Carl Behaim

24 ❦ Georg Wilhelm Pömer to Stephan Carl, 17 March 1630

Greetings "from the fount of salvation [Christ, who comes] with favors and without deceit."

Dear cousin Stephan Carl, not unreasonably are you annoyed that I had the coat of arms itself and not a part of it sketched for you. However, I can assure you that I have had neither your coat of arms nor any part, in a word, not a heller's worth, sketched for myself,[82] and this is as certain as I am resolved to live and die an honest fellow.

Dear cousin Behaim, recognize my true heart, and do not let any delirium of false opinion blind you [to it]. Since [your departure], much has transpired [against you here] because of your diminished reputation, and I have always tried diligently to avert it. [As the poet says:] "I did what I was able to do."

I rejoice to hear that things are going well for you there. It pleases me as much as it would if you were my brother or even my alter ego.

As for your [old] table companions here, I look on them all as dogs and my adversaries. They never show any true friendship for you, "whether you be present or absent." In a word, your enemy will always be my enemy and your friend my friend.

If you can be happy [there], then it brings a measure of joy to me in my own very sad and desperate situation here in the Fatherland, where I must watch my youth and the springtime of my dearest age fade, wither

---

81. Georg Pömer, a cousin, was Pfleger in Altdorf. See letter 25. "Excess" here has a double meaning: it refers both to Stephan Carl's "departure" from Altdorf and to the "extravagance" that caused it.

82. Stephan Carl and Georg Wilhelm are exchanging coats of arms, as students often did. Stephan Carl seems to have gotten more than he bargained for, and at his own expense.

and go to ruin in this obscure place.[83] "O, idleness! So often to die, and yet not to die!"

Ponder what I have written to you in the album.[84] There you will easily behold my thoughts as in a mirror, although my heart, which only death will be able to change, remains hidden to you. "But enough."

I wish as much joy for you as the sad moments I am now forced to have here in the Fatherland ("may the Spirit of the Fatherland forgive me"). Be as happy as I am sad. Have as much pleasure as I have displeasure. Be as joyful as I am melancholy. God willing, may it go as well for you as it goes ill for me. May your joy increase, as my sick heart slowly collapses in pain. I know, dear cousin, that my distress is loathsome to you. When, by your answer, I am assured of your sympathy, it will bring me great pleasure. That fortune should bring us together in foreign lands would be my fondest wish. Meanwhile, dear cousin Behaim, remain friendly, and do not forget the honorable Pömer. Speak every good of him. In addition to your well-established special familiarity [with me], you are also obligated to do so by the general law: "Of the absent and the dead, speak only good."

Be and live well, dearest of friends, and think often and again of him who, at the onset of fear, prefers an honorable death to a thousand irreverent lives.

> Y[our] L[oving] C[ousin] and good friend,
> Georg Wilhelm Pömer

[P.S.] In your reply (which I expect with the greatest possible speed), will you indicate the time of your departure from Dresden and your destination?

I do not know much news. Helena, the daughter of Frau Haller in Cronsberg, has died. Zainer and Huttfeld are being forced to move out of the house, the one for nonperformance, the other for lack of funds. Baumgartner has been examined and it went rather well.

Dated 17 March, on which day I [received] your letter of 26 February, 1630.[85] Remain true unto death.

---

83. The exact cause of Georg Wilhelm's moroseness is not immediately clear, but his days in Altdorf were numbered—perhaps because of mischief and unsatisfactory progress, as Stephan Carl's had been. Stephan Carl mentioned his troubles again in August 1630, when he expressed the wish that Georg Wilhelm go with him to the University of Angers. See letter 28. In 1634 Georg Wilhelm was with a Swedish military mission in Russia. He died in combat in 1639.

84. "Stambuch" or album amicorum, a kind of autograph book.

85. Letter not extant.

25 ❦ Stephan Carl to Georg Wilhelm Pömer, 17 March 1630

Again my greetings, much-beloved and highly esteemed cousin, Georg Wilhelm Pömer, Nuremberg patrician. From the following request you will be able to see that I continue to look on you as my best and most trusted friend and cousin. I certainly hope that you too are still favorably disposed toward me and will do me a very great service and favor, namely, formulate a Latin letter for my brother.[86] This is to be its content. (You can easily imagine how he writes to me, and you will know well enough yourself how to respond, but I want to provide you with a summary of what I think the letter should say.)

"I have read Brother's frank admonishment and correction, and I see that it comes from a true fatherly heart. For this, I sincerely thank him, as I do for all the good things he has done for me. My one wish is that God will give Brother a long life, so that I may continue to have such a father in him. I promise herewith to restrain myself, so that there are no complaints about me.

"Otherwise, I would like Brother's advice on whether I should learn French, Italian, or Spanish, while I am in Altenburg. And what else does he think I might learn here to prepare myself to travel successfully in foreign lands? Should I remain idle here and learn nothing, it will bode ill for my future. So I want to ask Brother and my other guardians most humbly to have me on their minds. I await their counsel and advice.

"Each month one gives [Herr von Bünau] two ducats and two upon entrance into his service. So Brother can send me what I should pay him. Otherwise, I have happily arrived in Altenburg with Herr von Bünau and his men, and everything is going well for me here. Brother will doubtlessly have learned this already from his royal highness.[87]

"May almighty God keep Brother and his family in continuing good health and may Brother please greet his much-beloved wife and dear children warmly on my behalf.

"Finis. Add this: I would like to know how cousin Hans Endres is doing."

This, then, is how I think the letter should go. Your wisdom and under-

---

86. Latin letters were considered the more authoritative. See Georg Wilhelm's advice, letter 15.

87. Duke Johann Philipp of Saxony-Altenburg.

Letter from Stephan Carl to Georg W. Pömer, 17 March 1630 (letter 25)

standing will know how to phrase it in correct and proper Latin. Write the letter as if you were addressing Albrecht Pömer.[88] I have every hope and expectation that you will do this favor for me and send the Latin version in the mail at the earliest. It is something you can do in a day. Just be sure that you choose a day when you are not daydreaming and disinclined. Then, you can do it quickly and still have time to write me a letter twenty-seven pages long! I wish I could repay you for this favor with a week's work. God as my witness, I would spare no effort, diligence, or labor. I am relying completely on you for this great act of friendship. If, in return, there is anything I can do to serve you (although I am too lowly to do much), do not spare me. Whatever you ask of me I will do gladly from the heart. Who knows, sometimes when one is in need, the least and poorest person can help. But, if not immediately, then sometime in the future there will be an opportunity for me to serve you.

Meanwhile, for God's sake (as I often, often, often ask in all my letters), answer me as soon as possible and at length, and send the Latin letter with it. Do take care that neither your father[89] nor anyone else learns anything about that letter, lest the Devil quickly become abbot. I know that you already understand this and that I need not write at length about keeping quiet and trusting no one, lest we be exposed.

Recently in Dresden I saw a beautiful, fine, delightful, ingenious piece,[90] which I was unable to buy at the time. I definitely hope to acquire it when I arrive at the Leipzig fair. Then, I will present it to you as an expression of thanks on Wilhelm's day.[91] Meanwhile, just answer my letter fully and put the Latin letter in the mail. If your Hieronymus cannot handle this, which I do not anticipate, then give it to another who can properly put it in the mail to Altenburg. But make sure this person is not someone who will let your father or another of my good friends pry into it, for then the Devil becomes abbot. Write clearly on the letter: "To be delivered to Herr Rudolph von Bünau, Altenburg warden." I believe one must give the letter to the Leipzig messenger or put it in the mail going

---

88. The reference is to Georg Wilhelm's powerful cousin Albrecht (1597–1654). Like Lucas Friederich he held several important positions, among them a seat in the *Rat* after 1628. Georg Wilhelm also had a prominent uncle named Wolf Albrecht (1597–1659), but he was out of Nuremberg in the late 1620s and early 1630s.

89. Georg Wilhelm's father, Georg Abraham, was of course one of Stephan Carl's guardians.

90. He probably means a sculpture or a painting.

91. Ostensibly the patronal feast-day, 28 May.

to Leipzig, for there is no special messenger or mail delivery [directly from Altdorf] to Altenburg. Mail reaches me here via Leipzig by another messenger.

Everywhere here, as in Dresden, the girls go about as you like to see them in Nuremberg. The breast-pieces of their dresses allow their breasts to go completely free, and they are covered only by a chemise. When the two brooches are removed, the breasts appear visibly in their own person[s]. And then you have a treat.

When you write cousin Georg Friederich,[92] please remember to give him my warm greetings. I would gladly have written to him, but I could think of nothing to say. If I get a letter from him, it will be most welcome.

As always, I want to know the good news of Altdorf. How does the Rector reward our little cousin after the boy tried so hard? How did it go with the wine merchant's wife? Who was the godfather? What did they name the child? Is it still alive? Is Herr Althöffer a bridegroom yet? With whom? Who is getting married in Nuremberg these days? In short, tell me everything I have asked you about in my previous letters. Then, I will be satisfied. And if you will write still more, I will be that much more pleased. Tell me about your father, your mother, your [brother] Philip, all your brothers, especially Georg Stephan,[93] and Hieronymus, and cousin Pfleger (is he now a bridegroom?),[94] and old widow Friederich Behaim (has she died yet?),[95] and Herr Dörrer and his beautiful wife,[96] and Maria Magdalena, Ursula Dorothea,[97] Georg Friederich, Georg Wolff,[98] and Tobias.[99] (How did his wedding go? Has he still not made a baby in his bedroom?)

You are no doubt thinking that I take my cousin to be a complete fool. "Next he will want to know what the emperor, the Nuremberg city council, the Swedes and the Danes are doing!" But take heart and do not

---

92. Georg Wilhelm's first cousin (b. 1612), who was at the time abroad in France. See letter 28, from Stephan Carl to him.

93. Georg Philip (b. 1613) and Georg Stephan (b. 1609).

94. Georg Pömer, *Pfleger* in Altdorf after 1620 and Georg Wilhelm's uncle. In September 1630 Maria Magdalena Paumgartner became his second wife.

95. The widow of Friederich VIII Behaim died in November 1632.

96. Christoph Dörrer (1596–1670) must be meant. His wife Helena died in 1634.

97. Maria Magdalena (b. 1624) and Ursula Dorothea (b. 1613) were Georg Wilhelm's first cousins.

98. Georg Wilhelm's first cousin (b. 1614).

99. Unclear who this is.

become angry. Do not curse, "May the Devil take him," or "May a thunderbolt strike him." What I have asked of you is not required work, and there is not much at stake in it. But if you do write to me about all these people and answer all my other questions, I may gather from it my place in your heart.

The esteemed servants of the [Altenburg] dukes get beer with all their meals, but they also swill plenty of wine when they wait on tables. I join them when I want, so I am swilling plenty of wine and stuffing myself with food.

Herewith God bless. Again (for perhaps the one hundredth time), please hear my most sincere and humble request and answer me as soon, as surely, and as fully as possible.

Be merry, cousin Georg Wilhelm. Some day I will acknowledge, honor, and reward your act of friendship. Altenburg, 17 March, 1630.

> Our cousin and friend always,
> Stephan Carl Behaim

[P.S.] I ask again most sincerely that you send me several proofs of the proposition: "Nuremberg patricians, like other nobility, are noble."[100] Write to me soon, post it early, answer fully, and let no letter [of mine] lie around [for others to read].

26 ❦ Lucas Friedrich to Rudolph von Bünau, 2/12 April 1630[101]

High, honorable, steadfast, gracious Sir and dear friend, sincere greetings to one I am and will always remain ready to serve to the best of my ability.

By letter and by word of mouth, I have learned with great delight from both my gracious lords, Johann von Blansdorf and Johann Christoph Oelhafen, in what measure my dear friend has not only graciously received my brother Stephen Carl, but, in accordance with his self-made reputation, is getting the best behavior out of him with less effort. On behalf of my dear family, let me first of all express most humbly my thanks for so favorable and accommodating a reception [of my brother]

---

100. This is a private joke about the way the boys were taught at school, and also a bit of teasing.

101. Letters are occasionally dated both by the old calendar and the new, Gregorian calendar (issued in 1582 by Pope Gregory XIII).

and also extend my steadfast assurance that my dear friend and his family will be remembered for this great favor. He shall always experience and should expect nothing but our every rightful duty [toward him].

I am distressed, however, to learn that my gracious lord and dear friend should have to be burdened with my brother before his appointed time of arrival. My intention had always been for Stephan Carl to return here [to Nuremberg] with Herr Oelhafen, should he arrive [in Altenburg] at an inconvenient time, and here await his scheduled [day of] arrival [in Altenburg]. But since it has nonetheless proven agreeable [to you to have him there early], I leave things as they are and remain even more indebted to [my dear friend].

Your above-lauded treatment [of Stephan Carl] gives me reason not only to express my most humble appreciation, but also to report in [the] established good trust [that exists between us] something of my brother's frame of mind. Because he was permitted all too much (and to me entirely unknown) freedom in Altdorf, he began to fool around with his friends in his house, to gamble, go off riding, and he apparently did little else. Moreover, he ran up many and considerable debts, which, to pay off, he feigned sundry necessary expenditures. Hence, the money, deviously totaled, as is customary with students, was deviously and dishonestly disbursed as well.

To anticipate such behavior and prevent his offending the other boys at court, I most humbly ask my dear friend, above all else, never to leave him idle. Arrange the most indispensable of his master's chores during his spare time. And keep a close eye on him so that he does not run up debts or otherwise behave frivolously. If it can be done without inconvenience, I also ask you to let him have money when he needs it, but only for his [basic] needs and nothing more. You will be reimbursed with appreciation at the Leipzig fair.

I have no doubt that in the beginning my dear friend will be somewhat patient with this still inept servant. On the other hand, I ask you most assiduously to inform me promptly should he ever in the least wish to be exempted from his duties. Then, although absent, I may write to him and admonish him.

Meanwhile, I and my family remain ready and willing to do what pleases my dear friend and those who are his. I commend us all most trustingly to divine care. Nuremberg, 2/12 April, 1630.

[unsigned]

27 ❦ Stephan Carl to Georg Ayermann, 6 May 1630

My readiness to serve you always to the best of my ability, honorable, highly esteemed, and very gracious Herr Ayermann.[102]

I am pleased to learn that my much-beloved brother has commended me to Herr Ayermann and asked him to recommend me to others in Altenburg and to give me money when I need it. I can truthfully report to my brother that my gracious lord [Ayermann] has faithfully acted on his request and commended me to one I rightly rejoice over.[103] I could not have been better recommended had I been his only child. It shall be gratefully remembered and one day repaid. Unfortunately, at the present time I am a person who has so far seen, heard, and learned nothing that is useful, so a lot of water will have to run into the sea before I am in a position to repay Herr Ayermann and his family. Meanwhile, I hope that my beloved brother will spare no effort to repay Herr Ayermann for his assistance whenever there is an opportunity.

It is my friendly request that Herr Ayermann send me twelve Reichsthaler at this time for my many great needs. Until I learned a few days ago that my brother had spoken with Herr Ayermann, I have relied on my dear mother to send me money from week to week. Because of the long move I have made [from Altdorf via Dresden to Altenburg], I have had to borrow money to buy new shoes and other necessary things for Easter Day, and now I must repay it. And if I am going to learn Italian, fencing, and other such things here, I am convinced that I cannot do so without twelve Reichsthaler. Hence, my sincere and humble request that Herr Ayermann send twelve Reichsthaler to me here at the earliest opportunity. I will then (as I will now write to my mother) ask that the money be reimbursed with gratitude in Nuremberg. Meanwhile, I very sincerely and humbly thank [Herr Ayermann] for commending me to Herr Sternenbecker, and I ask him to continue to recommend me to him.

Herewith I commend Herr Ayermann to the care of the Highest and wish him continuing good health. Altenburg, 6 May, 1630.

H[is] h[umble] and o[bedient] s[ervant] a[lways],
Stephan Carl Behaim

102. Ayermann was a merchant from Leipzig with offices in Nuremberg.
103. As becomes clear, this is Herr Sternenbecker, Stephan Carl's contact in Altenburg. When Stephen Carl later left Altenburg, Sternenbecker was the first person to whom he felt beholden. See letter 38.

28 ☙ Stephan Carl to Georg Friederich Pömer, 2 August 1630[104]

My sincere greetings and ready service [   ] always, noble, steadfast, friendly, much-beloved cousin and very eminent, worthy, and trusted friend. Often I have heard with great joy about your good and happy situation [in Angers]. I hope that cousin and his companion, Monsieur Grundherr,[105] are still in good health. As for me, I am, praise God, still well off. May the Divine Majesty continue to be gracious to both of us.

I could not refrain from visiting my cousin with a little letter and reminding him of our old friendship, although I hope that even without such a reminder cousin has not in the meantime let me fall completely from mind. For myself, I notice that the love between good and trusted friends increases all the more during the time they are apart. If that is also true for cousin, I hope he may find my letter and request all the more pleasant.

I am reporting privately to cousin that I have left the University of Altdorf almost a half-year ago for Dresden, there to visit the Elector's [military] camp. From Dresden, I betook myself to the princely court in Altenburg in the hope of discovering and learning something [useful] there. However, during the time I have spent there I have experienced almost the complete opposite [of what I set out to find]. So I have written to my Brother to ask that I not be kept here any longer, but sent instead to France. [My departure from Altenburg] will doubtlessly also come about because of the great destruction [here];[106] I will not say must come about. I have been advised by a wise and highly respected man here to betake myself above all and especially to the University of Angers, which he could not for many reasons praise too highly. Therefore, I am writing most sincerely and humbly to cousin, because [being in Angers] he can report and describe especially well to me the conditions at the University and tell me how much I must have to meet my annual expenses there. This cousin will best be able to judge from his own observations, although I will not be allowed [to spend] so much [as he]. Perhaps fortune

104. Georg Friederich (1612–59) was of the same age as Stephen Carl. At fourteen he traveled to France for schooling. Later he was in the Netherlands and pursued a military career before settling in Nuremberg.
105. Apparently a Grundherr from Nuremberg, but it is unclear who he was and in what capacity he worked. Possibly he was an accompanying tutor.
106. The Thirty Years War is going on.

may smile on me a bit and provide several Nurembergers as my companions, and (if fortune is good) my cousin Georg Wilhelm [Pömer among them]. Cousin will surely already have been informed about his situation by his dear brother Georg Wolff.[107] My wish is to meet cousin and Monsieur Grundherr in Angers.

I ask cousin most sincerely and humbly to report [this information] to me here at the earliest opportunity. In return, I remain devoted to serving him to the fullest of my ability.

Herewith I faithfully commend cousin and his beloved companion (whom he may greet most sincerely and humbly on my behalf) to the omnipotence and mercy of God, and I wish both of them continuing health, long life, and every wished-for and beneficial comfort, fortune, and blessing in both body and soul. Altenburg, in great haste, 2 August, 1630.

> H[is] C[ousin] R[eady-to-serve] Always,
> Stephan Carl Behaim

29 ❦ Stephan Carl to Lucas Friederich and his Guardians, 14 October 1630

Esteemed, honorable, prudent, most wise, and very gracious guardians. I am very happy to learn from the letters of my much-beloved and highly esteemed mother that my dear brother now says that my position [in Altenburg] has turned out to be far different that he had [originally] conceived, and that as a consequence my guardians have carefully considered a good and proper way [to end it, so] that I shall not be further deprived of useful experience and all the things that will help me advance. I can attest with good conscience before God and the world that nothing could be more harmful to me that to continue in the life I have known here. All who are familiar with court life will readily understand what I mean. I pass over the fact that Herr von Bünau, presently my commanding Junker, would now be entirely satisfied to keep house with few[er] servants. Not only has he sold all his possessions here, but he fully intends to sell those he has around Nuremberg as well. His creditors (who are

107. See letter 25.

many) harass him ferociously every day.[108] So in addition to being very harmful and destructive to me, [to the point that] I almost no longer know what I want to do, my remaining here also does not greatly please Herr von Bünau. I must truly confess with great disgust that I feel so deeply in my heart that my past year[s] and youth have accomplished nothing, as they reasonably should have done, and that were I now to let precious time slip away again in so useless and vain a manner, every hour and moment would become difficult for me. So it is my obedient and humble request that my much-beloved and highly esteemed guardians support my request to go to France next spring so that I can discover and learn something [useful]. Then, I may regain in my proper years[109] what I have neglected almost all of my youth. Then, I might still hope someday to become useful to my Fatherland and to walk in the steps of my late father, which can never happen if I remain here. The time of decision for me is clearly now. I am fully expecting my guardians to be favorably inclined to this request so that it is no longer delayed. My desire to honor God [in this way] shall bring joy to my much-beloved and highly esteemed mother and to all my family, and it will allow me, with God's help, to make the best of my life.

My guardians can bring this about all the sooner because a good opportunity has arisen for me [to go to France] with a very learned and experienced man, who has been to France and other foreign lands and knows many languages. He lives only a mile away with an eminent and very rich nobleman, who has instructed him to travel in France, to Tours, next spring with [the nobleman's] eleven-year-old son. Tours is a very merry place. The language is well spoken there, the board is cheap, and being German is not in the least a handicap. I have become good friends with this honest and respected man (they come often to us [at court]), and I have asked him to allow me to accompany him on the journey [to Tours], which he has promised to do, if I have the permission of my dear mother and guardians. So again, I humbly and earnestly seek, implore, and request that my guardians not hold me back from this good opportunity, which I do not think will soon come my way again. I ask this in the hope and with the promise to conduct myself in such a way that no

---

108. Two days after this letter (16 October), Stephan Carl wrote Lucas Friederich a brief note describing von Bünau's selling of his house and lands in Altenburg and his imminent resignation from the service of Duke Johann Philipp.

109. "Bei meinen zimlichen iahen." Stephan Carl had just turned eighteen.

one will have any reason to regret the decision, but rather, with God's help, will rejoice over it.

It is necessary that the decision be made soon, so that I may give the above-mentioned Herr Hoffmeister a definite answer. There are other noblemen in Leipzig who are now urgently petitioning him to let them travel with him. He wants, however, to take only me and one more [in addition to the nobleman's son], for, as he has told me, his nobleman is rich enough [to make it worth his while]. For my part, I would gladly see another Nuremberger go along, especially if Herr Jacob Welser or another [Nuremberg father] would send his son along on the trip.[110] I have already learned that Herr Jacob Welser wants to take his son out of Altdorf next spring and send him elsewhere. And his son himself, with others, has written to me to say how he regrets having conducted himself so badly for so long, and that he wants to do better from now on. So it would please me very much, if he or another honest and sober [youth] might share this good opportunity with me. If my guardians could look into this, they would do me a great service. For then we [two], as good and true fellow countrymen, could have true fellowship together [en route].

My guardians may perhaps have very different ideas and be planning to send me to another master. If so, they may be assured beyond any doubt that such would be as harmful to me as being here has been. For, my much-beloved and highly esteemed guardians, I have unfortunately learned nothing [here] that helps me. Should I now continue as before to serve a Junker, I could truly never attain any honor. I would be and remain only an idler and object of ridicule to everyone. I will not believe that my guardians desire this for me. I expect they would much rather spend the little [I have] entirely on me now, so that I may become an honorable man [able in time] thankfully to repay the same honorably (as my late father [would have done]). It would be far better for me to spend everything I have traveling, yet discover and learn something [useful], than to serve a Junker and learn nothing at all. For as [long as] I am a Junker's servant, I will learn nothing and come to nothing. Therefore, I again ask [my guardians] most urgently to consider the matter very carefully and above all, for my own sake, to allow me to do something [that is useful to me]. In return, I may then be able with honor and good reputation to earn [my own way] and serve other people.

I fully expect my much-beloved and highly esteemed guardians to grant

110. Welser (d. 1645) was a senator from Nuremberg whose son Jacob (1611–55) enrolled in Altdorf in 1627 and studied law.

my proper and humble wishes, "petitions no less honest than modest," and, as in the past, to "take counsel together on my welfare." For this, I remain always, God helping, as willing as I am obligated to repay my guardians and their own as best I can with my services, which, though few and small, shall always be obediently and diligently tendered. Meanwhile, I happily commend my highly aforementioned, greatly esteemed guardians (whom I herewith "submissively and most courteously" salute)[111] to divine Providence. Altenburg, 14 October, 1630.

> Y[our] C[ousin] a[nd] O[bedient] W[ard],
> Stephan Carl Behaim

30 ☙ Guardians to Stephan Carl, 12 November 1630

Our friendly greeting and obliging service, dear brother and cousin, Stephan Carl. We received your letter of 14 October on 5 November and have noted its contents as required. We must say, first of all, that it is not our hope that your time with Herr von Bünau should be spent idly and that you should be employed only as a household servant. Presumably he does not tolerate much idleness and inactivity among those in his very distinguished service, and he will use and employ each according to his abilities. So we can only conclude that, inasmuch as you do not yet write either pleasingly or correctly, he can, given your present skills, employ you in no more [demanding] jobs than the aforementioned household chores. You should now appreciate our many frank warnings to you about your willful behavior in Altdorf and here.

But inasmuch as we have learned on good authority that the aforesaid nobleman, your Junker [von Bünau], will leave the court and live privately on his own lands and will therefore not have need of your [services] so much anymore, we want wholeheartedly to pursue the best means by which you can get a lot of experience in writing, so that you may more gainfully serve an eminent princely counsel. In the meantime we most conscientiously instruct you to continue to serve your aforementioned Junker with all loyalty, diligence, and obedience, until we have reason to write directly to him ourselves and request your release.

As for your suggestion that you travel to France at this time, it is so childish, and also most harmful to you. We cannot deem it to be in your interest to spend your small paternal inheritance on French language,

---

111. "Submisse et officiosissime," a description of court conduct.

fencing, dancing, and tennis courts, only to return home broke. The aforesaid [trip] to France is such that it provides no opportunity for you to continue [your] studies, much less to resume them.[112] What one does not take with one [on such trips], one seldom brings back. The plan of study you propose serves only "practice" and not at all "theory."[113] It will prove much more useful for you to apply yourself in your youth to that which you will be as an adult, and primarily in the Fatherland. And this way, to your greater joy and profit, God also arranges for you to acquire what is necessary for your station in life at the expense of others and not out of your own pocket (which presently does not contain very much).

We fully expect you to show all due obedience to us, your appointed guardians, and to undertake nothing on your own without our permission or against our will, and always to keep us informed how we, in accordance with our duty and conscience, may best advise you. 12 November, 1630.

Your willing [guardians]

31 ❦ Guardians to Stephan Carl, 10 December 1630

Our friendly greeting and obliging will, dear foster son. From various of your letters to us,[114] as well as to your mother and Herr M. Steichen,[115] we gather that serving and waiting on others offends you less than the courtly life which, pro forma, you revile more strongly. As has been your custom in the past, you again allege a new reverence for God and emendation of life and soul. We would much rather believe that this has indeed happened to you than that you have fallen victim [again] to your prodigal ways. How painful it is, then, for us and for your good mother that you have again, without any previous report or request, much less with our foreknowledge and consent, wantonly taken forty-two Reichsthaler from

112. In his letter of 14 October to his guardians, Stephan Carl mentioned a trip to "merry Tours," not the university study in Angers he earlier proposed to his cousin Georg Friederich Pömer. His guardians considered the planned trip to France to be little more than a lark.

113. In other words, it is play, not serious academic work.

114. As becomes clear from its content, this letter is a response to a letter of Stephan Carl's (unfortunately not extant), in which he reacted negatively to his guardians' denial of his request to go to France.

115. Unclear who this is.

Herr Sternenbecker and Herr Ayermann between [   ][116] May and the
Michaelmas Leipzig fair. We consider your action all the more frivolous
because we know that you have not had the smallest [unmet] need or
deficiency either in clothing or in necessary board and support. By right,
you have not needed even ten or twenty, much less forty-two Reichsthaler. But now, in order to begin a fresh, new (namely) prodigal year,
you do not at all hesitate to demand still more money from us, even
though you have yet to account for and explain this previous amount.
When in this way you hypocritically refuse to be held accountable for
the money you spend, it deprives your mother and siblings of needed
support. So we shall expect from you in your next letter, without fail, an
accounting of the money you have received and a report on that which
you now desire. Specifically, what will the money be spent on, and how
much do you need? Otherwise, the absolute minimum will be drawn
and assigned to you.

Your wish to go to Jena or Tübingen is not unlike your last to go to
France.[117] Students like you who write a petition in such a silly way and
who are discovered with borrowed Latin and letters,[118] do not belong at
universities in either public or private lectures, but in places where they
may learn to write German and Latin orthographically, compose correctly, and construct finished and pleasing letters. With the assistance of
knowledgeable people we, for our part, are now wholeheartedly considering such a place for you. For your part, you can now be completely
free of premature worry [about your future]. Since the matter is in our
hands, and is one of duty, there is nothing at this time obliging you except
to show us due obedience.

The reason why we must place you in the service of a master has often
been explained to you. Several times, with candid warnings, we have also
threatened you [for your behavior]. We have not sent you to court for
the sake of eating, drinking, and idleness. Both here and in Altdorf you
had already practiced these more than we desired. Because your Junker
[von Bünau] had previously conducted a number of [princely] missions
and had held distinguished princely posts, we viewed your placement
there as an opportunity for you, with his assistance, both to learn some-

116. A space is left for an exact date, which was apparently given in the mailed version.
117. Jena is mentioned in a Latin letter of 22 November contrasting the nobility of the
university ("totius populi sit medicina") with the impiety and perfidy of court life.
118. His guardians have long recognized that Stephan Carl's Latin letters are not always
of his own creation.

thing [useful] and to advance to the service of other and more distinguished lords. Thus, [we hoped] you might experience and learn at court
what your dear father and his brother had learned there to their glory
and profit.

Once again, with good intentions, we remind you to show us due
obedience in all things. Provide us a true and accurate accounting of the
money you have already received, and report to us the purpose of the
money you now want and how much you will need. We also want you
to make the best of what we arrange for you with the help of good
counsel. And do stop your insulting fault-finding, demands, and irresponsible threats. In a word, prove yourself to us, as your duty and God's
command require of you. We have wanted in our reply, again with good
intentions, to withhold nothing from you. May God be with us all. Nuremberg, 10 December, 1630.

> Your caring and loyal guardians,
> L[ucas] F[riederich] Behaim
> C[onrad] Baier
> H[ans] H[einrich] Weiss

32 🦋 Stephan Carl to Guardians, 18 December 1630

My friendly greeting and due obedience always, very gracious, much-
beloved, and highly esteemed guardians. I received your letter [of 10
December] and I am very unhappy to learn that you harbor such evil
suspicions of me, as if I had returned to my previous prodigal life. From
Herr Sternenbecker's letter[119] and my own accounting [of my expendi-
tures], my guardians will see well enough that they have better to expect
of me. I do most humbly ask my guardians' forgiveness for not having
reported [this information] sooner. But I had thought it to be unnecessary,
inasmuch as my dear brother had written to Herr Sternenbecker and
asked him to give me money as required for my needs. That I did not,
as I reasonably should have done, write timely reports of [my use of] the
money I received during the period [you mention] occurred for no other
reason than that I had always expected my mother, in accordance with
my expressed wishes, to inform me how many Reichsthaler I had lately
charged to [her] account. So I now fully expect my guardians to hold me
blameless in this matter and to pardon me. God, my good conscience,

---

119. Not extant.

and people who know the facts can attest that I have not been extravagant, but have always conducted myself according to God's command.

It is truly no small disappointment that my guardians now give me so little hope of going to the university. My completely persuasive arguments [for doing so] have accomplished absolutely nothing. [It is still worse that] my very great desire to study should be thwarted by my guardians, who have always encouraged me in this direction, but will not now permit me even half a year to retrieve what I learned with so much effort and at such great expense (and also in the French language) and have since completely forgotten. My guardians themselves tell me that I cannot write orthographically and that I will truly not learn to do so here or at another court, and they wonder what I will do with my life without such a skill. Therefore, I ask my guardians again as urgently as I dare for God's sake to send me to the University of Wittenberg. And if not for a full year, at least for a half, so that I may have the opportunity to regain my Latin and French and, now that I am in my proper years,[120] to retrieve as far as possible what I neglected in Altdorf. My dear mother gave me so much before when I did not understand [what it meant], so I hope that she can even more easily give me a hundred thaler now without any harm to herself. By such assistance, God willing, she shall once and for all be free of spending money [on me].

I do not want much for board [at school]. My guardians may give me as little as they wish, and I will be satisfied with it so long as it allows me to make ends meet honorably. On the other hand, they may be assured that I will always show them due obedience and that this will be a decision they can rejoice over. Again, I ask my guardians for God's sake just to test me for a couple of months and see if I keep my promise. If I am only given the chance, they will discover for sure that I am truthful. I also ask my guardians to send me some money for the [Christmas] market (but only if they wish to do so; I leave it up to them). Then I may still have a suit of clothes made for myself and, my honor thereby saved, I will not have to hide out [during Christmas], for I cannot wear my other suit any longer. I also ask my guardians [again] to permit me with the new year to begin a new Christian life at the University of Wittenberg. I cannot live here any longer; I am completely incapable of playing the courtly game of flattery and deceit.

No more for now except to ask my guardians again most urgently to support me this one time and allow me to move from here to a university.

120. At eighteen, Stephan Carl has reached legal majority.

In humble obedience and daily prayer, I remain devoted to serving my guardians to the best of my ability, and I commend them all trustingly to the omnipotence and mercy of God and I wish them continuing physical health, long life, and every desired and beneficial comfort of body and soul. Altenburg, in great haste, 18 December, 1630.

Y[our] C[ousin] [and] O[bedient] W[ard] A[lways],
Stephan Carl Behaim

33 ❦ Guardians to Stephan Carl, 28 December 1630

Our friendly greeting and obliging will, dear foster son. We received your letter of 18 December on the 25th, and we understand well enough from it your defense [of the use] of the money you have received and your late accounting of it. But because your letter is so completely contradictory and bewildering, we have had great difficulty believing it, so let us again remind you to send us a detailed statement of all the money you have received during your entire stay in Altenburg, and [this time] indicate to us in an orderly manner, item by item, on a full or half sheet of paper, not on so many little tattered scraps, just how you have spent it. Then we can properly inform ourselves. Also, since you indicate that you are still in need of a suit of clothes, Herr Sternenbecker will be written to and instructed to accommodate you as economically as possible, if you do need it.

As for your wish to go to a university, indeed, to Wittenberg, we guardians, pursuant to our duty, have together and in consultation with your mother, carefully and fully considered it. We simply cannot in conscience find it advisable at the present time to grant your wish, considering that everything is now so corrupt and perverted in the universities.[121] Unfortunately, one now learns more evil than good there (even when one arrives with a good intention and is resolute). One could cite many and varied examples of such corruption of youth [in the universities]. In consideration of this one fact alone, we have unanimously decided that it is in your best interest to be placed instead with an eminent doctor of law and advocate at the imperial court in Speyer. There you will have the desired opportunity, by constant practice, not only to learn fine, elegant

121. Another reference to the turmoil created by the Thirty Years War, which spawned internal divisions and conflicts in the universities and made a disciplined course of study almost impossible.

handwriting and how to write orthographically and compose properly, but also with effort to acquaint yourself with imperial law and judicial procedure. Such knowledge will be useful to you in the future and give you an advantage over others not so experienced, should God want you to have a position in government. You need not in the least be ashamed of such [training]. Others of your rank, at great effort, have also spent time there. For example, your cousin who is now a forestry official,[122] Herr Georg Seyfried Kohler, and others. Indeed, a Harssdörffer, Haller, and a Schedel are now there.[123] One may hope that for you also [such training] will not defame your honor, but redound to your benefit. However, for the present, you must keep these plans to yourself and diligently serve [Herr von Bünau] and be loyal to your peers [in Altenburg], showing everyone there respect and avoiding bad company. If you conduct yourself according to God's commandments, there is no doubt that He will give you good fortune and success in all that you undertake, so that his divine honor and what is best both for you and for the common good may be served. All of which we wish you from the bottom of our hearts together with the start of a happy new year. May the divine omnipotence bless us all. Nuremberg, 28 December, 1630.

> Your willing and loyal guardians,
> Lucas Friederich Behaim
> Hans Heinrich Weiss
> Conrad Baier

34 ❦ Stephan Carl to Lucas Friederich, 5 February 1631

My friendly greeting and brotherly love and devotion always, much-beloved and highly esteemed Brother Lucas Friederich. I received your comforting letter on 4 February and learned with great joy that I shall at last gain release from my prison here. I now recognize how true and fatherly are the hearts of all my beloved and highly esteemed guardians. They have, of course, always been such, but on this occasion I am especially aware of it and can appreciate it anew. So it is no small sadness for me that I cannot, as would be fitting, express my thanks to you in a properly written Latin letter. But if God will now help me go back to a

122. Unclear who this is.
123. These are all prominent families in Nuremberg.

university, then, God willing, my guardians shall come to know well my grateful heart.

I have also learned from Brother's letter that [when I leave here] I am to betake myself [first] to Nuremberg with the Council's envoy. This is a command I would gladly follow and obey. But surely Brother and my other guardians can readily imagine how little respect people would have for me both here and in Nuremberg, if I now wanted to take Mother's milk again. Moreover, it would shame me to the bottom of my heart to return at this time to Nuremberg. For during my year [in Altenburg], I have made no notable progress in the acquisition either of skills or of good manners. I have rather forgotten the Arts and etiquette. Neither my gracious and highly esteemed guardians nor my dear and highly esteemed mother could take any particular pleasure in me at this time. So would my gracious guardians and my dear mother in this case excuse me [from such a visit]? In all the other things they want me to do, they will always find me, lifelong, an obedient and willing person. Perhaps my guardians have meant [only] that I should travel to Speyer via Nuremberg. But I can reach Speyer much sooner by going directly there from here.

Brother gives me too much credit when he thinks that I would not arrive in Speyer with much better skills and far greater respect, if I first attended a university for half a year and learned to write beautifully and correctly and [improved my] Latin. [It is not true, as Brother believes,] that all this could be learned just as well in Speyer. So again I ask Brother and my guardians, humbly and obediently, not to deny my wish to attend the University of Wittenberg, but to allow me to try it for just half a year. I assure them that it is a decision over which they will always have reason to rejoice and never to regret. I am not asking this for any superficial reason or for fun's sake. From the bottom of my heart and for God's sake, I ask my guardians to trust me when I say that my only motive is to learn. As God, who is my witness, knows, my great desire is someday to walk in the steps of my late father and to bring happiness to my troubled Mother and my entire family. I think especially of how much I can gain from a university. With God's help, I could learn enough there to become completely free of my mother's support. So I will gladly go to Speyer and become a clerk, if I can first prepare myself to do the job properly. For there I will be working not just for my daily bread, but also to make some money.

I urge Brother to hold firm on my early release from [Altenburg]. In return, my guardians shall always find me obedient and ready to serve. I am willing to invest money in this, my body and life as collateral.[124] So again, from the bottom of my heart, I ask my guardians to trust me just this one time. They will not regret it.

God bless. Altenburg, in great haste, 5 February, 1631.

H[is] O[bedient] [and] W[illing] Brother,
Stephan Carl Behaim

35 ❦ Stephan Carl to Lucas Friederich, 11 February 1631

My friendly greeting and brotherly love and devotion always, much-beloved and highly esteemed Brother. I had fully intended to go to Leipzig this week and discuss my situation with Herr Georg Volckhamer.[125] [I wanted to] ask him to write Brother a few words on my behalf so that my wish [to go to a university] might be realized all the sooner. But I have been unable to get permission from Herr von Bünau to do so, and so I must now wait until [Herr Volckhamer] comes here. Meanwhile, I cannot refrain from asking Brother again most urgently to oblige me just this once and not to deny my request. My desire to study in Wittenberg is very, very great. And if I do not first prepare myself at a university before I arrive in Speyer, it will be for sure to my very great detriment, as you can easily imagine. If Brother is thinking that I will be led astray again and my good plans thwarted, let me report here and now that there is no need whatsoever for such worry. I want to go to the university for only one reason and that is to learn. I have no desire whatsoever to become involved with a fraternity there.[126] I intend to stay in my room and to study, also to take my meals there, so that I will be completely safe from the students in the college. Just test me for as long as you wish; I will obey your command and withdraw when you desire. I ask Brother and all my guardians most sincerely to oblige me in this before the matter is closed altogether.

Meanwhile, I ask Brother to address my need by releasing the money that has been set aside for me from my youth by my dear Mother and to see that it is now paid to me. I can never put it to better use than now. If Brother loves me (as he surely does), then again I ask most urgently

124. Written above these words, apparently by Lucas Friederich, is "N.B."
125. This is Georg Christoph Volckhamer (1582–1632), alter Bürgermeister in Nuremberg after 1607. See letter 38.
126. "Mit der porsch gantz und gar nicht bekandt zumachen." He plans to avoid temptation by isolating himself from other students.

that he help me realize my desire [for a university education] and to write as soon as possible to Herr Ayermann and Herr von Bünau and to instruct Herr Ayermann especially how much he should give me for Wittenberg so that I can buy wood, trunks, books, and other necessities at the Easter market. No matter how little it is, I will be completely happy with it. Entrust it to me scrupulously, only write to me soon. My life will not be so painful after I have your answer. In return, you shall find me to be completely at your command in everything forevermore, and my humble and diligent prayer will always be to repay you.

Herewith I commit Brother and all his family to the care of the Highest. In great haste, in Altenburg, 11 February, 1631.

> H[is] O[bedient] B[rother] a[nd] F[oster son],
> Stephan Carl Behaim

36 ❦ Guardians to Stephan Carl, 15 February 1631

Our friendly greeting and obliging will, dear brother and cousin, Stephan Carl. From your letter of 8 February, written to me, L[ucas] Friederich Behaim, and to your Mother, we guardians must learn to our great astonishment and extreme displeasure that you not only will not abide by our well-intentioned, loyal, and even fatherly counsel, which we have earnestly discussed in advance with many knowledgeable people, but having been greatly displeased by it, you now stubbornly maintain your own pernicious and baseless opinion that you should go to the University of Wittenberg, and you will in no manner or way be turned away from it.

For our future justification, we always provide you clear reasons in writing for our decisions, whether they concern your service to a master, or, as in this case, why we cannot in good conscience send you to a university. We have now several times extensively and with sufficient argument addressed the last matter, and we do not consider it necessary to repeat ourselves here, nor are we able to spend the time required to do so. So, as is proper, we stand by our last, well-reasoned, and final decision. Under the circumstances, we could not have arranged a more pleasant or better opportunity for you [than the clerkship in Speyer], had you been our natural son. But if you want to continue in your Junker service, you can certainly follow your own obstinate head and do so, and we guardians, who have recommended a better course for you, will then be excused from any responsibility for it. But you should understand clearly that if you do, we will not give you one heller. You will then receive your board and clothes from your Junker and will not die from hunger or freeze to death. And you could then also relieve yourself of such unnecessary worries as your present shame over returning so soon to Nuremberg.

If you have had other things to be ashamed of in the past, you now have nothing to be more ashamed of than your disobedience and obstinacy toward us. If you will not return to Nuremberg with the Council's honorable envoy, and you remain convinced (apparently) that your own proud mind can arrange your transfer from Altenburg to Speyer more competently than your guardians, then in God's name by all means try your hand at it. We will not interfere. Arrangements have already been made on your behalf in Speyer, at great effort on our part, and we cannot change them at this point.

What you now owe us in this matter is simply proper obedience, which we remind you now with good intentions in response to your letter.

God be with us, Nuremberg, 15 February, 1631.

> Your caring and devoted guardians,
> Lucas Friederich Behaim
> H[ans] Heinrich Weiss
> Conrad Baier[127]

37 ❦ Stephan Carl to Lucas Friederich, 20 February 1631

My friendly greeting and ever ready obedience, much-beloved and highly esteemed Brother. I am very pleased that Brother has answered my last letter in timely fashion, although a different answer would have been much preferred and more pleasant for me. But since my highly esteemed guardians at this time find it in no way advisable to send me to a university, I am completely willing to submit to them, as I have promised and always intend to do, although I cannot deny that it would have been the greatest service to me to have been able to return to a university. But as this is not to be, I am completely willing to betake myself to Speyer in accordance with my guardians' loyal counsel. I am,

127. A note dated 9 March has been added to the letter, possibly in Lucas Friederich's hand, detailing an itinerary from Altenburg to Speyer with contacts along the way. This information was no doubt conveyed in neat copy to Stephan Carl.

however, surprised that no mention has yet been made of the kind of master I am to serve there.

My only request at this point, and I make it fervently, is that Brother and my guardians not force me to come first to Nuremberg. In all other respects I am willing to obey them completely. I expect, in return, to be obliged only in this one thing, as I have recently asked. Without any doubt, Brother will now say, "But it is impossible for you to go [directly from Altenburg to Speyer] without great expense," and this is no doubt true. But I ask Brother and all my guardians graciously to deem it a good thing, if I now present my view of the matter.

The loyal and, yes, fatherly hearts of my beloved and highly esteemed guardians are well known to me. I am sure they have been thinking that I can travel from Nuremberg to Speyer at no cost whatsoever. That, indeed, is why they think it may cost a lot [for me to travel directly from Altenburg to Speyer]. Again, I ask Brother and my other guardians to forgive me, but I do not believe that such opportunities [as the one in Speyer] are so readily arranged, and meanwhile it would also cost me money to be in Nuremberg.

The following [alternative] plan was given me by a wise and learned man here in Leipzig. Since I could travel as far as Naumburg with the honorable Nuremberg Council envoy, the better course of action, and the one he has recommended, would be for me to buy a horse here in Leipzig, [which I can do] for between twenty and twenty-four Reichsthaler. All of this money, and more, he has assured me, would be recouped when I sold the horse in Speyer, for horses are very cheap here. And I would be able to spare my mule, which should thoroughly please my guardians.

So I humbly ask Brother, all my guardians, and my highly esteemed Mother to oblige me in this and not force me to come to Nuremberg. Would they let me know their opinion promptly (as they did with their last letter)? And would Brother also write personally to Herr Ayermann about how much he should give me [for the journey]? Otherwise, I will get nothing from him.

I have delivered your letter to Herr von Bünau, and I have also written to him myself to request, most urgently, but also very humbly, that he release me from his service. I have no doubt that I have earned such a release by my constant and devout prayers for his health.

I know my debt [to my guardians] and I remain always completely at their command. I await your answer at the earliest possible time. God bless, from Leipzig, 20 February, 1631.

Again I ask to be forgiven for writing so wildly. If ever I do get away from here, I will be at my guardian's mercy if my writing does not improve.

H[is] F[riendly], O[bedient] B[rother]

Stephan Carl Behaim

[P.S.] I ran into my gracious lord, Herr von Blansdorf, here, and he is as fond of me as ever. I consider meeting him the best of luck.

Would Brother personally write a few words to Herr Ayermann? Otherwise I will get nothing from him. He says that he has been forbidden by Wimpfen [to give me any money].[128] Another request: if possible, would Brother deposit some money with Herr Ayermann's [Nuremberg] office? He says it is just as much as when he is there. He likes me a lot.

38 ❦ Stephan Carl to Lucas Friederich, 23 February 1631

My friendly greeting and brotherly love and devotion always, much-beloved and very respected Brother. No doubt Brother will by now have received my last letter of 20 February. Nevertheless, I could not refrain from writing another letter on this matter. As in my last, I remain completely willing to obey my guardians and betake myself to Speyer, although I had, to be sure, wished for nothing else than that I might go first to the University of Wittenberg for a while. But because it is my guardians' firm resolve that I change my mind about Speyer, I am obligated and willing to obey. For, apart from this [decision], I must acknowledge before God and the world that my brother and guardians have always meant the best for me.

My brother would, however, do me the greatest service, if he could arrange in advance by letter for me to have a room of my own [in Speyer]. Otherwise I fear my situation might turn out to be as bad there as it is here. Had I only had my own room here, I would have studied as much as at a university. So this would be a very great and pleasing service for me. The cost of a [private] room for a year will not be so much when it is taken into account how much I will gain from it.

Inasmuch as I am willingly obeying my guardians in this matter, I would again ask Brother most urgently for one favor in return and that is that

128. Another middleman in the chain of relatives and business associates who formed Stephan Carl's lifeline to his brother; perhaps a special messenger between Lucas Friederich and Ayermann, certainly someone very authoritative.

he not force me to come first to Nuremberg. I gladly obey my guardians in all other matters, but for many reasons I ask to be spared this one thing.

A very well-informed man here has given me the following advice, namely, that I travel with the honorable Nuremberg Council envoy as far as Coburg, then go either by foot, horse, or coach to Würzburg, then to Frankfurt (if possible, with the [Nuremberg] merchants' [convoy]), and finally on to Speyer. I would commit myself to making the trip on twenty Reichsthaler (assuming I have the use of my own horse). By contrast, eighty would not be sufficient to get there from Nuremberg by coach. But I will make do with whatever my guardians allow me to spend en route.

In accordance with [my guardians'] instruction, I have this morning ordered a suit of clothes to be made in Leipzig at a cost of thirty-seven thaler. Without new clothes, I dare not let myself be seen by the honorable Council's envoy. But the more immediate reason I have acted so quickly is that I would otherwise have had nothing to wear next week when we go to the Lord's Table.[129] Brother is certainly aware that at this time of the year the poorest youths in Nuremberg customarily bathe themselves and put on new clothes. How painful it would be for me to have to go [to the Sacrament] in my everyday clothes. If Brother desires, I will render him an accounting of the thirty-seven thaler heller by heller. Herr Georg Ayermann gave me this money most grudgingly, although I assured him of Brother's [forthcoming] letter. He said that he had no mandate to give me money and that he had been forbidden from doing so by Wimpfen.[130] But if Brother will only write me a few lines about how much he should give me, he will do so gladly.

I also humbly and obediently request that Brother consider writing to my very gracious lord G[eorg] Christoph Volckhamer,[131] and ask if I may accompany him as far as Coburg. Without such a request, he might not want me along. Would Brother also deposit soon with Herr Georg Ayermann's Nuremberg office the thirty-seven Reichsthaler [he has given me for new clothes] and the other [money due him], together with the total amount he should now give me for the journey [to Speyer]. Otherwise, he will give me nothing. As Brother can readily see, I will certainly need a lot of money. I hope everything can be properly arranged soon.

129. Apparently for the beginning of Lent.
130. This is the Wimpfen mentioned in letter 37.
131. See letter 35.

I plan to give goodbye presents to Herr Sternenbecker, who has done so many favors for me, my language instructor,[132] the six maids, and my coworkers. I must also have new boots for the journey, as well as a horse, which I trust I can get here for between twenty-four and thirty thaler. Without any doubt whatsoever the horse will sell for at least forty in Frankfurt. Brother will easily be able to figure out how much Herr Ayermann should give me. I await Brother's reply at the earliest opportunity.

God bless, Altenburg, 23 February, 1631.

H[is] L[oving] B[rother],

Stephan Carl Behaim

P.S. I have written Herr von Bünau myself and I am letting the discussion [about my release] take its course through H[err] D.[133] I hope to be released today. But I definitely do not want to come to Nuremberg. I would certainly like to know when the [Nuremberg] merchants will arrive in Würzburg.

132. Stephan Carl has been learning Italian.
133. Unclear who this is.

For more than a year Stephan Carl fell completely from view. Whether he ever made it to Speyer and trained for the clerkship is unknown. The subject of Speyer does not come up again in the correspondence, nor is there any dramatic improvement in the quality of his handwriting. It is however possible that he was in Speyer briefly.

In April 1632 Stephan Carl was a penitent military courier, under house arrest in Nuremberg. During the intervening months he had become attached to a German regiment in Frankfurt am Main serving with the royal Swedish army, then leading the Protestant side in the Thirty Years War (1618–48). This conflict was both political and religious. The English historian C. V. Wedgewood once described it as "the outstanding example in European history of meaningless conflict." She later recognized this to be an inaccurate generalization, for in its course the war did reshape the map and politics of Europe in important ways. But as Stephan Carl's experience makes clear, for ordinary people involved in it the war seemed utterly aimless and never-ending. To escape this "war without good fortune," Stephan

Carl fled to the Netherlands in summer 1635.

The war wreaked havoc on a scale unseen in Europe since the Black Death of the fourteenth century. The original antagonists were Bavaria, supported by Spain and Austria, and the Palatinate, supported by England, France, and the Netherlands, who believed it to their advantage to tie down Hapsburg armies in the empire. In 1630 the king of Sweden, with French and Dutch financing, picked up the Protestant banner after imperial armies under Maximilian of Bavaria and Albrecht of Wallenstein (in his teens a Protestant) had routed Danish forces in the empire and driven deep into Denmark. When Stephan Carl began military service in 1632, the war was well into its so-called Swedish phase, and the conflict concentrated in greater Nuremberg.

Stephan Carl first served in the company of First Lieutenant Johann Ludwig Wildeyssen in Frankfurt. Ordered to join the Frankish regiment of his cousin, First Lieutenant Hans Christoph Coler, a Nuremberger, in Kronweissenburg, he was prevented from doing so by the fortunes of war and ended up going instead to Nuremberg with Wildeyssen.[134] Nuremberg was providing money, weapons, and munitions to forces in the area led by Sweden. It was from Nuremberg that Stephan Carl undertook an unfortunate mission to deliver mail to the Swedish commander, Klaus Dietrich von Sperreuter, in nearby Eschenbach. Although emphatically ordered to ride in the company of troops when delivering mail, Stephan Carl dashed off alone on a borrowed horse.[135] A few miles outside Nuremberg he fell prey to riders, who took the horse and opened the mail. Wildeyssen claimed to have prophesied such an incident, recalling that in Frankfurt Stephan Carl had been warned several times about riding alone.[136] Apparently Stephan Carl's guardians had to compensate for the lost horse. For Lucas Friederich the incident proved to be the last straw, and in early May 1632 he prepared to resign as his brother's guardian after more than a decade in that capacity.

Stephan Carl proved as resourceful as ever. Before the year was out he managed to reach Coler's regiment, then in Mainz. For the first time he declared soldiering his true "profession" and he deeply admired Coler, his new mentor. But despite Coler's promises to curb Stephan Carl's spendthrift ways, he indulged the young man's fascination with military dress by taking him on a shopping spree in Frankfurt that cost seventy-three Reichsthaler, imperiling once again Stephan Carl's vow to his mother of financial independence.

Stephan Carl was spared none of the war's horror. By 1634 his company ran patrols in the heaviest areas of conflict in Bavaria. Twice he was ambushed and almost lost his life. After the first ambush, by imperial Croatian and German soldiers, he was taken captive to Kronach, where he escaped a citizens' mob only because his captors also were the mob's target. The second ambush, near Nördlingen, left him seriously wounded. The ambushes cost him his clothes, his horse, and, most irreplaceable, his aide. Stephan Carl also found the enemy within his own company and within himself. He became involved in a nasty rivalry with a hot-headed herald that resulted in

---

134. Coler (1589–1637) had been a member of Nuremberg's Rat until 1629, when he resigned to command the Frankish regiment. He was also a Pfleger and commandant of the Nuremberg fortress of Lichtenau. He married Elenora Scheurl in 1622.

135. Lucas Friederich to Johann Ludwig Wildeyssen, 1 May 1632.

136. Wildeyssen to Lucas Friederich, 4 May 1632.

the herald's death. And having several times lost virtually everything he had in the petty engagements of war, he again borrowed well beyond his means.

Stephan Carl's vow to his mother of self-sufficiency never lay more on his conscience than when the scope of his indebtedness lay before his brother Lucas Friederich. Yet as his debts soared, he was more confident than ever of finding ways to repay them all himself. He directed his creditors to his brother, while at the same time instructing his brother to redirect them back to him.

39 ❦ Stephan Carl to Guardians, [16] April 1632

My due obedience, love, and devotion to the best of my ability always, noble and most wise, very gracious, much-beloved, and highly esteemed guardians.

It is very well known to my gracious guardians with what great patience, heavy and troubled heart, and no little pain I have lived as an imprisoned man for the last two weeks. [I have endured it] only so that my gracious guardians might truly perceive and know my willing obedience toward them and release me all the sooner from my misery here. But since I am so far unable to experience or even to hope for such a happy hour, I could not withhold writing this letter and asking my gracious, highly esteemed, and dear guardians most humbly for my release, and that they graciously accept as a sufficient [punishment] my demonstrated patience and proven obedience during this time [of confinement]. They may easily observe that because of the violent theft of the horse I have been sentenced to such imprisonment as a completely innocent man. However, inasmuch as I might have earned such [punishment] on another occasion, I have not let it totally annoy me, but I have rather very humbly and gratefully accepted it as a punishment to discipline and better my life. Since I have not stolen, plundered, whored, or committed any other such wanton act for which such painful imprisonment and tedious confinement would be deserved, and since valuable time is passing and, because of the horse, I cannot now work and earn anything or report to First Lieutenant Coler, whom I still could not join without great effort, time, and expense, I look to my gracious guardians to comply fully with my humble request and have me released from my prison without fail. For such grace and great favor, I will remain, as always, obliged, willing, and ready to serve my guardians obediently and gratefully. I now commend them most humbly to the care of the Highest and wish them every good fortune under His continuing great favor. April, 1632.

> To my gracious Herr guardians,
> your life-long obedient foster son,
> Stephan Carl Behaim

40 ❦ Stephan Carl to Guardians, 30 April 1632

My due obedience, love, and devotion to the best of my ability always, noble and most wise, especially gracious, much loved, and highly esteemed guardians.

Yesterday I learned that First Lieutenant Wildeyssen's secretary had been here and asked urgently to talk with me. I have no doubt that the noble First Lieutenant had enjoined him to discuss several matters with me at this time, especially since my letter to him remains unanswered. So again I ask my gracious, much-beloved, and highly esteemed guardians, first of all, to forgive me for everything I have done improperly and against them over the last two years. As in my 16 April letter, I again repeat my sure promise henceforth to do every good thing [for them] to the best of my ability. And because of my great need still to speak with the aforementioned secretary, I ask them now for God's sake and for my own best interest graciously to release me from this month-long imprisonment. Otherwise I fear I will fall into complete disgrace with First Lieutenant Wildeyssen. God bless. Nuremberg, the last day of April, 1632.

> My gracious Herr guardians' obedient
> foster son for as long as I live,
> Stephan Carl Behaim

41 ❦ Stephan Carl to Lucas Friederich, 3 May 1632

My due obedient service and brotherly love and loyalty to the fullest and best of my ability, much-beloved and highly esteemed brother and true guardian.

Since it is entirely your wish and intention to resign your guardianship over my person this afternoon, I shall therefore name a new trustee. To be sure, my heart aches that you should now discharge your abundant and loyally exercised care and effort [on my behalf] because of my so ill-led life. Nevertheless may you always without fail place in me the sure and certain hope that, with the passage of years and by the grace of God and the assistance of the Holy Ghost, and at their good pleasure, amends will be made for what now, because of my folly and blindness, I unfortunately neglect.

By letter, word, and deed, I have always perceived my gracious, much-beloved, and highly esteemed brother to have a true fatherly heart and mind toward my small person, so much so that I could not wish for a better trustee than he. With this in mind, I would, if I may, ask him to reconsider. Inasmuch as he has administered the guardianship for more than ten years with such great, unceasing effort and care, and because he also still thinks it is fitting that we please and honor our mother, it is my most humble and earnest inquiry, petition, and request that Brother continue as my trustee. If he agrees, he shall lighten all my hardship. And he shall not be burdened again by any contrary efforts on my part, especially now that I do not know how long God may allow me to live.[137] I am, moreover, ready and willing—and I here and now pledge myself to it—not to ask or demand so much as a single heller from you until I have made good on all that I have foolishly and excessively squandered up to now. In short, with God's help, I will henceforth conduct myself in such a way that Brother shall not regret any effort he makes [on my behalf], but come instead to rejoice over it.

Here awaiting Brother's concurring answer.[138] God bless. Nuremberg, 3 May, 1632.

> In humblediligentmostwillingservice[139] to my
> gracious, much-beloved, and highly esteemed
> brother,
> Stephan Carl Behaim

42 🐝 Stephan Carl to Conrad Baier, 20/28 December 1632[140]

My greeting and due and diligent service to the fullest and best of my ability always, high and honorable, very much-beloved and highly esteemed cousin.

My position [as your foster son] obligates me to report that we all made

137. Because of the increased dangers of his military service.
138. He is still in his prison in Nuremberg.
139. So written.
140. An identical letter was sent at the same time to Lucas Friederich.

it happily and safely to Frankfurt and to Mainz, thanks to God's grace.[141]
And everything went very well en route. We were shown every honor
and good will in Remlingen at the court of Her Grace, the countess of
Castell. [This was in gratitude for the assistance given] Her Grace's son,
who was injured outside Nuremberg and now lodges there with Dr.
Fetzer. Everywhere of course we have had to travel through plague-
infested places, but we have by God's grace survived well.

My "little fox" behaves so well that many high officers have praised
it.[142] It goes as boldly from its stall in Mainz as in Nuremberg. I truly do
not regret spending a single heller on it. I have already had offers of
twenty-six Reichsthaler for it.

Now we are doing nothing but making the rounds of our camps,
namely in Hardenburg and Bochenheim in the Leiningen earldom,[143] and
also in Weissenburg.[144] Once I am in my quarters in Dürkheim, I am
going to make some money, although the total amount will not be as
much as I might wish. Still, it is enough, praise God, that I can confidently
say that I will cause my mother no further expense for half a year.

Day after tomorrow, God willing, I will travel to Strasbourg, because
neither Lieutenant Coler nor I met with Dr. Lucas Gollen in Speyer, nor
have we been able to get an answer to our letters. I will certainly make
the best possible effort to get this money from him.[145]

I am, praise God, now with a man who has all the virtues of a true
leader.[146] With him, I have it as good as he does. So I have good reason
to pray diligently that almighty God may let me continue in my present
condition for a long time. By this earnestly desired opportunity, I may
now make amends for the wrong I have done for so many years. I have,
praise God, gotten off to a good start, and cousin shall hear of many
more.

All of which I had to let cousin know. Would cousin kindly convey

141. Stephan Carl is now on maneuvers in the Palatinate with Coler's regiment.
142. Stephan Carl is referring to his horse.
143. Stephan Carl's regiment is traveling southward along the Rhine from Mainz.
144. In Alsace.
145. In the itinerary prepared for Stephan Carl's journey to Speyer (see n. 127), he was
to report to Gollen on his arrival. The money here mentioned seems to be either a
refund of what Lucas Friederich had paid Gollen in anticipation of Stephan Carl's arrival
(assuming Stephan Carl never arrived) or a partial refund of money paid in advance
(assuming Stephan Carl was there only briefly).
146. This is Lieutenant Coler.

my sincere and humble greetings and all love and good wishes to his dear wife and children and his entire family? I commend all of you to continuing health and every peace and comfort under the care of the Highest. From my camp in Dürkheim on the Hardt, 20 December, 1632.

In the humblediligentmostwillingservice of my
cousin,
Stephan Carl Behaim

P.S. After returning from Mainz, I find my letter is still here in the castle. Because the precious new year now stands at the door, I wish my cousin and his dear wife and children a happy, healthful, peaceful, joyous, profitable, and successful new year from the bottom of my heart. And I pray daily from my heart that almighty God will graciously spare one and all from any horrible evil and misfortune and that like a father He will compensate you in this new year for all the great trouble, hardship, and sadness you have had to endure, and bless you richly with spiritual and temporal goods. Amen. Amen. Amen. Hartenburg, 28 December, 1632.

In the humblediligentmostwillingservice of my
cousin,
Stephan Carl Behaim

43 ❦ Stephan Carl to Lucas Friederich, 11 March 1633

My due and diligent service to the best and fullest of my ability always, noble, most wise, very much-beloved, and highly esteemed Brother . . .

I have learned from my dear mother's letter, which I received here [Mainz] after arriving from Dürkheim, that she wants to know whether I received twenty-five Reichsthaler from Herr Thenn.[147] I recognize that I am obligated to report such [transactions] not only to my much-beloved and highly esteemed mother, but also to my much-beloved brother, so I herewith acknowledge that twenty-five Reichsthaler were indeed sent by Herr Thenn from Augsburg to me in Nördlingen, but, as God knows, only to meet my great and most pressing needs when I was ill. Cousin Georg Friederich Pömer will have to vouch for me on this. My hope had all along been to repay Herr Thenn without Brother's knowledge from the money I received from Dr. Lucas Gollen and to hand it over to him at the latest by the time we had decamped. But in the meantime, I have not been able to collect the money from Dr. Gollen. Almost all the money

---

147. A merchant in Augsburg and another of Stephan Carl's middlemen.

I have made in the camp has gone to spare my dear Mother any [further] expense, as will be shown by the accounting I am sending with my next letter. So it is my very humble request that Brother not blame me for the delay [in repaying Herr Thenn]. Should the money remain unpaid [by Dr. Gollen], I am ready to make the fullest effort to see that these twenty-five Reichsthaler and the [additional] six [I have since received] are repaid at the earliest possible time. This I will do as soon as I reach Donauwörth, for it is impossible for me to do so here. I shall keep Brother informed.

God be with us all. Mainz, 11 March, 1633.

> Brother's obligated servant,
> Stephan Carl Behaim

44 ☼ Stephan Carl to Lucas Friederich, 19 March 1633

My due, devoted service to the best and fullest of my ability always, noble and most wise, very much-beloved and highly esteemed Brother.

Brother will without doubt remember very well how often I have earlier given assurances that I would spare my dear mother any further expense, if only I might be so fortunate as to reach Lieutenant Coler. He will also have understood from my first letter that I had not expected to ask my dear mother for a single heller for a half-year.[148] That I have so far not done so, and that Brother has truly witnessed it, pleases me greatly. But that I cannot now keep my promise, as I might wish, is very painful to me. But if Brother would observe, first, that I have until now not had any way to make money in this garrison, [then he may appreciate] how sparing and frugal I have had to be, if my weekly board were not forthcoming at the mustering camp. From the enclosed list of my expenditures to date, Brother can easily judge that I have nonetheless saved more than thirty-six Reichsthaler.[149] He can also see that I have made every possible effort to keep my promise and avoid all [unnecessary] expenditures. If I still had my previous [prodigal] disposition, I truly would not have spent this money in such a [responsible] way. Considering this, I hope Brother will look all the less askance at the following request: For inasmuch as I have until now made the best possible effort to keep my promise [to Mother], I very humbly ask Brother to show me his favor and do his best

148. See letter 42.
149. Enclosure not extant. It is clear from letter 43 that Stephan Carl was at least thirty-one Reichsthaler in arrears.

to put in a good word for me with my dear mother on this matter, so that enough money [to meet my needs] may be made available to me at the upcoming Frankfurt fair by way of Herr Abraham de Braa.[150] Then, like my comrades, I may be able to attire myself honorably. By no means do I prescribe any set amount. Brother will be able to learn from cousin Gammersfelder what his son has been given, likewise from Herr Gugel at the Registry what his cousin has received to date in clothing from Lieutenant [Coler],[151] and thereby confirm my request. I am counting on Brother personally to see that I lack nothing that I need and that I am not handicapped now that I have this opportunity. When I move among counts, lords, generals, first lieutenants, and other cavalrymen, as I now must do daily, I should not have to do so dressed contrary to my profession, namely, that of soldiering. I need to buy clothes for myself at this time, both in preparation for Easter and for the impending summer. God helping, Brother should certainly expect me to keep my expenditures for the rest of the year at a minimum. Because of my great need now, I have held nothing back from Brother.

I humbly commend Brother and his dear wife and children, whom I ask that he greet warmly on my behalf, to the continuing care and favor of the Highest. From Mainz, in haste, 19 March, 1633.

    In due service to Brother,

    Stephan Carl Behaim

P.S. Just as I am sealing this letter, Lieutenant Coler is being notified to make ready, for we will shortly have to go on maneuvers. So again I ask Brother to act now so that I may receive this money at the earliest.

[P.S.] Much-beloved and highly honored Brother, I have just now [29 March] returned from Hardenburg, again to find my letter still lying here.[152] Not only does this give me heartache, but inasmuch as this also happened with my first letter,[153] Brother, my dear mother, and my highly esteemed cousin Baier will think that such [delay] occurs only because of

---

150. De Braa was an influential banker in Amsterdam who from this point was Stephan Carl's main contact for money there and in Mainz. His name is variously given as de Bra and de Bray.

151. The reference is to youths from Nuremberg who also are serving with Coler's regiment in the royal Swedish army.

152. A completed letter often did not get mailed immediately, and in the meantime several additions might be made. Stephan Carl's experience suggests that personal mail to and from military camps was especially slow.

153. Letter 42.

my sloth and carelessness. But God knows, and may He punish my soul [if I lie], such letters were written long ago. If Brother will only consider that, because of the delay, the opportunity to give Herr Ab[raham] de Braa verbal instructions to provide me the money I need has now been lost,[154] then he can easily deduce that this must also be happening against my will.

So it is now my very humble and urgent request that Brother and cousin Baier, together with my dear [mother], make arrangements by return mail for either Lieutenant Coler or Herr Ab[raham] de Braa to be asked to give me at my request as much money as I will show them I need for the fair in Frankfurt so that I can clothe myself honorably. [I ask this also] in the awareness that if clothes are not bought at this fair, and we should break camp before Easter, for such is imminent, then you would truly regret it, for my clothes will cost twelve Reichsthaler more [if I buy them later]. So I look forward to all the more helpful and certain compliance. I am willing to earn and repay such [money as you give me] by dutiful and obedient service.

May I ask Brother to let my dear and highly esteemed mother and cousin Baier also read this postscript? Otherwise, I would have to open all the other letters again.[155] May God be with us. Mainz, in haste, the 29th.

45 ❦ Hans Christoph Coler to Lucas Friederich, 11 April 1633

It is always my pleasure to serve you willingly, noble, esteemed, prudent, wise, very gracious dear friend and brother.[156]

I have received your letter of 11 April by the new [Gregorian] calendar, together with your enclosure. Having carefully noted their contents, I can report to my dear friend that I am indeed well satisfied with his brother. But I hold him to a strict discipline. After he had run away from me once, I wanted to turn him over to the military police the second time (only

154. Apparently the opportunity existed while Lucas Friederich and de Braa were meeting in Nuremberg.
155. Stephan Carl has written separate, identical letters to each, none of which got mailed in his absence.
156. Close friendship is meant. Hans Christoph and Lucas Friederich were distantly related by Coler's marriage to Elenora Scheurl.

pro forma). However, he pleaded so earnestly to be spared and promised not to do it again. To this day he has kept his promise. My dear friend may also be assured that I tolerate neither his nor the other boys' getting drunk outside my lodging. When someone wants a drink after a meal, or when an ensign or another officer comes to [one of] my guards, my guards have orders to give them enough to drink, and I overlook the bill. I do find, however, that Stephan Carl goes to the barber too often. I really know nothing about his laundress, except that I certainly regret it when I have to pay six heller to have a shirt washed. Because the burghers must make such heavy contributions [to the war], in addition to quartering [soldiers], the smith and the other artisans here are doubly expensive.

[Beyond these expenditures], I have given Stephan Carl [a total of] nine Reichsthaler over the six months [he has been with me], but always on condition that he first tell me what he needs the money for. His clothes have become completely threadbare. Because all the boys must do four watches and sleep on benches, they wear out more clothes than they otherwise would. His sword [also] has not been of much use. Since Stephan Carl is now away from Nuremberg, and my dear friend writes to me that I should buy him clothes only as he needs them and not merely for show, I will, God willing, go with him and [his fellow musketeer] Gugel to Frankfurt next week and buy them clothes as their need requires. Stephan Carl gave me the enclosed specification of what he needs, all of which I observe he truly does need. What I spend on him my dear friend can repay me through my brother-in-law Christian Scheurl.[157]

As for military exercises, Stephan Carl got on awkwardly at first with the muskets, but he is now getting better. My good friend may be assured that I will neglect nothing that serves his brother's advancement, [and he will be treated] as if he were my very own child.

I will write to you each week any news here, just as if my dear friend were privy to the council minutes. But my dear friend will learn from my deeds, not words, that I am his servant and friend.

Commending [you] to God, with sincere greetings I remain
the servant of my dear friend and brother,
Hans Christoph Coler, First Lieutenant
Mainz, 11 April,
by the old calendar,
1633

157. Christian (1601–77) was an official in Nuremberg and Elenora's brother. See n. 134.

46 ❦ Hans Christoph Coler to Lucas Friederich, 22 April 1633

It is always my pleasure to serve you willingly and as a dear friend, noble, esteemed, prudent, wise, very gracious dear friend and brother.

I am sorry that Stephan Carl's frugal brother must spend so much money [on him]. But now that he has been very well clothed you may be assured that I will ride herd on him. He shall incur no debts beyond those he makes with me. When he needs money for laundry, the smith, or the saddler, I will give it to him. No longer may he go so often to the barber. I will give him a handsome haircut myself. He has been in need of a suit of clothes, so I am having a good, sleeved elk leather jacket and a pair of gray trousers made for him. The [new] sword costs six Reichs-thaler, but it is beautiful and of good quality. If that is too expensive, I will gladly keep it [for myself] and buy him a lesser one and deduct the money for it. Altogether Stephan Carl will [have] run up seventy-three Reichsthaler on my dear friend's account, which I ask you to deliver to my brother-in-law Christian Scheurl. I have not had so much money that I could help both my dear friend's brother and [young] Gugel [at the same time]. So I have had to borrow sixty Reichsthaler from Herr Elischbein.

Commending you to God and with humble greeting, I remain
> my dear friend and brother's
> w[illing] s[ervant],
> Hans Christoph Coler, First Lieutenant

47 ❦ Stephan Carl to Lucas Friederich, 17 April 1634[158]

My due and willing service and brotherly love and loyalty to the best of my ability always, noble and very wise, very much-beloved and highly esteemed Brother.

With great sadness, I cannot let go unreported that on the fourth day of Easter, namely 9 April, between four and five a.m., we were unfortu-nately attacked in Neustadt an der Heid [near Coburg] by imperial forces, four hundred cavalry and two hundred infantry strong, drawn from all the regiments around Eger [Cheb] and Hof in Vogtland. They plundered us utterly, and I was taken captive to Kronach with my Lieutenant and other riders. To a man, we lost our horses, clothes, and other things. In

158. A year has passed since Stephan Carl's last letter. He is now with a regiment in Bavaria.

one hour everything was gone. May God have mercy. I could, indeed, have escaped this great misfortune, for I was on the verge of mounting my horse in the very minutes when the Croatians struck my street, a misfortune I was, of course, completely unaware of at the time.[159] Without doubt, it was God's special will and destiny that I too fall into the hands of the Croatians and have to suffer extreme punishment and chastisement.

As great as this misfortune has been for me, I have still richly experienced God's special help. As the Croatians and Germans quarreled for a long time [over whose prisoner I was], and it dawned on the Croatians that the Germans outnumbered them, a Croatian behind me wanted the rest [of the Croatians] to depart. Having observed this, a German menacingly proposed to give the Croatians a bullet. While this [wrangling] went on, the Germans led me away, and thus I have been their prisoner. But to tell the truth, every honor and courtesy has been shown me in Kronach, and God knows, I have not been able to marvel over it enough. For on Sunday the thirteenth of April, the burghers of Kronach became completely rebellious and, to the amazement of all, wanted to storm the castle there and, above all, to slay me and my Lieutenant. I owe my life to Herr Heuss, the captain of the cavalry, whose prisoner I was, and to all his riders, whose good instruction allowed me to escape unharmed the [mob's] hands and clubs.

This rebellion occurred because the commander of the castle had at another time (not unreasonably) arranged to bring our herald, who had been sent [to Kronach] on our behalf, into the castle without consulting the burghers. Suspecting some trickery, the burghers not only knocked our herald from his horse and beat him to the point that he now lies near death in Coburg, but they also wanted to destroy the castle completely and by all means drag out and kill its commander, whom they call the black captain. At this point, the commander summoned his company together and wanted to ride down those responsible. But knowing their devilish tricks, he dared not.

There is still another reason why I must see God's special help in this. At first, on the recommendation of my countrymen who serve on the imperial side, my ransom was set at two hundred Reichsthaler. In the end I arranged with cavalry captain Heuss to be freed on the fourteenth of this month for twenty-five Reichsthaler, and these on my word, and escorted a mile away by six riders.

159. The Croatians were mercenaries fighting with imperial forces.

So I have had great misfortune with my imprisonment, but also not a little luck, for, praise God, I was confined for only six days and all that time I was treated very well. God's grace also saved me from various threats to my body and life. Indeed, I experienced things for which I would not soon take twenty-five Reichsthaler.

As for all this, I can easily imagine that my much-beloved and highly esteemed mother is now very much concerned, saddened, and dismayed by the loss of all my possessions and fearing that she will be asked to help me replace these things. However, recently in Nuremberg I very much obligated myself henceforth to cause my mother no further expense whatsoever, and I will not now break that promise, even to help myself in this [my hour of] greatest need. The Burghermeister and council [of Hülburg where we are now quartered] have desired a letter of safe conduct, and I have already spoken to my cavalry master about entrusting it to me. He has promised it to me and another rider as soon as we march from here to [our camps in] Straiffdorf and Rossfield. [For such service] the city will gladly restore my ransom and, in addition, fittingly resupply me with the things I have lost. So it is now my most fraternal request that when the occasion presents itself Brother explain my present situation to my mother and assure her that she will for sure not have to give me the smallest heller at this time of my greatest loss. I still live entirely in the hope of someday coming to her aid. I also expect to regain very quickly all that the enemy has taken from me, and with interest.[160] I would gladly have written to Mother myself, but for many reasons I felt Brother should first learn about this.

I wish Brother, his very dear wife, his dear sons and daughters, and all other relatives and acquaintances continuing health and all the comforts of good fortune under the care of the Highest, and I ask him to greet everyone warmly for me and freely extend to each my love and kindness.

From quarters in Hülburg, in great haste, 17 April, 1634.

Brother's loyal and most obligated servant,

Stephan Carl Behaim

P.S. Much-beloved and highly esteemed Brother, I know for sure that my Hans has neither been captured nor shot.[161] So I fully suspect that he has returned to Nuremberg with the mailman. I simply cannot do without him at the present time. So if he is in Nuremberg, it is my most fraternal request that he be instructed to send me a good passport as soon as

160. That is, by way of booty.
161. Hans was a personal servant or aide.

possible [   ] and that he be told that I might well wish to have him come back to Coburg with the carters who transport grain to Nuremberg. In Coburg, he will be able to learn from Herr Ayermann, who lodges at The Swan, where our company may be found. Provided we are not again, as happened in Neustadt, put to flight by the enemy, there is reason to believe that we will not soon be leaving the Coburg area. If, however, against all hope, my Hans should not be there, then I ask that an answer |to my letter| be vouchsafed here as quickly as possible and sent only to Herr Ayermann in Coburg. Write on it: "Inquire among Herr cavalry master Adolph's company." Ayermann will already know how to transmit it to me promptly. Dated as in the letter.

48 ❦ Stephan Carl to Lucas Friederich, 24 May 1634

Much-beloved and highly esteemed Brother. I am writing this quick note only so that these two riders, who are being sent in a hurry to the cavalry master in Nuremberg because of the death of my lieutenant here, will be able all the sooner to deliver the enclosed letter to Mother. Because they say they know absolutely nothing of Nuremberg, I fear they will be unable to find either the cavalry master's or Mother's house. So it is my sincere fraternal request that Brother direct these two riders to my cavalry master's brother's house, so that they do not ride around the city for a long time.

I also urgently ask Brother, as before, to remember my humble person in the best way to my cavalry master whenever the opportunity presents itself, for I very much need his help at the present time to resupply myself.

I wish Brother, his very dear wife, and his dear sons and daughters continuing health and all the comforts of good fortune under the care of the Highest, and I ask that he greet them all warmly for me and extend to each my love and kindness.

In great haste, from quarters in Rossfield, 27 May, 1634.
Brother's most obliged servant,
Stephan Carl Behaim

49 ❦ Stephan Carl to Lucas Friederich, 14 July 1634

My due obedient service and brotherly love and loyalty to the best of my ability always, noble and very wise, very much-beloved and highly esteemed Brother.

With not a little sadness, I must unfortunately learn from my dear sisters, Frau Thomas Tucher,[162] Magdalena, and Maria Helena, that someone in Nuremberg, very much to my detriment, has taken it upon himself to tell people there how I, in a completely blameless way, stabbed a herald to death. Because this person knows nothing at all about the incident and is telling it all wrong, and I have a duty to demonstrate my innocence, I am herewith in great haste reporting the entire matter to Brother.

When I last rode from Nuremberg with my cavalry master, I was invited with others to dinner by Commander Brincken outside Anerbach, which was at the time under siege by General Major Vitztum. After dinner, the now dead [herald] Valentin had spoken these words to me: "Now, once again, Behaim has warmed and stuffed himself and played the toady to the full." Because I had other business to attend to under orders from my cavalry master, I replied that he should "address me respectfully" and that he did not know what he was doing. He then asked me if I was speaking to him. I answered, yes. Whereupon he lashed out at me, as a drunken man does, with these irresponsible words: "It is no honest fellow who demands this of me, but rather a scoundrel." He said he would rather not carry the trumpet [than to address me respectfully]. The stench about him was such that I left.

Because he was drunk and still a youth, I thought it best to report the incident to the cavalry master. But because he had a very important commission from General Major Vitztum, it could not be done either on the same or the following day. My cavalry master had to depart hurriedly on the mail coach from Bayreuth to meet with our princes. [While away] he entrusted his horse to my care, and I did my best to accommodate him. But mindful of the crazed mind of the late Valentin whenever he got drunk (a vice to which he easily let himself succumb), I took [new] quarters with another burgher in town as a precaution against very serious conflict.

The next morning I could easily see that the day would not pass without a brawl. I was completely alone and, by no fault of mine, had made many enemies within the company, especially our Herr First Lieutenant Herald [Valentin]. So, in God's name, I went first to church and there I prayed humbly to God for his help and sure support against my enemies

162. Stephan Carl's sister Susanna Sabina (1600–1667) became Frau Thomas Tucker on 3 February 1634.

and I most faithfully commended my soul to Him. Then, in the Lord's name, I set forth [with my company].

As we came to Kulmbach, Duke Bernhard [of Weimar's] quartermaster, valet, and other princely servants stopped for a drink. It was at this [moment] that my good late Valentin slipped away from me and got drunk out of his mind. I waited a long time for him to return, but he would not come back with the horse, so I rode to the inn where he was. I said not a word to him, but spoke only to the cavalry master's youths and to the other riders he had sent me. I told them they should make haste, that it was time to go, that we would otherwise not reach our quarters outside Kronach today, and, failing to do so, would have to explain ourselves to the cavalry master. The late Valentin then began to speak these rude words (to paraphrase them honorably): "He who will not wait, let him lick this and lick that," gesturing all the time as if he would at any moment strike me in the neck. I did not acknowledge him, but acted as if I neither heard nor saw it. Then I climbed back on my horse. He followed me all the way out the door and called out the same words after me.

As we reached the outskirts of town and I rode somewhat behind the others on my cavalry master's horse, the late Valentin came riding toward me, completely unseen, at full gallop, his pistol drawn, and he took a shot at me. As the bullet passed through my coat and I realized I was in the greatest danger, I grabbed my pistol. But then I thought how hard it would be for me to live with the knowledge that I had in such fashion executed this drunken man outright in all his sins. So I returned my pistol and set my sword to his heart and said to him, "Do you now see that, after God, your life is in my hands? Tell me now if you still hold me to be the scoundrel you earlier said I was." At this, he again answered most obstinately.

Now, my highly esteemed Brother, tell me who could treat such irresponsible and intolerable insults and expressed violence as unintended and ignore them? I ask all reasonable people whether I acted wrongly when I then brought my sword down on his head. I did not do so with any intention of taking his life, as his wounds have since proven. As God knows and is my witness, I struck him only to accomplish two things. First, so that those present would have no reason to dread drinking out of the same can with me or elsewhere proclaim me to be [the scoundrel] the late Valentin had unjustly accused me of being; secondly, so that I might be spared such irresponsible insults [from Valentin] until we had rejoined the cavalry master.

This, then, is the entire incident as it actually happened. To respond to that person in Nuremberg who now most falsely and untruly relates the incident as if I were responsible for Valentin's death, I say to one and all that there is no basis in fact for such a statement. For (as I shall now report) when the aforementioned late Valentin first became deathly ill, it was due neither to the wound I had inflicted on his head nor to any he had inflicted on himself [during the conflict with me]. To be specific, on the very next day, as we approached Kronach, he paid no particular attention to his wounds, and he made his rounds for the most part. He did the same in Coburg. There the wound I had given him healed right away. But the one to his hand, which he had inflicted on himself by grabbing my sword, would not at first heal. It finally did so, however, under the care of a new bath surgeon. As I sat imprisoned in Kronbach (so I have been told), he returned to the company and forthwith made his rounds again. He also continued to drink all too much, in spite of warnings from a good friend. He said it did not matter any more, for who knew when he could avenge himself. Thereafter, he reopened the wound in his hand and returned to Coburg. It was there, more than two months after [his conflict with me], that he passed away to God, his life having ended.

From my telling of the whole story, I hope everyone can now readily conclude that I defended myself only after very considerable provocation and that I was justified in doing so, also that no one will now attribute any great wrong to me because of the incident, much less hold me responsible for his death. Consider also that I have told this story to various reasonable people, both clergymen and laymen, and the clergy always comment that if the incident truly occurred as I have said, then [my role] notwithstanding, the death was much more the fault of the deceased and, after him, without any doubt, the attending physicians. Laymen [to whom I have recounted the story] respond that I acted very properly and that I am to be praised for my long-suffering and proven discretion, also that they would not have blamed me in the least had I, in self-defense, run him through with my sword immediately. I assure Brother that my cavalry master would definitely not have let me walk away from the incident unpunished, had he not weighed it carefully and well. As many must attest, he is truly the kind of conscientious cavalryman who would most certainly not let the spilling of innocent blood go unpunished.

My entire hope now is that, having heard this true account of the incident, Brother will by his great discretion easily conclude that my action was necessary both for my own self-defense and to prevent the regiment from continuing to mock and ridicule me to the great dishonor of my entirely praiseworthy family. I hope Brother will now dismiss completely his unquestionable but also premature anger, displeasure, and disapproval of me. And if, against hope, my highly esteemed mother should have learned of the incident, I hope Brother will now share with her, in the most positive way for her own consolation, my justification of my action. And may Brother, too, as he has [always] done, continue to hold me in fraternal favor and affection. I ask this above all and without the slightest doubt that it will be done.

I know for sure that when Brother reads this letter he will have the [following] thoughts, [namely] that if all of this is true, not only can no blame whatsoever be assigned to me for the death of the late Valentin, but one must rather rejoice that I turned away such expressed violence and slanderous insults with so much discretion, while at the same time safeguarding the purity of my conscience.

There is no surer way to force a person to confirm something than by having him swear an oath. My absence [from Nuremberg] makes it impossible for me to do this now. In the meantime, I swear before God the Highest that as truly as I desire to enter the Kingdom of God and be saved, not a single untrue or false word has here been written. The same [story] can also be heard at any time from my cavalry master and from others here [who know the facts]. I have not neglected to tell Brother the truth.

I commend Brother and all his loved ones to the care of the Highest and myself to his continuing kindness. In haste, from quarters in Straiffdorf, 14 July, 1634.

    Stephan Carl Behaim

50 🐌 Stephan Carl to Lucas Friederich, 12 September 1634

Much-beloved Brother Lucas Friederich.

I must herewith briefly report to Brother that I have been shot. During the most recent engagement with the enemy near Nördlingen, my cavalry master, a few riders, and I came upon Croatians, and I received a near-fatal wound in my left side near my heart. My cavalry master was also very seriously wounded in his stomach. I would scarcely have escaped had God the Highest not stood by me and strengthened my arm and hand. An entire enemy regiment surrounded me; one had me by the throat, another by my left arm, and a third around my waist trying to wrestle me from my horse. But God the Highest and Strongest stood by me, so that, praise God, I valiantly resisted them all. Many have praised God and honored me for my valor and are still doing so now.

But with my great good fortune has come also not a little bad luck. Now that I am again, with great difficulty, somewhat able to clothe myself and to ride, I can no longer wear the clothes I was then wearing. They were so filled with blood that they are now completely stiff and it is impossible to put them on or to wash them out any more. And not only my clothes. I had no money whatsoever [after the incident], but because of my wound, I could not forgo any expense. I had to pay eight Reichsthaler a week in Stuttgart for my medicine, three for my board, and two to feed my horse. As a result, I was forced to sell my white horse in Heilbronn. Since it was impossible for me to go on from there without him, I then had to take a coach and travel [by boat] on the Rhine and Main to Frankfurt, until, praise God, I arrived today at our quarters in Obernburg in rather good physical condition.

I wanted to inform Brother of these events as soon as possible and leave absolutely nothing out. I would gladly have reported the entire course of events from beginning to end immediately, but, as God knows, I have been too weak to write or even to dictate until today.

I ask Brother very sincerely and urgently to report these events to my mother and [to tell her] that I am, praise God, no longer in any distress. Praise God, I now have no further need, if only I can come by a horse and some clothes. Because over the last half year almighty God has helped me, I have been able, praise God, to meet all my needs adequately without burdening my conscience, [that is] without a single act of theft or plundering, or deceiving a single person (which I can in truth write and say, praise God). I live entirely in the hope that my gracious God and Father will also not forsake me now, but will impart to me in my [hour of] greatest need everything my survival requires and inspire good people to help me. If He will do such a work of mercy for me, I will not be forced again against my promise to ask my much-beloved and highly esteemed mother for money.

Beyond this, I can report to Brother that I saw our cousin, Hans Endres. This occurred at daybreak when on order from our General, Duke Bernhard [of Weimar], my cavalry master rode alone with his company to engage the most recently arriving enemy troops. It was, however, impossible for me to speak to him. Whether he remained with Colonel Lorwald (with whom I saw him stop) and subsequently died with him at that place [Nördlingen], I cannot say. (The imperial soldiers buried Colonel Lorwald with much ceremony.)[163] I always keep an eye out for [cousin Endres] and ask about him, but I can get no information.

Finally, I very urgently ask Brother, if possible, to find me a proven loyal servant and send him to Duke Bernhard's army and regiment immediately. I have written sister Maria Helena about this several times, but my letters accomplish nothing. I have to this very hour had to live at no small disadvantage [for want of a servant], and it is impossible for me to go on without one. I assure Brother that nothing could be more useful and beneficial to me at this point than a loyal servant. If I should not get one soon, not only can I not continue, but I will be forced to end my military career, and I do not know what I will do then.

My entire hope is that Brother will oblige me in this as soon as possible both in writing and by action. Just send the person to Frankfurt or Obernburg. Forgive me for writing at this time so confusedly and poorly. Hopefully my next letter will be better.

Herewith, in great haste, I commend all to God in complete trust. Obernburg, 12 September, 1634.

S[tephan] C[arl] Behaim.

51 ❦ Stephan Carl to Lucas Friederich, 8 November 1634

My due and obedient service to the best of my ability always, noble, high, most wise, and very much-beloved Brother.

On 2| |October, Georg Philip Pömer delivered Brother's dear reply to me, written on my birthday, Michaelmas, and it has given me very great joy to read his expression of sympathy for my misfortune. For this, I want, first of all, to thank Brother very much. I am also especially grateful to Brother for having made the effort, when an especially good opportunity arose, to honor me with a letter during these (may God have mercy) very dangerous times. God knows, there is nothing in the world that could please me more than to live to see the happy hour when I learn that my much-beloved mother, my esteemed brother, his dear wife, sons and daughters, my dear siblings, and our entire family, excepting our dear sister Apell,[164] who now rests in God, are still alive and in good

163. The battle at Nördlingen cost the Swedes an enormous number of lives. It was customary for opposing sides to honor high-ranking officers; hence the ceremonial burial of Colonel Lorwald.
164. Apollonia (1603–34).

health. I pray from my heart that God the Highest will continue to give our family such grace. I also ask God daily to allow my much-beloved mother and my entire family to know honor and joy in me before Mother dies. To this end I will definitely not spare any effort, day or night, to the fullest extent of my industry and ability. I live entirely in the hope that God will not forget me and that He will someday exalt me to [a position of] honor.

I also live entirely in the hope that my much-beloved brother will all the sooner forgive me when [I tell him that] I have, with the greatest reluctance (God as my witness), borrowed much more money than he prescribed for me. Considering that I have now and again had to spend the [allotted] twenty Reichsthaler, I have begged thirty [more] from several merchants. Few indeed were willing to give me money for my most pressing and persistent needs, indicating that they feared Brother's anger and severity if they did, even though it would have been impossible for me at this time to outfit myself more humbly and simply than I have. I certainly would not have gotten a horse at the great horse fair, where one customarily pays in Bohemian groschen, had I not [borrowed beyond Brother's limit], paid in advance, and paraded myself [properly attired] on horseback. But, praise God, I have not the slightest doubt that, God helping, I will recover what I have in this case twice lost.[165] With my cavalry master as my witness, I will now devote the greatest energy to repaying all this [borrowed money], so that you may continue to know by my deeds that there is nothing I want more than to honor my pledge to do what is necessary [to spare Mother further expense]. I would gladly from my heart simply have suffered [and not have borrowed any money], but the shortness of time made it impossible. You should not have the slightest doubt, however, about my firm resolve to repay this money.

As for my present situation, it is not without reason that Herr Ochsenfelder's son reported [to you] that I was definitely dead and, according to others, buried in Heilbronn. However, by God's grace, I am already so well and strong that I have, praise God, nothing to complain about. May God the Highest always graciously be with us all.

In my letter of 28 September, from Frankfurt,[166] I informed my much-beloved brother about our dear cousin Hans Endres as soon as I had learned the circumstances and reason [of his death] from the late Colonel Lorwald's surviving troops. [According to them] he was shot repeatedly

165. First by being shot, then by borrowing heavily.
166. Not extant.

through the head near Nördlingen, after having gone there under orders from Colonel Lorwald to alert a captain of impending danger. He ended his life on the [battlefield] with his colonel . . . I have never been able to catch sight of his servant, but I am told, again by the late Colonel Lorwald's surviving troops, that he sold everything cousin Endres left behind and is now living in Frankfurt. I thought it fitting that I should let Brother know all these matters again.

I dutifully and urgently ask Brother to dispatch with forbearance and assurance all those who present to him my signature for money I have received. My entire hope to God, in which I constantly live, is to repay all these bills myself. I can easily imagine that it would now be impossible for Mother to pay off such bills. I assure my brother that I am now truly resolved to become something or nothing, to put it briefly.

Would my brother at his convenience safely deliver the enclosed letter for Herr Adolph Dümler? He attaches a great deal of importance to it. He lies still at this hour in Worms in the same place. Unfortunately there is little hope for him. Inquire about Frau Baumgartner at St. Lorenz's [church].[167]

In great haste and with complete trust, I herewith commend Brother and all my relatives to God's care. From Bischofsheim,

8 November, 1634.

> Brother's most obligated and obedient servant,
> Stephan Carl Behaim

---

167. Herr Dümler's letter apparently concerned Frau Baumgartner.

Stephan Carl quit the war in Bavaria and made his way to Amsterdam in the summer 1635, where the plotting and prodding of his brother and Abraham de Braa led him to sign on with the Dutch West India Company for service in Brazil. He went as a low-ranking officer in a musketeer unit, but with the promise of an opportunity to become a cavalryman in the New Land. In late November he boarded a ship called the *Harlem*, which made its way north to Texel. There the ship joined a convoy of other vessels, some going east, some west, to await a favorable wind down the English Channel to the Spanish sea. The wait proved long. The *Harlem* lay at anchor in Texel for more than two months, not leaving for Brazil until February 1636. Stephan Carl passed his time fighting illness and amassing the necessities of a voyager to the New Land.

Amsterdam was among Europe's most expensive cities, and Stephan Carl was a willing player. Before boarding the *Harlem* he spent a Reichsthaler a day by de Braa's accounting. De Braa recognized Stephan Carl's profligacy and his family's desire to be rid of him; he sent Lucas Friederich a final bill for 194 Reichsthaler. There is every evidence that Stephan Carl's family did not soon reimburse de Braa for this considerable sum,[168] which had been spent over not much more than four months, and despite all of Lucas Friederich's precautions. When Stephan Carl arrived in Amsterdam the word was already out not to lend him money. The plan was to have him sign on with either the Dutch East India Company or the Dutch West India Company; this would have made him self-sufficient, for each company paid its employees monthly wages in addition to board. But de Braa had received such negative reports about Stephan Carl from Lucas Friederich that he did not at first take his inquiries on his brother's behalf seriously, with the result that his efforts to find Stephan Carl employment developed only slowly, notwithstanding his disclaimers. De Braa's surveillance of Stephan Carl seems also to have been tardier and less conscientious than he maintained in his letters to Lucas Friederich. A widower, de Braa was in these months understandably distracted, for he was contemplating a second marriage. But neither was Stephan Carl himself in any hurry to

---

168. See nn. 195, 223.

trade the sure pleasures of urban life for the uncertainty of life at sea. He dawdled and played for as long as he could before a mountain of debt forced him to seek employment. Rebuffed by his customary middlemen, including de Braa, he was soon in full cry against them. He blamed all his troubles and shortcomings on greedy merchants and stingy lenders. His reluctant creditors forced him to do again what he said he liked least, yet clearly did best: beg his mother and brother for more money and understanding of his unauthorized borrowing.

52 ❦ Abraham de Braa to Lucas Friederich, 27 March 1635

My willing service to the best of my ability always, noble, esteemed, prudent, wise, very gracious, and dear Sir.

I have read your letter of 21 February and learned with much sorrow about the deteriorating military situation there, for which I have heartfelt sympathy. I pray that dear God will so manage affairs there that the enemy may not do as he pleases. The good imperial cities are certainly poorly led. May God stand with them and with all who are oppressed. May he also forgive those who now, for the sake of their own shameful gain bring such misfortune upon so many thousands of people.

I am also unhappy to learn that your brother, Stephan Carl, conducts himself so poorly and that you wish my humble advice on how he might find a place on a scheduled voyage from [Amsterdam] and also how he might [best] be brought here from [Frankfurt]. I can tell you that people are taken into service here for the East Indies twice a year. They must promise to serve seven years there, and the voyage is toilsome, requiring six or seven months at sea. Because ships from the East Indies are expected here in June, no ships will set sail [after then] from here before October or November.

The voyage to the West Indies or Brazil is shorter and more tolerable, with approximately two months at sea. [Those who hire on] pledge themselves to only four years of service. Both companies provide board and pay wages. And both have so many applicants that it requires a very great effort to accommodate them all. I will, however, have an edge in finding Stephan Carl a place. But I can offer him little hope of going as a shipman because he has no previous service [at sea]. He will have to go initially as a soldier. But if he conducts himself well, he will advance easily once he is there, and much sooner in the West than in the East Indies.

Given the present situation in the empire, I do not know what advice to give you on moving him here. If he is coming from Frankfurt, I would think he could not do so without Prussian, Swedish, French, electoral Colognese, and Dutch letters of safe conduct, which will cost plenty. Then, once here, should he not choose to report freely to one of the companies and enlist, he will be forced by circumstances to do so. For as long as he does not sign on and get paid, he will be without income, while having to live here [in Amsterdam], where everything is very expensive. Last summer a Tucher [from Nuremberg] settled here and signed on with the West India Company, but thereafter did not want to go.[169] So the chairman called a meeting of the Commission,[170] and many people had to trouble themselves to force him to go on board. Otherwise, there would have been a debacle. So everything had to be reconciled by mediation.

If you want to attempt to send Stephan Carl here now, and can constrain him to enlist freely [once he arrives], I will gladly do my part to help him in this and much more. I can advise him on how to keep his expenses at a minimum, and I will see that he does not flee [Amsterdam], but goes on board ship.

As for my own situation, I am now living alone and poorly with my one daughter, who is fourteen, and a servant, who is my cousin. I take my board with a widow, who treats me very well. I must learn to get used to it and be patient, until I arrange my affairs better and can venture forth again. The war now dictates everything. But because it pleases God, I accept it from his hand. May he also help bring it to an end. Into his gracious care and protection I herewith commend you and your family.

Remaining your diligent servant always,

Abraham de Braa

Amsterdam, 27 March, 1635

53 ❦ Stephan Carl to Mother, 21 August 1635

My due, obedient service and inborn filial love and loyalty to the best of my ability always, noble, very honored, richly virtuous, much-beloved, and highly esteemed Mother.

169. Perhaps this is Moritz Tucher (1621–1637).
170. The reference is to the so-called Heeren XIX, or nineteen directors of the West India Company. The company was incorporated on 3 June 1621 strictly as a mercenary venture, after a decade of successful Dutch poaching to Iberia's detriment in Brazil. Sugar was the main object, along with cotton and wood.

If I may learn from my mother that she, my dear brothers and sisters, and the entire family have been healthy and all has gone well for them over this very long period of time when I have heard not a word about them, then that is for me a joy greater than any I can know on earth (next to spiritual joy). As for myself, ever since the wound I received in Nördlingen quickly healed, I have remained to this very hour in good health, thanks to God, although I have been all this time in very unhappy circumstances. May God the Highest graciously be and remain with us all until our last and blessed end.

Dear Mother, to make for you and report to you more joy than suffering would be the fairest and most dutiful thing I could do. I shall remain the world's most unhappy person until this happens. Someday I hope to send Mother a happy letter about the great good fortune God has bestowed upon me. But I must now again, unfortunately, write far more about misfortune than about good fortune. I had hoped that fleeting and fickle fortune would by now somewhat have raged itself out against me. Since my youth I have wanted just once to experience such good fortune that my mother might know true joy [in me]. This was foremost in my mind when I fought in the war with the infantry (I entered military service solely for that reason). For a long time, I have thought that just as a mild and pleasant summer customarily follows a hard, severe winter, so God might bestow somewhat better fortune on me in the cavalry—like the examples in history books and in my present experience. Unfortunately, I have been deceived in this good hope. [Since joining the cavalry], I have twice been taken prisoner and three times I have lost everything. And it is easy for me to see that my mother has been extremely inconvenienced by the not small number of [financial] transactions I have had to make each time to replace what I lost. I can only say that heaven, earth, and all the elements have conspired to bring this suffering, cross, and misfortune upon me, [and such will continue] as long as I remain in Germany and in the Swedish war, which has brought me nothing but misfortune. I have, therefore, been forced to choose between two evils.[171]

Often I have wished and proposed to end once and for all the expense I cause my mother. But as much as I have wanted to do this, I am always prevented by the greatest misfortune. But so that my mother may see and recognize that nothing has been more on my mind, I have in God's name and with the foreknowledge of Herr Tetzel and Herr Löffelholz,

171. Namely, to remain in the cavalry or to flee to the Netherlands and take passage to the West Indies.

and after notifying Brother Lucas Friederich, quit the Swedish war, which has never brought me any good fortune whatsoever.[172] And fearing no danger, misfortune, or effort, I have now betaken myself to Holland to seek my fortune among the most powerful of cities. [Here I shall] make myself strong so that Mother may truly know that this time I am for sure and without any doubt making the supreme effort never again in my life to be a burden to her.

I am disinclined to serve [again] on land, for getting reoutfitted would cost a lot. So I have in the name of the Lord decided to enter service at sea in the West Indies. The Lord has wondrously led me here not only through an enemy who surrounded me on all sides and against the ever-treacherous Rhine, but also past the wanton and godless peasants of Koll and Trier and around deserted soldiers who murder and plunder people everywhere in the woods. Despite the loss of my sword and coat, the awful food I have had to eat, and the twenty-eight miles I have had to go by foot through enemy territory, the Lord has accompanied me here from Frankfurt with very good fortune. I hope now to sail with the next ship to the West Indies and I will seek a recommendation from Herr [Ludwig] Camerarius.[173] As I have had prior service as an infantryman, I may be able to obtain an ensigncy.[174] [If so] I am sure I will not have to request a single heller from home for at least three years. Such a position not only pays regular monthly wages, but [as an ensign] one has also not to pay the smallest heller for food and drink. And beyond this, all reasonable unexpected expenses are covered when one has only a little money and the smallest of means. This does not include unexpected losses from gambling, a pastime I have renounced anyway, as I am against spending money I can never have. I can imagine no better way in the world to curtail all my expenses and pay off my accumulated debts [than by gaining such an ensigncy].

Although the voyage [to the West Indies] is very dangerous, it is one many thousand honest youths cheerfully undertake. I hope my plans do not displease Mother, but gratify her very much. I am doing this solely for our mutual gain and well-being. With God all things are possible. He has helped me make my perilous way here over land with much good

172. Tetzel and Löffelholz were authorities in Nuremberg deeply involved diplomatically in the war.
173. The Swedish ambassador to the Netherlands and a friend of Lucas Friederich. See n. 216.
174. The status or position of a junior officer.

fortune, whereas many cavaliers had told me it would be impossible to do so. Surely my God, who saved my life more than a hundred times while I was in the service of the Swedish crown, can by his gracious and fatherly will protect me from all the mischief, howling, and tossing of a mad, raging sea. And if with [my expected] good fortune and greater well-being, I am able to return home and serve Mother, my brothers and sisters, and the entire family as I have often wanted to do, then may all my plans and actions now be devoted to that end.

It is not without reason that people say such a voyage is as dangerous as a journey can be. No one knows if I will be permitted to write to Mother again in my lifetime. Unfortunately, it is not unknown to me that my excessive borrowing has often distressed Mother in the extreme, even though, as God knows, I have always borrowed money with extreme reluctance, sadness, and inconvenience to myself. And no one other than my dear fellow countrymen is to blame for this.[175] It is for God to have mercy on them. If I did not now have good friends in the city to whom, God willing, I will go in the morning [and there await] Mother's answer to my letter and the sailing of the West Indies ship, I could easily have experienced the same misfortune here all over again. For had I been able to save my soul and body with it, I could not get a single heller [from my usual German contacts].[176] So, for God's sake, I very sincerely ask Mother mercifully to forgive and forget all that has happened up to now in Germany. As a great evildoer and sinner can do nothing better than betake himself to a cloister, there to make amends for his evil works and to serve God alone by doing good works and surrendering all his worldly desires and actions, so I am now entering the best cloister of godliness.[177] There all worldly luxury is forgotten, and because there one best recognizes one's greatest need, no one is better served than God. I know of no better way to make amends for all that has happened in the past than by this voyage.

I live entirely in the hope that my highly esteemed mother will kindly forgive me from her heart for all the distress I have caused her in the past and not speak of it again. May she now see that I neither fear nor hesitate

175. Apparently, in Stephan Carl's mind, because they refused to give him all the money he needed to live honorably, forcing him to expand his creditors and indebtedness.
176. The word was out among Stephan Carl's well-established contacts (like de Braa) not to lend him money.
177. Stephan Carl means his voyage to the "New Land" and his tenure in a primitive new world, not the cloister of the Church fathers and Christian tradition.

to do anything humanly possible to free her of expense, make amends for her suffering, and bring her joy. While God alone knows whether I may live to read another word from my mother, I know that as soon as she receives this letter, she will write me sincere maternal congratulations and tell me how my dear Fatherland and family are faring, also who is still living and who is now dead. Since it will be at least four weeks before we sail, such a thoroughly pleasant letter can still reach me here in good order.

I could earn not a little traveling money, if I had twenty thaler to invest here in cheap goods to take with me to the West Indies. Unfortunately, I am completely broke. Also, at the very least, I must provide myself with linens, a coat, and other necessary articles [before we sail]. I have no idea where I will get a heller for this. So I want to ask Mother, in complete filial trust, and urgently, to send me twenty thaler via Abraham de Braa, if it is possible for her to do so. In return, I shall arrange for my monthly wages to be sent to Herr de Braa every quarter- or half-year (assuming God lets me live so long), and he will then transfer the money to Mother for her support and compensation.

It had very much been my hope this time to send Mother an especially well-written letter, but the shortness of time and [my need] still today to compose a letter for brother Lucas Friederich has made this impossible. I will send such a letter with the next mail. Meanwhile, I commend Mother, my dear brothers and sisters, and my entire family in complete trust to the care of the Highest and wish them all continuing health and prosperity. Amsterdam, 21 August, 1635.

Mother's obedient son for as long as I live,

S. C. Behaim

[P.S.] Because I very much need some money before we sail, and not only for my spiritual and physical needs,[178] I earnestly ask Mother to do her utmost.

54 ❦ Stephan Carl to Lucas Friederich, 10 October 1635

My due and willing service and brotherly love and loyalty to the best of my ability always, noble, high, very wise, very much-beloved, and highly esteemed Brother.

On 3 September, I very happily received Brother's dear reply of 26

---

178. Money was also needed to pay outstanding debts.

Letter from Stephan Carl to Lucas Friederich, 10 October 1635 (letter 54)

August from de Braa.[179] I have read it and, with the help of the Highest, I will truly observe its friendly brotherly reminders and admonitions,[180] as is just and fair. If the heavenly God will now just help me avoid any further dealings with merchants, I have a sure trust in God that you shall not again hear of a single borrowing [of mine] and that all past debts will be satisfied with good and gratifying letters. Again, I can only say that merchants alone are the cause of all my past misfortune and great unnecessary expenditures. They are also the reason I have been unable so far to keep my oft-made promise [to spare Mother expense]. And it is not only in Germany that I have such [difficulty]. With pain and no little dismay, I have also run into it here in Holland. For when I asked Abraham de Braa, both by humble letter and personally, for a mere four Reichsthaler to cover all my various needs so that I might travel to the camp[181] and spare myself the mounting expenses [of the city] until letters [approving additional funds] came from Brother, I could not get those four Reichsthaler from him, had I been able to save my soul with them. So for the entire time I have been here, I have had to live as a virtual prisoner in my lodgings in the city. He has not given me so much as [to be able] to wash a shirt or repair a shoe, while expense has nevertheless piled upon expense. Apart from the fact that he held Brother's letter for a long time before giving it to me,[182] I still have yet to get a good word from him on [the subject of] moving out of my present lodging and paying off my expenses, not to mention any money. The only word he has given me is that he will provide money according to need as he sees it, so that when I want money, I should make a case to him for it. I assure Brother that I would much rather talk with the greatest prince than to have to deal with him again. He thinks he is so high and mighty here; he completely ignores [my] proposals.

I am in such bad shape and so ill-equipped to keep my promise to do enough to unburden [Mother] that I must now put all my hope in God and trust that by the help of the All-Highest I may yet set sail next week with the departing ships on my West Indies voyage. Had de Braa wanted to be a help rather than a hindrance in [getting my passage], he could

179. Neither Lucas Friederich's letter nor Stephan Carl's to which he replies is extant.
180. Namely, to cease all unauthorized borrowing from merchants (as becomes clear from the letter).
181. Apparently a military camp outside the city.
182. De Braa held the letter for a week.

have done so a month ago. He has, in short, treated me in a very unreasonable and inhumane way.

Were God not with me, I would not now know what to do. I have ended the twenty-third year of my life with misfortune, but I have begun the twenty-fourth with God, fervent prayer, good hope, and resolution. If God now grants me life, with His help you will never again hear anything dishonorable about me. You are going to receive a different report on me in the future than you have gotten in the past. May God the Highest be with me and bestow his divine blessing and success upon all my good plans. Amen.

In complete trust I commend our beloved Fatherland, my highly esteemed brother, his very dear wife, his dear sons and daughters, and all our relatives, old and young, to the all-powerful care and protection of our true God and heavenly Father. From my heart I wish and ask that the merciful God himself become Regent and Housekeeper in our dear Fatherland and at all times preserve the true, soul-saving Religion[183] from corruption and turn aside and drive out all foreigners and people intent on our destruction, so that precious peace may come upon the Fatherland like a flood, and my brother, his family, and devout people everywhere may live in peace and tranquillity and good health and prosperity, until our joyful reunion some time in the future. Amen.

About our late cousin Hans Endres's death, I have learned from captured officers in the same regiment who have since returned, as well as from the late Colonel Lorwald's surviving troops, that he had been ordered by his aforementioned colonel to ride out and alert a captain of danger and assure him that more troops were on the way. But while en route to do this, our late dear cousin was shot through the head. Whether it came from a cannon or a musket, they could not say. I may never learn any more about the incident, but this much is certain.

Amsterdam, in great haste, 10 October, 1635.

S. C. Behaim

P.S. As de Braa well knows, the boatman who brought me here from Cologne received the six Reichsthaler for which I gave de Braa a receipt. Henceforth, when Brother wants to send me a letter, please address it to me here in care of Herr Hans Heinrich Bilgrom.[184] He will then arrange to have it delivered to me in the West Indies. I will not fail to send another

---

183. He means Protestantism, whether Calvinist or Lutheran.
184. Unclear who this is.

written [report] before I sail. Meanwhile, I commend [Brother] to God in complete trust.

55 ❦ Stephan Carl to Lucas Friederich, 18/28 November 1635

My due and obedient service and brotherly love and loyalty life long, noble, high, very wise, much beloved, and highly esteemed Brother.

Hopefully Brother will by now have received my reply to him and Mother, which I sent in October via Hamburg. As I then promised to write Brother before my voyage to the West Indies, I am herewith reporting that we could not get under way any sooner than last Saturday, 14/24 November. The delay was quite apart from Brother's very useful and gratifying letter to Herr de Braa, which put everything in such good order here that I have gotten everything I needed from the aforementioned Herr de Braa. For this graciously arranged command to him, I thank you most sincerely from the bottom of my heart.

However, in the intervening time, as my boarding-house keeper's bill indicates (and as I, too, can readily see), a lot of money has been irresponsibly and extravagantly spent, very much against my will and to my very great sorrow.[185] As painful as [such spending] has always been for me, and as much as I regret it, I cannot explain it. As one who is very judicious, Brother can easily see that this is very much out of character for me and has happened contrary to all my plans and against all odds. Had I run up such incalculable expenses gladly and intentionally, I would not be a Christian or have a single honorable vein in my body, and, because of the unspeakable grief such would cause my mother, God would punish me in soul and body here on earth and even more so in eternity. May God graciously protect me and everyone else from such a fate!

With the help of the Highest, I shall make amends for what has unfortunately already happened and repay the money. God willing, you may then see by my act and deed that my heart has always been very differently inclined than you may now perhaps think. This (God knows) is my final resolution: before you shall ever again pay any expense of mine, or

185. The bill was no doubt submitted directly to de Braa, who probably discussed it with Stephan Carl before sending it on to Lucas Friederich for reimbursement in Nuremberg. It came to 225 guilders, or about eighty-nine Reichsthaler. See letter 56.

otherwise be billed for any improper spending, I shall sooner suffer and endure all that a person can, yes, even death.

But so that the money that Abraham de Braa has already advanced me might be repaid to him as soon as possible and other money that has been designated for me not now be withheld and applied to these unnecessary expenses,[186] would Brother (if it can be done and he thinks it advisable) borrow the sum [owed de Braa] at interest or take it out of my own little capital? With the help of the Highest (and if He lets me live so long) I plan to explore, experience, and learn so much in the West Indies that I may make my own way honorably without [any need of] my patrimony and satisfy the merchants for the many unnecessary, but still very great, expenses I have so quickly run up [in Amsterdam]. I leave everything to Brother's discretion. I only wanted to let him know my heart and mind and to make the sincere brotherly request that he not show Mother the little bill Abraham de Braa has sent. It will depress her entirely too much, and she may read it as Reichsthaler [rather than as Dutch guilders].[187] I should also report that the extra [expense] written [on the bill] is not for wine, but for my contributions to the [poor] box on the dinner table and at church. My boarding-house keeper had set aside some money for me [from the poor box when I first came], since at that time I received absolutely nothing from Herr de Braa.

As for my voyage to the West Indies, it began in the name of God on the same Saturday, 14/24 November. We now lie at anchor here in Texel and, God willing, hope to set sail in the morning, as the east wind is beginning to blow. As for my service, I have agreed conditionally to sail to the West Indies as a corporal[188] in command of fifteen chosen musketeers on the ship *Harlem*, which carries thirty cannon. The West India Company has agreed to write a recommendation to its general there,[189] instructing him to advance me before the others according to merit into either the cavalry or the infantry, as I desire. They have given me everything I asked for. And everything at sea suits me very well, praise God. I

---

186. That is those he had run up at his boarding house.

187. At two and a half guilders to the Reichsthaler, this would make it seem more than twice as great as it was. The reference is presumably to the boarding-house keeper's bill mentioned earlier.

188. "Gefrieder," the lowest-ranking noncommissioned officer.

189. Crestofle d'Artischau Arciszewski (1592–1656), an exiled Polish nobleman and successful mercenary, joined the West India Company in 1629 and was in Brazil from 1631.

hope to God to be somewhat happier in the West Indies than I have so far been in Germany and there, at last, to be able to keep my promise [to Mother]. May God grant me his grace, blessing, and good fortune to that end. Amen.

Meanwhile, I again commend Brother, his very dear wife, his sons and daughters, cousin Baier and all his dear ones, Aunt Baumgartner, and our entire family into the care and protection of the All-Highest. When there is an opportunity, would Brother greet them all warmly for me and wish them all well? I commend myself and all the little I have to Brother's continuing fraternal favor, kindness, and sure hands. And I pray daily that God will keep one and all in true peace and comfort, continuing good health, and prosperity and that by his divine will we may at some time in the future meet again in good fortune, honor, and joy. May God grant it; I wish it from the bottom of my heart. Amen.

In great haste, from Texel, on the ship named *Harlem*, 18/28 November, 1635.

> Brother's true and obedient brother for
> as long as I live,
> Stephan Carl Behaim

P.S. If possible, I urge Brother to send the enclosed letter to my former cavalry master Adolph, and with it to ask him on my behalf if I may now receive my honorable discharge from him. I fully expect he will act as if I had been obligated to him [when I left Germany].[190] I only desire his answer. When Brother wants to send it to me, would he just address it to Herr de Braa (who now, at last, shows me great friendship and has gone to a lot of trouble for me). By our agreement, he will have it safely delivered to me. And would Brother also let me know whether he got my most recent, October letter, and if cousin Georg Wilhelm and sister Madel got theirs?

56 ❦ Abraham de Braa to Lucas Friederich, 27 November 1635

Noble, esteemed, prudent, wise, and very well-beloved Sir. With the offer of my ready service, let me inform you that your esteemed letters of 14, 17, and 21 October arrived safely on 10 and 17 November. From them I learned for the first time that you and your mother are indeed in

190. The suggestion is that Stephan Carl was effectively absent without leave.

earnest about finding Stephan Carl a position in the service of the famous West India Company. (I had previously very much doubted your intentions in this regard, since you had written so very ill of your brother to me.) I have also understood that until he has accepted such service, I am not to pay his boarding-house keeper or anyone else anything.

I will not withhold from you that I began work on this as soon as I received the [first] letter, and I explored every possibility. But I could not get him signed on with the company any sooner than 12 November. Contrary to the company's custom (but at my wish and with my money and in the hope of obligating Stephan Carl all the more to his service), a Reichsthaler was placed in his hand at the signing.[191] I then provided him with all kinds of things, but only as they were truly needed. The same day I paid his boarding-house keeper two hundred and twenty-five guilders and arranged another lodging for the remainder of his stay here, providing him six guilders a week allowance. With good beer there to drink, [I thought] he should be well treated. However [I have discovered that] he took only one meal there. Without my knowing, he returned to his old lodging and, as he had done before, spent a Reichsthaler every day up to the 24th of this month. When the call came on the 24th for him to go by cart with the other soldiers to Texel, I went with servants to his new lodgings to fetch him so that he might get to the ship. To my astonishment, I learned that he had taken only one meal there, notwithstanding that he repeatedly told me he was staying at his new lodging. At this, my servant and I began to ask everywhere for him before finding him back at his old lodging. We then hurried him to throw his things together and come with my servant to the West India House. There he was given his musket and two months' pay (at four Reichsthaler per month), and he boarded ship with the other soldiers. I convoyed him to the very end, fearing he might make for Posen,[192] as he was at the time looking for every excuse to get out of the voyage (which he had never taken seriously). He tried to deceive me in a variety of ways and with all kinds of untruths. He wanted me to give him one hundred Reichsthaler on the spot, promising that he could easily satisfy his boarding-house keeper with it and also find another good lodging, and would thereafter not need any more money from me. I always told him that as long as I had sure knowledge that he had not signed with the West India Company to sail on their first departing ship, I would pay not a heller or a pfennig

191. A ceremonial symbol, akin to the ring used in marriage.
192. That is, that he might flee.

[of his expenses]. Since he was being harassed and threatened over money [by his creditors], he finally had to act. He came to me and said that, as he saw that it could not be otherwise, he would accept service with the company. At that, I went with him to the West India House and there persevered so successfully with the directors that they gave him a junior officer's position, as they did not at the time have any higher positions open. They also wrote a recommendation for Colonel Christoph Artischau,[193] a Pole who commands the militia in Brazil, instructing him to assist Stephan Carl and see that he gets a mount. Stephan Carl hopes to make his fortune better [in the cavalry than in the infantry]. He is now in Texel, awaiting wind on the ship called *Harlem*. It has thirty-three cannon and is departing in the company of [fifteen or sixteen ships], eight bound for Brazil, two or three for the East Indies, four for the straits,[194] and still another going west. He will have no difficulty before Dunkirk. His relatives are now free of him for four years. In addition to paying him wages, the company provides his board, which will certainly not be a Reichsthaler a day. He will now learn to manage for an entire week on one Reichsthaler. This will keep him very sober and give him an opportunity to examine himself and choose a different life. If his family would like to see him remain in Brazil for a longer time, the means can be found here to arrange that he must.

I could not have done more for him at this time, had he been my own brother. As will be seen from my accompanying bill, I have spent money on him most exactingly, and he has been outfitted with not a few clothes and linens. I will itemize all my expenditures on him, if not with this, then with the next mail, so that payment can be made to my account.[195] If I may again serve you here in other ways, I shall do so with great pleasure. I have been rather scrupulous this time because I saw that he

---

193. See n. 189.

194. Apparently the straits of Gibraltar. These ships would have been headed for the Mediterranean.

195. The total came to 479 guilders, which was 191 Reichsthaler. When everything was totaled de Braa's final bill came to 194.75 Reichsthaler, or close to three hundred gulden. Later De Braa twice wrote to Lucas Friederich (on 18 December 1635 and 1 January 1636), to enquire about paying the bill still outstanding. Stephan Carl's family could not have been pleased with de Braa's supervision, and they may have washed their hands of both him and his charge. Sixteen months later in Brazil, Stephan Carl was still pleading with his mother and brother to reimburse de Braa. See letters 58, 60 (postscript), and 61.

was so extravagant, and I worried that his mother and family would prefer to see him in jail rather than have to pay his expenses. This time the best opportunity to confine him at small cost would have been through his boarding-house keeper. But he will now be disciplined well enough. May God grant that he better himself by it.

I thank you for the congratulations on the occasion of my second marriage. Your comments on its circumstances and worry over [my ability to] command [her] were unnecessary. The arrangement has none of the difficulty you imagine. She is thirty-nine years old and was born in Frankfurt, and so she wanted to spend her time in the future both in Germany and here.[196] If only God will now give us such time. Then we can see what will become of the beautiful Saxon peace.[197] We are hoping for the best.

Meanwhile, I commend your grace to the favor of almighty God and all of us to His grace.

> Remaining your willing servant always,
> Abraham de Braa
> Amsterdam, 27 November, 1635

57 ❧ Stephan Carl to Johannes Morian, 30 December 1635[198]

Very gracious and much-beloved Herr Johannes Morian.

With the offer of my most willing service, let me say that I wrote Herr Morian from here three weeks ago to report that I had received in good order the cellar and other items I had asked for.[199] I sent your bill for eight Reichsthaler to Herr de Braa no less than two weeks ago. I was very happy to receive all these things also for the sake of my health. Being pretty weak at the time, I had no small need of them. I still have not been able to regain my full strength and health on account of the unrelenting bitter cold and the food, which I have not yet gotten used to. Because I thought

196. De Braa seems to have entered into a seventeenth-century version of a commuter marriage, which disturbed Lucas Friederich.
197. Saxony led the Protestant side in making peace with Emperor Ferdinand at Prague in 1635. The Swedes, with French and Dutch backing, did not join in, and the so-called Swedish-French phase of the war commenced the same year.
198. Morian was de Braa's cousin and a direct supplier of Stephan Carl.
199. The cellar refers to wine and liquor.

I should not take any short cuts with my health, I had pills and other things that were available in Texel (although not a lot was to be found there) brought to me on board ship. Hence, few of the ten Reichsthaler that Herr de Braa gave me still remain. I would not like to touch the eight the company gave me and which I have since exchanged for Rosenobel in Enkhuizen,[200] because as soon as I get to the [New] Land (if God helps me do so in good health), I want to invest them in a horse.[201] I have learned from soldiers who recently returned from the [New] Land and who will now go there again with us, that one no longer captures horses in the wild, but buys them from the Portuguese. So that I do not arrive in the [New] Land totally broke and may still buy a couple of pieces of smoked meat, some lemons, and biscuits for myself before we sail, would Herr Morian at his convenience by all means ask Herr de Braa to send a slip for five Reichsthaler to my mother and then, without delay, send me two ducats in cash and some candied ginger through Herr Morian?[202]

I very sincerely ask that you let me know without delay whether you have received my two letters[203] and whether your cousin [de Braa] will oblige my request and accommodate me before we sail. Herr de Braa can easily imagine the condition I must be in after having lain at anchor for such a long time and still again for so long. In case a letter should arrive here for me after we have sailed, please write on it to inquire after me in Colonel Artischau's lodging. He will certainly know where I will be.

May God be with us, 30 December, 1635.

In Texel, on the Ship *Harlem*,
Stephan Carl Behaim

58 🍷   Stephan Carl to Mother, 4/14 January 1636

My due obedient service and inborn filial love and trust as long as I live, noble, very honorable, richly virtuous, much-beloved, and highly esteemed Mother.

200. Rosenobel are English gold pieces bearing the figure of a rose.
201. Probably because he had been told that horses must be purchased from the Portuguese, Stephan Carl foresaw a delay in obtaining a horse and wanted to set the process in motion immediately on arrival.
202. The slip for five Reichsthaler is a charge to his mother of the money to be made available to him (apparently five Reichsthaler worth of ducats).
203. He means this letter and the one of three weeks earlier, still unanswered.

By the grace of God (and there is nothing else I hope for from the Highest) we have ended the year 1635 in good health and prosperity and are now beginning 1636 in the name of the Lord. As duty requires me, I want to wish Mother, my much-beloved brothers and sisters, and our entire praiseworthy family a happy, peaceful, joyous, and very blessed New Year from the bottom of my heart. I shall each day humbly ask the Almighty and All-merciful to bestow His grace generously on Mother and on all those we hold dear, so that Mother may spend not only the coming year in good health and prosperity, but many more such years as well. I also pray that we may continue to write to one another in good health and under the happy circumstance of peace in our beloved Fatherland. And I pray that in compensation for the abundant sorrow I have regret tably caused Mother, I may now bring her honor and happiness and be a consolation and joy to her in her old age. Amen.

I had not imagined when I recently wrote brother Lucas Friederich from Texel about my present condition and concerns that I would also be reporting such things to my much-beloved and highly esteemed mother. I had not expected to write such a letter until, with God's help, I had reached Pernambuco. But a contrary daily wind unfortunately still prevents us from sailing. So I remain in Holland (we have put into Den Helder on the Gat), wishing for nothing more than that God finally save us from the bitter cold and gladden our hearts with a good east or at least northeast wind, and that He bring us safely with good fortune and as quickly as possible into the warm [New] Land. So I now have additional things to report to Mother.

I should directly inform Mother that at my continuing and urgent re- quest Herr de Braa has several times sent me sundry items I very much needed for the recovery and preservation of my health. [I mean] such [things] as candied ginger, assorted brandies, lemons, lemon juice (for refreshment), several pounds of fresh butter and plums, ham, smoked meat, herring, and the like, also four Reichsthaler in cash, and linens for lighter clothing in the [New] Land [all of which] Mother will be discov- ering from my bills. [Such expenditures] will not, however, continue in the future, even if we should be forced to lie at anchor here another two months and longer (may God graciously spare us that). I promised Herr de Braa in my last letter that I would not ask for the smallest item to be sent after me, and I herewith likewise obligate myself to Mother. I will henceforth receive [from the company] all that I need during the voyage, and once I am in the [New] Land, God helping, I hope easily to earn within a year all that my needs require.

Mother can easily see that I wish nothing more now than to spare her any and all expense. Had I not, with Herr de Braa's help, boarded this ship two months ago, I would, like others, have preferred not to suffer the bitter cold and the many other not small inconveniences on board ship, but to have had a good time on land at Mother's inconvenience and expense until our departure. Mother can readily imagine what I would have spent [had I been on land] during this period of time. But the above-mentioned items were very necessary, and I had to have them. I assure Mother that if Herr de Braa had refused me these things, I could not have survived the illness I brought with me when I boarded ship. Indeed, at one point I was completely resolved, before my end came, to have a letter written to Mother and signed [by another] with my [weak] hand. But now, by God's grace, I am again in rather good health. May almighty God (if it be his fatherly will) continue to keep me so.

Meanwhile, it is my very earnest filial request that Mother not delay in reimbursing Herr de Braa, and with much gratitude, for the payments he has made [on my behalf].[204] Then, he will no longer have an excuse to place every obstacle he can before my every move, as he now does. Also, it is a lot of wasted work and effort for me to write Herr de Braa and ask him to buy this or that for me and to send it out at a good opportunity, when I know that he has these [unrefunded] expenditures.

For my part, I assure and promise [Mother] that as long as I live in a foreign land I will for sure not ask her for a single heller. I now serve masters whose monthly wages are paid more surely than those of the crown of Sweden. If God the Highest will only grant me his divine blessing and good health, I have no doubt that I shall someday return home and that Mother will not regret the expense of this voyage or think any more about all she has spent on me in the past. If God helps me reach Pernambuco with good fortune and in good health, I shall write Mother as soon as I arrive and tell her about the city and my condition and service there.

Meanwhile, if Herr de Braa asks for the money he has spent on mail and ship fees, would [Mother] pay him immediately? I have sent various [items] and many letters from here, and it costs a lot to send mail back and forth. I also ask Mother very kindly to write to me as soon as possible and often, if it is to her liking. Just send the letters to Herr de Braa, who will then have them safely delivered to me in Brazil. Mother can easily imagine what great joy it would give me to hear about this or that going-

204. See letters 56, 60, and 61. Stephan Carl is eager to keep de Braa as a willing creditor.

on in our beloved Fatherland or family. I would certainly also like to know whether Mother, my much-beloved cousin Georg Wilhelm, and sister Ebner have received the letters I sent them from Amsterdam via Hamburg.[205]

Herewith I trustingly commend Mother, my dear brothers and sisters, and all our relatives and acquaintances, both old and young, into the care of the Highest and I [wish all of them] continuing health and well-being. Would Mother also greet them warmly on my behalf and wish them a happy, healthy, peaceful, and joyous New Year. Written in Den Helder on the Gat, aboard the ship *Harlem*, 4/14 January, 1636.

        Mother's obedient son for as long as I live,

        Stephan Carl Behaim

P.S. Just now, on 8/18 January at midday, we are in the name of God departing into the North Sea with a good east wind. Now at last, with the help of the Highest, our voyage joyfully begins. May God grant us his grace so that we reach Pernambuco in good health and with good fortune and happiness. Meanwhile, I again commend Mother, my dear brothers and sisters, and the whole family to God's care and protection and send warm greetings to them all.

59 ❧ Stephan Carl to Johannes Morian, 6/16 January 1636

My wish for a happy, healthy, and joyous new year and my ready and willing service to the fullest extent of my ability always, honorable and eminent, very gracious and much-beloved Herr Morian.

When I last wrote Herr Morian, I did not intend to burden him still again with my tiresome letters. But I am now forced to do so because several knowledgeable people familiar with Brazil have advised me about the things I will need most when I arrive in the [New] Land. Some I cannot get there, and some would cost as much there as in Amsterdam. So I am writing with the very earnest request that Herr Morian show me this one act of friendship without delay and convey to his cousin [de Braa] the two enclosed lists, along with my most willing service, and ask him kindly, but firmly, to send me the items on the lists. Thereafter I will want nothing else, either large or small, sent to me for as long as we remain in [Texel]. I would gladly have done my own shopping in Texel with one or the other of the two and one-half Rosenobel sent me, but

---

205. Maria Helena (1617–80) married Wilhelm Ebner on 26 October 1635.

neither in Den Helder (where we lay for a day or two on the Gat before turning back) nor here in Texel was a piece of meat or anything else to be had. I have, therefore, written down absolutely everything I will need for the voyage as well as immediately upon my arrival in the [New] Land, so that Herr Morian and his cousin may not expect to be troubled again on my behalf.

So that your cousin may know why I want these various things, let me say that I need a light, thin suit of clothes because for the entire time we have been here, the constant bitter cold has forced me to wear both my suits of clothes day and night. My green suit did not have much wear before this, but as Herr de Braa can easily see, I will now arrive in the [New] Land with a worthless summer suit. Also, I have sure information from knowledgeable people that a suit of clothes that costs around six Reichsthaler in Amsterdam could only with difficulty be made for sixteen in the [New] Land.

As for the provisions I am requesting, Herr de Braa himself knows well that one cannot be too well supplied. When we reach the ocean proper, there is nothing I can more certainly expect than an illness for which our ship's remedies are ineffective. I want the ham, smoked meat, and cheese not for the voyage, but to take with me to the [New] Land, for these are things one cannot buy there. So it should not be taken amiss if I am somewhat better provisioned than young Tucher, who still lives in Brazil. Then, unlike him, I may not have to write home that I do nothing but go hungry. For the rations there shall not only be small, but also stale and half-rotten. So especially for the sake of my refreshment, additional provisions can do no harm. Also, shoes, slippers, hats, and white linen cloth are as expensive in the [New] Land as in Amsterdam. Herr de Braa will discover among my bills for linens that I did not buy a pair of stockings. I had believed at the time that I could get by with the ones I had, but I now discover that the reverse is true. I still have some of the water skins I brought along, but it may be difficult for me to make do with them for the duration of the voyage, for one cannot drink alone on ship, but [must] always [do so] with mates.

My brother Lucas Friederich now writes to me and without doubt to Herr de Braa as well that only your cousin de Braa and no one else should provide me what I still need for the voyage, and only such things as are absolutely necessary and indispensable and which, because of my ignorance, I failed to buy in Amsterdam. So Herr de Braa need have no misgivings that I will fail to write my mother in detail about the items on the enclosed list and tell her to reimburse Herr de Braa gratefully for them.

In great haste I commend Herr Morian in complete trust to the Highest. From Texel, on the ship *Harlem*, 6/16 January, 1636.

S. C. Behaim

P.S. We are just today, 8/18 January, putting out to sea in the name of the Highest, having waited out, praise God, a desired good wind. I ask Herr Morian most sincerely, if it is possible and can be done, to send me these items on the next ships going to Brazil. Just write on them: to be delivered to Colonel Artischau's lodging. I very much need these things and cannot get by without them, and I will have to pay twice as much for them in the [New] Land. There is no need to report to Nuremberg that I will receive them only after I arrive in Brazil; to do so also seems to be a criticism of my [ship]. I await Herr Morian's letter with the next arriving ships and, should mail arrive [from Nuremberg], my mother's letter as well. I commend Herr Morian to God in complete trust.

After their successful capture of the captaincy of Bahia in 1624, the Dutch sought to establish a permanent colony in Brazil and to challenge the Iberian monopoly on the sugar trade there. This ambition did not end with the subsequent recapture of Bahia by Portuguese and Spanish troops. Looking to the rich and more vulnerable captaincy of Pernambuco to the north, Dutch forces successfully attacked Olinda and Recife in February 1630. Despite their utter superiority on the sea, Dutch soldiers proved no match for the Portuguese and their Amerindian allies on land. They were simply unprepared for tropical warfare. They adapted poorly to the Brazilian climate, remained dependent on imports for basic necessities (even firewood), and were easy prey to malnutrition and disease. Malaria and dysentery claimed more lives than did the guerilla actions waged against them by the Portuguese and the Spanish.

By November 1631 Dutch forces had withdrawn south to Recife and neighboring Antonio Vaz, and north to the fortress of Oranje on an islet off the southern tip of Itamaraca. Colonel Cres-

tofle d'Artischau Arciszewski, a Pole, commanded Fort Oranje and remained the chief military strategist for the Dutch until 1639, when he fell afoul of the new governor-general, His Excellency Johan Maurits. When Stephan Carl arrived after a blessedly uneventful voyage at the Dutch fortress of de Bruijne, near Recife, in late March 1636, Arciszewski and his staff were eyeing the major enemy strongholds at Porto Calvo and the fortress of Povoaçao (Boverson).[206]

The beauty of the New Land overwhelmed Stephan Carl, as it had so many before him. He had to reassure himself that God had blessed the Fatherland equally well. He soon saw combat as an infantryman, although his desire to be a cavalryman remained strong, and to this end he believed he had the favor and support of Colonel Arciszewski. During his first months in the New Land he worried most about his family's failure to reimburse de Braa for the enormous bills he had left behind in Amsterdam. These unpaid bills effectively cut off his credit with the European homeland: so long as de Braa's debts remained unpaid, Stephan

206. C. R. Boxer, The Dutch in Brazil (Oxford, 1957), chaps. 2–3.

Carl could not readily borrow on his family's good name through his customary channels.

Within a year the Brazilian venture had turned sour. Now truly on his own in a strange land and bereft of the relatives and middlemen who had always provided him with a safety net, Stephan Carl soon had deep misgivings. The mere receipt of a letter from Lucas Friederich in March 1637 brought on a torrent of thanksgiving.[207] Judging from Stephan Carl's repeated plea for repayment of de Braa's loan (now sixteen months old), this may have been his first and last mail from home. And he had little else to rejoice over. He likened himself to Joseph, sold into slavery in Egypt by his jealous half-brothers. Stephan Carl hoped that just as the Lord made Joseph the ruler of Egypt, He would yet crown his life with honor after so much adversity. Stephan Carl resolved to be heroic in battle, even if it meant sure death, so that he might gain the recognition and in-

dependence that had eluded him all his life. Forced by personal circumstance and external conditions to remain a musketeer, he saw action in the major engagements of the Dutch war for Pernambuco and neighboring captaincies.

Stephan Carl's last letter ends where his earlier letters so often began. He had found a new creditor in Recife, a fellow Nuremberger purported to be of exceptional humanity (who happened also to know nothing about Stephan Carl's bad debts and alienated family). During a reportedly serious illness Stephan Carl had borrowed money from this man, with the promise that Lucas Friederich would repay his family in Nuremberg. Allegedly willing to die gloriously in battle before begging money again from his mother, Stephan Carl was not prepared to die ingloriously on a sickbed to spare her still another reimbursement.

60 ☙ Stephan Carl to Lucas Friederich, 3/13 May 1636

My due, obedient service and brotherly love and loyalty to the best of my ability for as long as I live, noble, high, and most wise Brother.

It is my duty to inform Brother that by the grace, help, and assistance of the Highest, I completed my West Indies voyage to this land of Brazil in nine weeks and three days. As my heart had wished, I remained healthy

207. Letter not extant.

throughout and we had an extraordinarily good, steady wind and beautiful weather all the way from England. We saw many marvelous fish, whales and flying fish, among others. Although Brazil is still a very long way from India,[208] it can in no way be compared to our European countries. One may even call it a completely different world.

As I first observe the land, it is, in a word, true wilderness. There is not a single cultivated acre, field, or meadow, only dense brush and untillable forest everywhere. It is also utterly without bread, wine, and barley—almost everything needed to sustain life.

2. The people here, namely, the Portuguese, the Brazilians, the black[s], and the savages, are not completely unlike ourselves in their appearance, intelligence, and customs, nor in their way of life and even to a degree in their religion (excepting the savage or *tapojer*, who relies more on Satan than on God). Brother will already have enough information about them in [Sebastian] Münster and others.[209]

3. The climate and weather here are also completely different from our own. While you are now having summer, we are having winter, which is as hot as a German summer. During this half-year, which is called the rainy season, it rains more here than it ever does in Germany and (so I am told) also more than it does here during the summer months. Also, when it is evening in Germany, it is midnight here.[210]

Fourthly, I seldom find [in Germany] the enrapturing vegetation, animals, and birds, which God has bestowed upon this land, and when I do, they are very rare. As Brother will discover in my letter to sister Ebner, I praise Brazil and everything in it to the sky. But I dare say that the riches of God are also manifest in the splendor and glory of our own dear Fatherland in the same gracious gifts.

As for my own situation, I can report to Brother that I am fully resolved to seek my fortune in the cavalry. Colonel Arciszewski wants me there,

---

208. For Stephan Carl, India was the most far away and exotic of lands. See letter 23.

209. Münster (1489–1552) wrote *Cosmographey oder Beschreibung aller Länder*, a very popular description of foreign lands and peoples that was first published in 1544 and that saw many later editions. In addition to the Portuguese colonists were the friendly Amerindians (called "Brazilians" by Stephan Carl), the black slaves from Africa, and those whom Stephan Carl called savages ("wilde") and *tapojer* (tapuyas), a fierce, hinterland, Stone Age tribe whom he considered in every way different from Europeans, and whom Münster portrayed as cannibals dominating the whole of Brazil.

210. Stephan Carl obviously means the reverse, for the sun sets four hours later in Recife than in Germany.

and there are magnificent horses running around in the forests here which one can have for free.[211] [Military] pay is eighteen gulden a month, to which is added my regular plunder. Last month, April, the Portuguese here guided the enemy to St. Lorenz, thinking to strike us again from there, but God helped us counterattack [successfully] while the enemy was en route.[212] However, until the above-mentioned Colonel [Arciszewski] presents me with my own sword and I am able to support myself by it, I will remain with the infantry in Fort de Bruijne (which is the main fort on the seacoast lying between the once beautiful, but now ruined, city of Olinda and the populous market-town of Recife). While the enemy was breathing down our necks, there was much movement back and forth from the fort. Now there is nothing to do but keep watch, which for a young soldier like myself will not be entirely glorious.

Soldiers here are provisioned according to need. I still receive each week enough bread, meat, bacon, plums, beans, berries, barley, vinegar, olive oil, and sometimes wine to get along rather well. These foods one cannot get here. They must be imported from Holland and Seeland by the West India Company at great cost and peril. So far, praise God, I find that one gets on better in these [soldierly] duties when one has neither money nor livelihood.

I felt obliged to report these things very hastily to Brother and to make a sincere filial request that he acknowledge receipt of this letter by return mail, if it can be done conveniently, and also send me news of our beloved Fatherland.

I commend Brother, his very dear wife, sons and daughters, and all our relatives to the care of the Highest. When the opportunity arises, would Brother also greet them all warmly on my behalf, give each my love, and wish them every good thing? I will pray daily to the Highest that He give you every peace and prosperity, and that we may meet and talk again in the future in true peace, abiding health, honor, and joy.

Written in great haste, 3/13 May, from Fort de Bruijne, 1636, in Brazil.

My Brother's obedient servant for as
long as I live,
Stephan Carl Behaim

P.S. If the money given me by Herr de Braa [when I was in Holland] has not yet been fully repaid, I urgently ask that it be done as soon as possible.

211. Contrary to his earlier, "expert" information.
212. The enemy was fresh Portuguese and Spanish troops, who came at irregular intervals from Iberia.

The New World, by Sebastian Münster (1439–1552), from the French translation of the original German edition of 1544, La Cosmographie universelle, contenant la situation de toutes les parties du monde, avec leurs proprietez & appartenances (Basel: Henry Pierre, 1565). Münster portrays the "new Atlantic island of Brazil" as a land of cannibals, something Stephan Carl does not attest. Reproduced by permission of the Map Library, Harvard University.

SCA

C. Britonum

Coreres

Exteriores

Hispania

Oceanus occidentalis

Medera

Fortunatæ inſ.

Antilla

Inſ. Heſperidum

AFRICÆ pars

Dominica

S. Iacobi

Sinus Atlanticus

Canibali

w

7. inſulę Margueritarũ

You may truly be assured that not a single bill from me will reach you as long as I am in this land. However, I will have to trouble Herr de Braa on many occasions for one thing or another, as Brother may learn from my letters to cousin Baier.

There is nothing new to report from here beyond what has been said.[213] Almost every week our ships bring [captured] Spanish vessels and yachts into Pernambuco harbor. Our armada sails with the next [tide] to Alko, where the enemy has built his strongest fort, protected by thirty-six cannon.[214]

61   ❦   Stephan Carl to Lucas Friederich, 25 March 1637

My obedient service, brotherly love, and what inborn loyalty otherwise obligates me always to do, noble, high, most wise, well-beloved, and highly esteemed Brother.

On 22 March I received with great joy Brother's very pleasant and dear reply. I have read the letter with still greater, even indescribable, joy. I thank Brother most sincerely for his true fraternal concern. With my whole heart I will sing the praises of our good and powerful God, and I will thank Him hourly for as long as I live for the inexpressibly great grace He has shown in keeping Brother in good health, and also by caring for Brother's own loved ones and my very dear mother, brothers and sisters, and our entire family (apart from those few who have died, to whom, as to all of us, may the good God some day grant a happy resurrection). God could not have given us greater joy and happiness. I will call on Him daily from my heart to be your protector and shield. May He spare you every misfortune in soul and body and allow you to live always, day after day, in peace and quiet, good health, and complete well-being, so that one day I may find you again and talk with you in joy and exultation. Amen.

As for myself, I too have all this time been in good health, thanks to the grace of the All-Merciful, whom I cannot thank enough. Although in every land nothing is more noble than a healthy body, it is especially true here, where for many reasons good health is deemed the greatest blessing. Here provisions have all too many ways of going bad, and each day

213. The postscript was added some days after the letter had been written.
214. Stephan Carl probably means Alagoras, just south of the enemy's strongest fort, in Porto Calvo. See letter 62.

there are very many high mountains to climb. Nonetheless, the true God has all this time graciously helped me do my duty honorably like the other soldiers. Here I cannot, as I could in the Fatherland, depend on the good will of others or turn to good friends and known acquaintances. Here the rule is: "If you will not, then you must."[215]

I have been all this time in the infantry. For many reasons, I changed my original resolution to join the cavalry. The forests here make it impossible for horsemen, and there is no grass in the summer. In addition, I could not at the time equip myself with a saddle, armor, and pistol with the hundred gulden I had. I still have scarcely more than that now. And to borrow on my wages would very much thwart my resolve [not to incur debt], and should an emergency occur, it might also do me great harm. So I am not inclined to borrow a single heller. I have lived all this time in the hope that God (as He has always done in the past) will again help me overcome my present want and distress and lead me to honor, as He did with Joseph [in the Bible]. In this regard, Brother's letter was very consoling.

I still wish to receive Herr Camerarius's previously mentioned recommendation as soon as possible. When God helps me rejoin the army, which, with a good wind, I hope to do in six or eight days, I will ask the Junkers at His Excellency's court if they know whether Herr Camerarius might already have remembered my humble person to His Excellency.[216] For about a week ago, at around the same time I received Brother's letter, the army detached me to Recife. I was not there long, however, having spent [almost] all my time either at sea or in camp.

In sum, I assure Brother that if God lets me live, Brother and his family shall receive my future letters with greater joy than they have any to date. As far as borrowing money goes, Brother may be assured that before I allow him to pay a single heller on my behalf, what I have long and often promised him shall now, with God's help, resound in my own ears. My only urgent request is that Brother deal with Herr de Braa as soon as

215. "Wilt du nit, so must du."
216. Stephan Carl has been sent to Recife on an unexplained mission. He suspects (or perhaps hopes) that his selection is the result of Herr Camerarius's direct recommendation to His Excellency Johann Maurits, count of Nassau-Siegen (1604–79). Maurits, who arrived in Recife in January 1637, was the first and last Dutch governor-general of Brazil. Thanks to Lucas Friederich's influence, Camerarius was in a position to comment favorably on Stephan Carl to Maurits, with whom he had personal contact before Maurits sailed from the Netherlands.

possible and satisfy him. Also that he ask cousin Lieutenant Coler at his convenience how twelve Reichsthaler can be paid to Junker Antonio Neuner von Montebaur. Junker Neuner paid this amount to General W. Boninohausen for my ransom after General Boninohausen had captured me near Boppard.[217] So great an act of friendship must be properly acknowledged by grateful repayment. I would gladly transfer these twelve Reichsthaler to Brother, but there is no one here to receive payment [on his behalf]. I also ask Brother to write Junker Neuner, greet him warmly, and thank him on my behalf.

Here are the [major] items of news here. Shortly after His Excellency's happy arrival in this land, he marched with all our troops on Boverson,[218] the enemy's strongest fort in Brazil, where they had placed all their hope, soldiers, and munitions. As we approached, the Count of Bamola and his three thousand soldiers worked themselves into the bush and swamp of a mountain pass through which we had to travel and there awaited us in ambush. After an hour's fighting, we could not marvel enough at the great fear God put in them, for they all fled at once to the bay. Seven companies had remained behind to defend the fort. After ten days of fighting, they were forced to agree to a surrender. In the fort we found twenty-five cannons, mostly half-kartanen,[219] four excellent small field cannons, fuses, and more of the same beyond number. His Excellency will next march on Alko and Porto Francisco.[220]

No more for now, except in complete trust and greatest haste to commend Brother and our entire family to God. The boats now want to sail. Recife, 25 March, 1637.

S. C. Behaim

62 ❦ Stephan Carl to Lucas Friederich, 14 May 1637

Much-beloved and highly esteemed Brother.

I have learned from my present experience that the old, remembered

217. On the Rhine, northwest of Mainz. This is another long-standing, unpaid debt. Stephan Carl's motive is unclear, especially because he would seem no longer to need Junker Neuner's services as a creditor. Perhaps he has sensed the loss of de Braa as a creditor and wants to have the option in the future of turning again to Neuner.
218. Maurits's forces first attacked the Portuguese stronghold in Porto Calvo on 18 February before beseiging the fort of Povoação (Boverson). Boxer, The Dutch in Brazil, 70.
219. A small, heavy cannon that shoots balling weighing about twenty-five pounds.
220. By pushing farther south through Alagoras and into Sergipe.

proverb, "man proposes, God disposes," is true. My much-beloved brother will recall that I said in my last letter that [he and his family] shall read my future letters with particular joy. When I wrote that, I had resolved to prove at the next opportunity that His Excellency may necessarily have reason to favor me over the others. For I had decided that it would be better to die an honorable and manly death now than to live any longer in my present wretched condition. But shortly after my resolution, God, by his divine will, visited me with not a small illness and robbed me of seemingly every helpful cure. I could not enjoy a penny of my wages.[221] However, He did not choose to let me waste away and die. As my true helper and assistant, He raised up the honorable Herr Christoph Ayrschedel from Nuremberg, who, in sympathy, showed me very great friendship. He honored me with Spanish wine, and to help me regain my health, at my request he advanced me cash for all my needs. After God, I am most grateful to him for the health I presently enjoy. Were it not for him, the only food I would have gotten to lift me to my knees again would have been stale bread, coarse, hardened beans, and barley—a fare so wretched that they serve it here to horses as well as to people. In sum, I have learned to endure poverty beyond description. But thanks be to God for helping me regain my health.

Meanwhile, I very sincerely ask my highly esteemed brother to show me this one great brotherly favor and before all other [obligations] to reimburse Herr Ayrschedel's brother [in Nuremberg] on my behalf without delay for the fifteen Reichsthaler [Herr Ayrschedel lent me]. In Brazil, with one gulden in cash one can honorably get four or five more. And Herr Ayrschedel also acted out of great sympathy and friendship, when he had [new] cloth and linen clothes made for me. Remember that here during the present rainy season one must march three, four, and more days in the rain.[222]

Because this letter not only goes against my promise [to Mother], but against all my own good plans and intentions as well, I ask Brother not to say a word about this loan to Mother or to anyone else. In the future I will be no less diligent in my efforts to spare Mother a single additional

221. A *Stieber* (or *stuiver* or *stiver*) was a Dutch penny. There were twenty to the guilder or florin.
222. In the margin of the letter is written "N.B. obsecro": "Note well, I am imploring." It is unclear whether this was written beseechingly by Stephan Carl or mockingly by Lucas Friederich.

expense. It breaks my heart that this has happened. But it could not have been otherwise, unless I had been willing to take my own life.

I must now conclude in great haste and much fatigue. I ask Brother to thank this man [Ayrschedel] by letter and to recommend me to him when he does. I ask this simply because he is such an honorable man, not because I want to get any more money from him; no indeed. Tomorrow, God willing, I [begin a] journey that will take me a hundred miles away from him. Brother may be assured that I am now, by God's grace, a different man.

Recife, Brazil, 14 May, 1637.
S[tephan] C[arl] Behaim

❦ EPILOGUE

Stephan Carl died on 14 January 1638, in Recife from wounds received two months earlier. It is not known whether he received them heroically in combat, as he had contemplated, or ingloriously in an ambush or even a brawl. The last surviving information about him from his own hand is the announcement in his last letter, eight months before his death, that he was setting out on a journey that would take him "a hundred miles" from Recife. He could have been referring only to the expedition to Elmina (São Jorge de Mina), which the Dutch successfully besieged in August 1637. Later he was very likely involved in raids in Sergipe in November.

In April 1639, after not having heard from his brother for a year and a half, Lucas Friederich wrote to de Braa in Amsterdam to ask whether he had any information; de Braa responded with a report from one Caspar Stör, a fellow German and former judge advocate in a Brazilian regiment, who had known Stephan Carl well. Stör had seen Stephan Carl in Fort San Francisco in November 1637, two months before his death. Ac-cording to his report, Stephan Carl was then already a broken man. He was filthy and fevered, wore a tattered coat, and went about without stockings and shoes. A festering toe, half-rotted and dangling from his foot, caused him constant pain. Stör exhorted him to wash and care for himself, but Stephan Carl did not have the heart to do anything. He was taken from Fort San Francisco to the garrison hospital in Recife, where Stör promised to visit him soon. But fourteen months passed before Stör could keep his promise. At that time he learned that Stephan Carl had died from blood poisoning a year earlier. According to Stör, the conditions in the garrison hospital were such that even a healthy man could not long have survived there.

Stephan Carl's company then sent de Braa twenty-three gulden, ten kreuzer, the sum total of Stephan Carl's possessions after his obligations in Brazil had been paid; de Braa dutifully forwarded this money to Lucas Friederich. At the request of Stephan Carl's mother, it was used to place a memorial to her son at St. Sebald church in Nuremberg.[223]

---

223. Ernstberger, *Abenteurer*, 86–90. The account is preserved in the copybooks of Lucas Friederich for 1639. That de Braa sent the twenty-three gulden on to Nuremberg suggests that he had by this time been reimbursed for the money he spent on Stephan Carl in Amsterdam.

Edited Sources on the Behaims

Anton Ernstberger, ed. "Nürnberger Patrizier- und Geschlechtersöhne [Lukas Friederich Behaim, Raimund Imhoff, Konrad Baier, Hans Wilhelm Kress]," Mitteilungen des Vereins für Geschichte der Stadt Nürnberg (hereafter cited as MVGN) 43 (1952): 341–60.

———. "Liebesbriefe Lukas Friedrich Behaims an seine Braut Anna Maria Pfinzing 1612–1613," MVGN 44 (1953): 317–70.

Theodore Hampe, ed. "Die Reise des jungen Nürnberger Patriziersohnes Georg Hieronymus Behaim an den Hof des Fürsten Bethlen Gabor von Siebenbürgen (1614)," MVGN 31 (1933): 133–62.

J. Kamann, ed. "Aus Paulus Behaims I. Briefwechsel [1533–35]," MVGN 3 (1881): 73–154.

———. "Aus Nürnberger Haushaltungs- und Rechnungsbüchern des 15. und 16. Jahrhunderts: II: Aus Paulus Behaims I. Haushaltungsbüchern 1548–1568 (1576)," MVGN 7 (1888): 39–139.

———. "Aus dem Briefwechsel eines jungen Nürnberger Kaufmanns [Paul I Behaim] im 16. Jahrhundert," Mitteilungen aus dem Germanischen Nationalmuseum (1894), 11–22.

Wilhelm Loose, ed. "Brief des zehnjährigen Friedrich Behaim an seinen in Leipzig studierenden Bruder Paul," Anzeiger für Kunde der deutschen Vorzeit (1877), no. 10, pp. 339–40.

———. "Deutsches Studentenleben in Padua 1575 bis 1578 [Paul II Behaim]," Beilage zur Schul- und Universitätsgeschichte (Meissen, 1879), 11–38.

———. "Briefe eines Leipziger Studenten [Paul II Behaim] aus den Jahren 1572 bis 1574," Beigabe zum Jahres-Bericht der Realschule zu Meissen, no. 480 (Meissen, 1880): 1–23.

Monetary Values (1550–1650)

1 gulden	8 pounds, 12 pfennigs (or 252 pfennigs)
1 pound	30 pfennigs
1 batzen	16 pfennigs
1 schilling (or groschen)	10–12 pfennigs
1 kreuzer	4 pfennigs
1 heller	½ pfennig
1 Ducat	1½–2 gulden
1 Reichsthaler	1½–2 gulden
1 Thaler	1½–2 gulden
1 (Italian) Crown	1½–2 gulden

Altdorf School Ordinance

1. Students shall attend worship services on Sundays and holidays.
2. They must go to school daily.
3. They must speak [only] Latin [in school].
4. They shall arrive at school punctually.
5. They shall study diligently and behave honorably in their rooms.
6. They shall dress honorably.
7. They must be peaceful among themselves.
8. Quarrelsome students will be punished by either confinement or expulsion.
9. Bearing weapons is forbidden.
10. Weapons brought to school are to be given to teachers or to those running the boarding houses.
11. He who wounds a fellow student with a weapon will be thrown into the city prison and expelled from school. He who strikes a fellow student with his fists will be punished at school.
12. Bad company is to be avoided.
13. Inns and pubs are forbidden.
14. All students have to go to church on Sunday.
15. Students who live in the city must also attend school choir practice and appear at school worship services.
16. Quarrels between students and burghers will be resolved by the rector and the burghermeister.
17. Students may not tear down posters in their classes.
18. Students may not post or distribute lampoons.
19. Students may not go about the city without permission from their parents and the rector.
20. Students permitted out [of the city] must return at an appointed hour.
21. Students who are gone longer [than the permitted time] must present a written explanation.
22. Local youths should set a good example for students from outside the city.
23. Teachers are responsible for the supervision of boarders and private students within their homes. Transgressions against teachers [in private homes] are punished as transgressions at school.
24. Private students have to observe house rules.
25. Students may not leave the city or spend the night outside their rooms.

This ordinance is given in Mertz, *Das Schulwesen*, 596.

Stephan Carl's Poem on the Occasion of Lucas Friederich Behaim's Birthday

For the Birthday of the Generous, Noble, Native Bud, Herr Lucas Friederich Behaim, A Lover of Shining Virtue and of the Higher Muse, my Sweetest and Deeply Beloved Brother.

a[lpha]-o[mega]

He who asks poetry from me asks water from a stone, for I am scarcely able to rhyme words.

True Brother, my Honey, fraternal Crown of my Head, my Life, and Salvation of my Life!

The advent of your birthday exhorts me to pour forth a few verses for you.

If any day ever should be marked [on the calendar] with little white stones,[1] if any day ever was to be applauded and celebrated,

That day, surely, is one to be marked on the snowy tablets, a day to be embraced in our prayers,

That day [is the one] on which you, emerging into the heavenly light, began to gladden the patriarchal hearth.

O Lucas Friederich, greatest part of my heart, glittering truly within my soul like a little gem,

If old Rome celebrated the birthday of the Trojan Quirinus, and the Cretan land the birthday of Jove,

Surely it is fitting to celebrate worthily in the Austrian light[2] the day the Fates wished my brother to be born.

I am deceived! That she might sprinkle her locks with lustral waters Mysta has bid us be present at the rites of the little church.[3]

Clotho, the very greatest of the three Fates, stood by your cradle, Brother, [at the hour of your birth], and sang these words:

---

1. A mark for something deemed special; see letter 4.
2. "In Noridae lucem." Surely "Noribergae" was meant; Nuremberg, not Austria!
3. Mysta was a priest of divine mysteries. Here Stephan Carl is apparently offering an excuse for not being at home on his brother's birthday; the ecclesiastical authorities required children to be in church in Altdorf on St. Luke's day.

"Be born, my Lucas, child most longed-for by the gods! Come, be born, O glittering gem of your Fatherland!

"Arise, Hyantian Honey, from the very womb of his pious mother, and shape his entire genius and wit,

"Ready to carve great names in mighty characters upon the flowering bark of the fragrant cedar.

"Soft threads of our own loosing are spun out for you, and I attend the long coil wound in accordance with your destiny.[4]

"No deceiving Fortune of men shall harm you; she who is swift shall show you favor in every way.

"Although she may fling troublesome cares at you, yet shall they not be equal to your strength.

"Your prudence shall overcome all things and you shall be strong in the face of all that men must endure.

"You shall prescribe laws [and be] the pillar of [your] Fatherland, and you shall choose temperate over unfair motions of the mind.

"Let neither drunkenness, implacable anger, nor an avaricious spirit make you its prey."

Thus is Clotho said to have predicted at your cradle when you were born, sweetest brother.

Add (since I felicitate you now with a snowy heart): I wish this to be a happy and special day [for you]!

Ah, thou happy day, return again with the too-oft revolving year[s], and bring back my brother unharmed!

For my part, I hope your happy children, with your wife, will celebrate this day, Lucas Friederich.

I wish that the One-in-Three and Three-in-One will long preserve this very day under the happiest possible auspices.

So move I who favor you, my most longed-for brother.

Stephan Carl Behaim

4. Vergil, *Georgics*, IV.348.

THE BEHAIMS

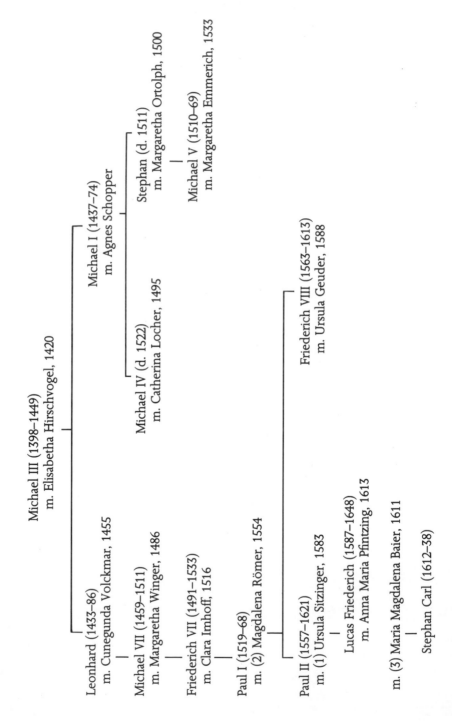

Michael III (1398–1449)
m. Elisabetha Hirschvogel, 1420

Michael I (1437–74)
m. Agnes Schopper

Stephan (d. 1511)
m. Margaretha Ortolph, 1500

Michael V (1510–69)
m. Margaretha Emmerich, 1533

Michael IV (d. 1522)
m. Catherina Locher, 1495

Friederich VIII (1563–1613)
m. Ursula Geuder, 1588

Leonhard (1433–86)
m. Cunegunda Volckmar, 1455

Michael VII (1459–1511)
m. Margaretha Winger, 1486

Friederich VII (1491–1533)
m. Clara Imhoff, 1516

Paul I (1519–68)
m. (2) Magdalena Römer, 1554

Paul II (1557–1621)
m. (1) Ursula Sitzinger, 1583

Lucas Friederich (1587–1648)
m. Anna Maria Pfintzing, 1613

m. (3) Maria Magdalena Baier, 1611

Stephan Carl (1612–38)

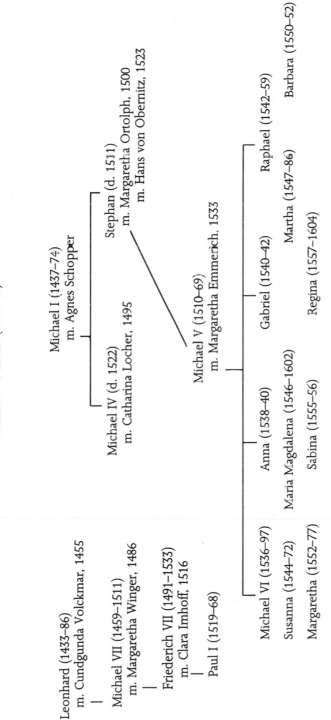

Michael V Behaim (1510–69)

Michael I (1437–74)
m. Agnes Schopper

Stephan (d. 1511)
m. Margaretha Ortolph, 1500
m. Hans von Obernitz, 1523

Michael IV (d. 1522)
m. Catharina Locher, 1495

Leonhard (1433–86)
m. Cundgunda Volckmar, 1455

Michael VII (1459–1511)
m. Margaretha Winger, 1486

Friederich VII (1491–1533)
m. Clara Imhoff, 1516

Paul I (1519–68)

Michael V (1510–69)
m. Margaretha Emmerich, 1533

Anna (1538–40)

Gabriel (1540–42)

Raphael (1542–59)

Maria Magdalena (1546–1602)

Martha (1547–86)

Barbara (1550–52)

Michael VI (1536–97)

Susanna (1544–72)

Sabina (1555–56)

Regina (1557–1604)

Margaretha (1552–77)

Friederich VIII Behaim (1563–1613)

Paul I Behaim (1519–68)
m. (2) Magdalena Römer (d. 1581), 1554

Magdalena (1555–1642)

Clara (1561)

Sabina (1556–1639)

Christoph (1562–1624)

Paul II (1557–1621)

Friederich VIII (1563–1613)
m. Ursula Geuder, 1588

Catharina (1560–1638)

Maria (1565–1600)

Albrecht (1589–1636)

Friederich IX (1594–1619)

Maria Magdalena (1605–42)

Alexander (1590–1624)

Sabina (1596)

Anna (1607)

Ursula (1591–1629)

Susanna (1598–1632)

Magdalena (1593–1652)

Wolf (1604–28)

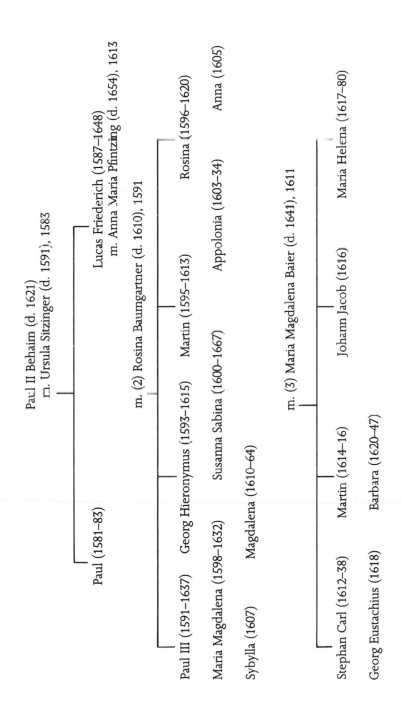

APPENDIX 6

Genealogical and Other Aids

Johann Gottfried Biedermann, *Geschlechtsregister des Hochadellichen Patriciats Nürnberg* (Bayreuth, 1748; repr. Nuremberg, 1982).

Alfred Goetze, *Frühneuhochdeutsches Glossar*, 7th ed. (Berlin, 1967).

Jacob and Wilhelm Grimm, *Deutsches Wörterbuch* (Leipzig, 1854–1860).

Handbuch der historischen Stätten Deutschlands, vol. 4, *Hessen*, ed. Georg W. Sante (Stuttgart, 1960); vol. 5, *Rheinland-Pfalz und Saarland*, ed. Ludwig Petry (Stuttgart, 1959); vol. 6, *Baden-Württemberg*, ed. Max Miller (Stuttgart, 1965); vol. 7, *Bayern*, ed. Karl Bosl (Stuttgart, 1961).

Julia Lehner, *Die Mode im alten Nürnberg. Modische Entwicklung und sozialer Wandel in Nürnberg aufgezeigt an den Nürnberger Kleiderordnungen* (1984).

Matthias Lexers Mittelhochdeutsches Taschenwörterbuch, 23d ed. (Stuttgart, 1966).

Gerhard Pfeiffer, ed., *Nürnberg: Geschichte einer europäischen Stadt* (1971).

Ernst Scholler, *Das Münzwesen der Reichsstadt Nürnberg im 16. Jahrhundert* (1916).

Schwäbisches Wörterbuch, ed. Hermann Fischer (Tübingen, 1901–26).

Georg Steinhausen, *Geschichte des deutschen Briefes*, vols. 1, 2 (1889).

Georg Steinhausen, *Der Kaufmann in der deutschen Vergangenheit* (1899).

Ernst Walter Zeeden, *Deutsche Kultur in der frühen Neuzeit* (1968).